AF716897

Copyright © 2026 by Dr. Mark Porter

All rights reserved.

No part of this book may be reproduced, stored in a retrieval system, or transmitted in any form or by any means electronic, mechanical, photocopying, recording, or otherwise without the prior written permission of the author, except for brief quotations used in reviews or scholarly works.

This book is a work of non-fiction. Names, characters, organizations, and events are either the product of the author's research or used in a representative manner. Any resemblance to actual persons, living or dead, or actual events is coincidental.

The concepts, frameworks, and methodologies described in this book are presented for educational and informational purposes only. The author makes no guarantees regarding outcomes or results from the application of these ideas. Readers are responsible for their own decisions and actions.

Dedication

For the people whose effort was real when the system was not.

For those who carried the weight when structure was missing.

Acknowledgement

This work was shaped by a small number of people whose contributions materially improved its clarity, rigor, and reach.

Almeen Bano played a central role in bringing this book into form. Her editorial work, leadership on illustrations and cover design, and guidance on launch and positioning significantly shaped how the ideas are expressed and experienced. Her background in neuroscience also served as a continual, if informal, stress test of the psychological and cognitive foundations of the work.

Dr. Kevin Gazzara, my doctoral dissertation chair, colleague, and mentor, influenced the way I think about systems, structure, and organizational architecture. His insistence on disciplined reasoning and coherent design continues to inform my work and is evident throughout these pages.

Gord Stephens provided sustained intellectual challenge through engaged reading and critique of the manuscript. His questions and pushback sharpened the arguments and helped clarify what mattered most.

I am also grateful to those close to me for their patience during the long process of writing and refinement.

Table of Contents

Prologue: The Breaking Point

Every leader arrives at a moment they would rather avoid. For Reg, it came on a gray Tuesday morning in the boardroom. The light through the high windows was pale and cold, washing the long table in sterile gray. The quarterly deck glowed on the screen. Polished. Rehearsed. Perfect on the surface. But the room was silent. No one smiled. No one nodded. The numbers had slipped again, and this time there were no explanations left.

Reg forced his jaw into a confident grin. He had been celebrated for years for his energy, his vision, his ability to rally a room. He had learned how to fill silence with optimism. He leaned forward, hands spread on the table, and declared that the organization would recover, that agility was still their edge. The words came out smooth, but even as he spoke, he felt the hollowness beneath them. His executive team stared back politely. One adjusted his pen. Another glanced at the clock. The air felt heavy, the stale scent of old coffee lingering.

What Reg could not yet see was that this silence was not simply a failure of energy. It was the absence of design. Design is the disciplined enactment of governing architecture translated into culture and behavior that sustains clarity and performance.

As he stood there, Reg's mind flickered back to another moment in the same room, years earlier. Back then, he had stood at the head of the table with fire in his voice. He had announced a bold new strategy and painted a picture of a future that felt electric. The applause had been thunderous. Hands slapped the table. People rose to their feet. He had believed then that charisma and courage could carry the company anywhere. The memory glowed like a flame in his chest, and then, as he scrutinized the faces now staring at him, the flame flickered and died.

Later, in his office, Reg closed the door and collapsed into the leather chair. The silence pressed in. His breathing was shallow. Sweat collected at his temples. He loosened his tie, but it still felt like something was choking him. He stared at the charts again, willing them to shift, to rise, to reflect on the story he kept telling. They did not move. He rubbed his forehead, but the pressure would not release. The applause was gone. The slogans no longer inspired. This unraveling was Drift.

Drift does not announce itself. It creeps in silently. It appears in the erosion of confidence and clarity. Reg had seen the signs, but he had ignored them. He did not recognize Drift for what it was: the slow collapse of culture where no deliberate design holds it together. Design is the architecture of the structure leaders choose to build. And where architecture is absent, Drift advances.

The Shape of Drift and Rationalizations

The first sign came in a highly regarded mid-manager named Tara. She was brilliant, charismatic, a favorite in meetings. She nodded enthusiastically when new initiatives were announced. She echoed Reg's words back to her team. But deadlines slipped. Promises were not delivered. Projects hung unfinished, leaving others scrambling. One afternoon, a frustrated teammate muttered under his breath, "We are building fog, not strategy." Reg brushed it off as an isolated issue. He gave Tara another pep talk. But Drift had already advanced.

The second sign was Miguel, the rising star. Young, ambitious, the kind of employee recruiters chased. One evening Reg overheard him in the lobby on the phone. His voice was low, cautious, but the words were clear: "I want to make an impact, but I do not see how here." A week later Reg noticed Miguel standing by the glass doors, badge in hand, staring out at the city lights. He left a month later. Reg convinced himself it was about salary. But deep down he knew there had been no design, no structure that gave Miguel a reason to stay. Unraveling had whispered that there was more out there, and Miguel had listened.

And then there was the project team, talented, dedicated, burning the midnight oil to hit an urgent deadline. Reg admired their effort. But the night before delivery, their inboxes filled with confusion. "Are we using version A or version B?" "Who owns this?" "We just found three conflicting reports." The fluorescent lights buzzed overhead, the musty odor of boxed leftovers lingering like defeat. By morning, the team was exhausted and ashamed, their work a tangle of contradictions. They had given everything, but without clarity, their effort collapsed into failure of execution.

These were not abstractions. Drift was alive. Reg saw it. He lived with it every week. But he kept telling himself it was temporary. That the market was tough. Competitors were ruthless. He pushed the blame outward, anywhere but inward. Leaders always do, until they cannot.

Denial only deepened the crisis. Leaders pretend Drift is external. They blame markets, talent shortages, or impatient boards. They push responsibility down to managers or across to HR. They convince themselves that next quarter will fix it. Reg was no different. These were his rationalizations, his shields. But Drift thrives on rationalizations. Decline spreads in silence, fed by avoidance. Drift always wins where leaders refuse to design.

Excuses bought time, but time only fueled the unraveling.

Reg's Reckoning

The unraveling sharpened. Departments broke into turf wars, each defending its budget like territory. Promises of agility collapsed into chaos as teams tripped over one another. Customers called, frustrated by delays and broken promises. Turnover spiked. Even the most loyal employees seemed worn down, moving mechanically, avoiding eye contact.

One afternoon, Reg walked past two senior managers in the hallway. Their voices were low but sharp. "I am not cleaning up their mess again," one muttered. "Let them fail." The words hit him like a punch. He kept walking, pretending not to hear, but inside he felt a chill. This was not the company he had built. Something had shifted. And he could not explain it away.

Still, he clung to his rituals. He scheduled more meetings. He sent out messages filled with bold language: "We will win by outworking the competition." "We are resilient." "Our culture is our edge." He said these words with force, but each repetition sounded thinner, weaker. Even he no longer believed his words.

At night, lying in bed, he stared at the ceiling. His mind replayed every failure, every awkward silence in the boardroom, every resignation email. The slogans echoed in his head, hollow. His chest felt tight. He whispered to himself: Maybe it is me. Maybe I am the problem. He carried that fear silently, until Imara, his mentor and guide, broke through his denial.

Imara's Confrontation

A heavy silence lingered in the room. Reg sat alone for a long moment, feeling the gravity of his failures gather around him like fog. The air was still, the hum of the building faint, as if the world itself was holding its breath before the reckoning.

"Reg," she said, sitting across from him in his office, her voice calm but unyielding, "you are not losing to talent or markets. You are losing to Drift. And Drift wins because you have no design."

Reg bristled. His fists clenched. His jaw tightened. "That is not fair. We have worked harder than ever. I have given them vision. I have kept the story alive."

Imara's eyes did not soften. "Your emphasis on inspiration has become your excuse. Drift does not care about speeches. Drift only yields to intentional design."

He leaned forward, desperate. Sweat gathered on his brow. "But people need inspiration. They need to feel energy. That is what leadership is."

Imara shook her head. "No, Reg. Leadership without design is theater. You are putting on shows while the foundation collapses beneath you."

She leaned closer, her tone sharper now. "Excellence is engineered. Mastery is never an accident. It is constructed step by step, with structure that cannot be faked."

Her words cut. He felt exposed, as if she had stripped away the image he had built for years. Still, he pushed back. "Structure slows us down. Discipline kills agility."

Imara's reply was sharp. "What slows you down is Drift. Chaos is not speed. Confusion is not agility. Drift devours energy in every direction. Only structure creates freedom."

Reg slammed his hand on the desk. "I cannot just kill the energy. People look to me for inspiration. If I stop giving it, they will give up entirely."

Imara's voice rose. "They are already giving up. Look around you. They nod, but they do not act. They stay late, but they do not deliver. They smile, but they are already listening to recruiters. You are losing them, Reg, not because you failed to inspire, but because you failed to design."

Reg's chest tightened. His breath came shallow. His eyes narrowed. His shoulders slumped. He swallowed hard, the knot in his throat refusing to move. Imara leaned closer. "You must face the truth. Energy fades. Charisma cracks. Drift consumes every gap. The only thing that endures is design."

The Threshold

Every leader arrives at the threshold. It is not marked by applause, but by silence. Reg stood there, exhausted. He saw Drift everywhere, in disengaged managers, in eroded trust, in disappearing talent. He saw it in himself, in his avoidance, in his excuses.

He wanted to find a compromise, some middle ground between speeches and structure. But there was none. Imara had left him no space to pretend. The silence pressed in. His throat was dry. His hands trembled slightly as he realized that this was the true weight of leadership. Not applause. Not recognition. But the courage to design when Drift was already advancing.

Imara's words were final. "Drift or design. Fragility or strength. Excuses or mastery. There is no middle ground. Mastery may unfold step by step, but Drift is never patient. Every delay is Drift advancing."

Reg closed his eyes. He could continue pretending, or he could face himself and build what he had always avoided. And the same threshold now stands before you.

Leader's Challenge

Drift is not abstract. You are either designing or collapsing. You must decide: will you continue excusing fatigue, mediocrity, and silence as temporary setbacks; or will you name Drift for what it is and confront it with design? There is no neutral ground Drift advances unless you stop it. You must choose now whether to confront or collapse.

Maxim: Design is destiny; Drift is surrender

Introduction

This book is written for leaders responsible for sustained performance; not episodic success. If you are tired of rebuilding what keeps collapsing, if you feel the weight of Drift but refuse to accept it as inevitable, this book is for you.

You now stand where Reg once stood. The threshold between Drift and Design.

Leaders are drifting. Sharpness dulls. What was inevitable now feels fragile. Drift is silent but relentless. Without architecture, it wins.

Performance Mastery Culture (PMC) is that architecture. It is not philosophy, not a ghost, not a mystery. It is the definitive architecture of organizational culture: original, authoritative, enduring. This book is The Architecture of Excellence: both an executional standard and a practitioner manual. Its pages hold architecture and application, conviction and practice. It is not meant to be admired. It is meant to be used.

I am the originator of Performance Mastery Culture. My role is not to entertain you, nor to overwhelm you with theories borrowed from elsewhere. My role is to lay down the architecture of sustained excellence so you can build it inside your own organization. My voice here is not that of an observer but of an architect. What follows is not suggestion; it is design.

As you witnessed in Reg's story, the weary CEO, the weight of unraveling pressing on his shoulders; Drift creeps silently. His unraveling was not unique. It is the norm where design is missing. Here begins the design that offers a way out. If Reg is the caution, Marcus is the mirror.

Enter Marcus: a skeptical middle manager, pressed by the same weight, resisting the same truths. He will accompany you as mirror and guide. His confrontation with Drift is yours. His structure is your structure.

The tension in his chest mirrors yours. His tight jaw and restless hands declare the battle within. Marcus is your proxy. His transformation must become your transformation.

Marcus's conflict is not hypothetical. Picture him in the meeting room: the team gathered, the agenda bloated, the real issues untouched. Standards are slipping. A bold idea lies silent on the table, unspoken. He senses Drift tightening its grip, but he stays quiet. He knows something is wrong but does nothing. That paralysis is Drift. Marcus must learn what you must learn: silence is surrender. Design demands courage.

Later that evening, Marcus sits at his kitchen table, laptop open, shoulders slumped. He replays the meeting in his mind. The excuses he accepted. The accountability he avoided. The words he should have spoken. His spouse asks how the day went. He forces a half-smile: "Fine." But he knows it wasn't fine. Drift had won another day. Marcus feels the erosion inside. The battle is not abstract. It is lived, moment by moment, decision by decision. And so is yours.

What is Mastery

Mastery is the engineered permanence of excellence; architecture embedding clarity when inspiration fades.

It is the alignment of structure, behavior, and meaning transforming performance from fragile bursts into sustained precision. This alignment is constructed, observable, and repeatable.

Mastery is observable, trainable, measurable, and scalable.

It is the opposite of Drift. Drift erodes; Mastery endures.

Mastery is not design, development, or resilience alone; it is their convergence, made structural and sustained through architecture.

Mastery is not a pursuit; it is architecture.

It is engineered permanence sustained through deliberate repetition; each act of design reinforcing the architecture that anchors excellence.

Resilience, discipline, and clarity are not traits; they are structural outcomes.

When architecture is absent, these qualities erode. When it is present, they endure.

Mastery is not maintained by inspiration; but by designed mechanisms.

It is the disciplined recurrence of design preventing drift and renewing excellence.

This is the difference between performance that fades and enduring excellence.

These are not theories. They are non-negotiable principles of performance. They define why Drift consumes even the seemingly strong, and why PMC stands as the only structural countermeasure.

The Enemy Revisited: Drift

Drift is the silent collapse of culture. Invisible erosion. Subtle at first, then devastating. It feeds on sentimentality, bureaucracy, mediocrity, fragility. It requires no decision, no dramatic moment. Drift whispers complacency while it stealthily collapses your structure.

Every culture drifts.

Only deliberate architecture prevents collapse. Where it is absent, Drift is absolute.

Drift is not theoretical; it is present, waiting, patient. You have seen it before, even if you refused to name it.

Drift is visible if you choose to see it: the meeting where truth goes unspoken, teams where standards fade, leaders avoiding conflict. Drift thrives where leaders look away.

It begins quietly. A missed deadline excused. A promise forgotten. A voice silenced. Soon, politics replace honesty. Mediocrity replaces discipline. Drift never arrives with fanfare. It arrives as fatigue, avoidance, resignation. And then collapse feels unstoppable.

Every culture pays the cost of Drift: wasted talent, broken trust, lost opportunities. The brightest employees leave, suffocated by mediocrity. Innovation stalls under bureaucracy. Leaders once admired grow weary and hollow. The culture becomes fragile, unable to bear pressure. Drift is not neutral. Drift is loss. And loss compounds.

Look beyond your walls. Promising companies, once hailed as innovators, vanished within a decade because they mistook speed for strength. Nations faltered, not from invasion, but from the erosion of integrity. Championship teams, built on bursts of performance, dissolved when cohesion faltered. Drift is universal. The silent predator of every human system. Left unchecked, Drift always wins and every leader who denies it becomes its accomplice.

Global Vignette

Empires once stretched across continents. They commanded armies, wealth, and brilliance. Yet they collapsed, not from invasion, but from Drift. Discipline eroded. Standards softened. Integrity frayed. The fall of a nation mirrors the fall of a company. Drift consumes what is not designed for permanence.

Consider social movements that surged with passion and momentum yet faded into obscurity because no structure held it. Passion without architecture is fragility. Inspiration without design is exhaustion. Performance without architecture is temporary.

Drift is not confined to boardrooms or balance sheets. It is the undoing of nations, the collapse of dynasties, the silence of movements that should have endured. Drift always wins unless design intervenes. PMC is the only architecture that prevents collapse and guarantees permanence.

Every moment.

Every decision.

Surrenders to Drift.

Or forges Design.

There is no neutral ground.

Whether you lead a company, a community, or a nation, Drift obeys the same law, and only deliberate architecture resists it.

High-Performance Culture Within PMC

Much has been written about high-performance culture. It drives results, sharpens execution, inspires belief, but remains fragile. They rise quickly, but often collapse under pressure, fade into mediocrity, or fracture when leaders change.

Performance Mastery Culture does not compete with high-performance culture. It completes it. PMC transcends performance as an outcome; it establishes performance as a condition. High performance is not discarded in PMC; it is absorbed, one of many outcomes engineered by architecture. Within PMC, high performance becomes structural permanence.

High-performance culture is necessary, but never sufficient. PMC transforms the sprint of high performance into the marathon of mastery; replacing speed with stamina, effort with engineering. It makes resilience and sustainability constants, not variables. PMC is a design for enduring excellence withstanding disruption and change.

PMC engineers mastery beyond inspiration and episodic bursts; it secures relentless endurance and structural dominance.

Other organizational cultures offer moments of strength, but remain vulnerable to Drift. They rely on inspiration, charisma, or bursts of execution. They fade when pressure mounts, when leaders change, or when markets shift. PMC anchors excellence permanently. It is not one option among many. It is the only path to sustained excellence.

PMC is not a cultural preference. It is a leadership necessity. It is the must-have architecture of performance. Without it, Drift wins. With it, excellence becomes permanence.

All other culture models are fragments. PMC is the whole. It is not inspiration. It is not a trend. It is the blueprint of mastery.

PMC is the architecture of excellence. Every other model is decoration.

Consider the company that surged in a booming market. It grew fast, hired fast, and won awards. Leaders celebrated high performance. But when disruption hit, cracks spread. Confidence vanished. Silos hardened. Politics replaced progress. High performance collapsed into Drift. High performance without PMC is a sprint to exhaustion. High performance within PMC is sustained dominance.

Reg thought he had built strength. In reality, he built speed. For three years, his company hit record numbers. But beneath the surface, people were exhausted.

When one leader left, performance deteriorated. Trust faltered. Politics grew. Morale collapsed. What had been hailed as high performance dissolved almost overnight. Reg's failure was not a lack of effort; it was the absence of design. Drift rewarded his speed until it consumed his strength. PMC would have anchored that performance in resilience, individuality, and structure. High performance would have been permanent.

Your Role as Reader and Leader

This book speaks directly to you. Whether CEO, board member, vice president, or director, you shape architecture. The choice is stark: design with intent, or watch Drift dismantle what you built.

Your leadership today will either surrender to Drift or forge Design.

This book will unsettle you, it must. Excellence is forged in discomfort.

Halt and consider.

Which truths can you no longer deny?

What discomfort stands between you and mastery?

Drift is visible now. In the initiative that began sharp but grew diluted. In the team that once upheld standards, but now tolerates mediocrity. In the leader who once inspired but now avoids conflict. Drift does not wait, it is already working.

Leaders fear what confronting Drift might cost: conflict, change, discomfort. But the greater cost is invisible: the loss of excellence, the erosion of trust, the decay of mastery. Drift steals silently, but its theft is total.

The truth cuts deeper: every leader carries Drift within. It lives in compromise, in silence, in every standard allowed to fade. To confront Drift, you must confront yourself. Until you do, Drift rules you.

Drift's Human Toll

Drift is not just structural; it is personal. It begins in the silence of fatigue, in the leader staring at the ceiling at 2 a.m., wondering why the fire is gone. It lives in the high-potential employee who resigns quietly, exhausted by politics. It lingers in the whispered frustration of teams who know the truth, but dare not speak it.

Drift corrodes courage and hollows resolve. It erodes integrity until avoidance becomes habit, and habit becomes identity. Drift is not only the erosion of systems; it is the erosion of purpose. Every day Drift wins, leaders lose a piece of conviction, a piece of clarity, a piece of themselves. The longer Drift rules, the more leaders become strangers to their own potential.

Every organization collapses the same way; starting silently within its leaders.

The purpose of this book is to stop Drift and replace it with deliberate architecture. You cannot wish Drift away. You cannot inspire it away. You must design against it. Only PMC provides the design.

Every decision is Drift or Design.

No neutral ground exists.

How to Engage This Architecture

This book is structured deliberately.

The opening chapters expose the patterns that quietly erode performance. You will recognize them, perhaps uncomfortably. This is intentional. Before anything can be built differently, the problem must be seen clearly.

Next, you will be introduced to the core principles that prevent collapse. These are not abstract ideas; they are practical foundations you can apply immediately. From there, the book moves into execution. You will examine structure, authority, behavior, and the decisions that determine whether excellence holds under pressure or slowly erodes. Each chapter builds on the last. This is not a collection of insights; it is a deliberate design.

Do not rush it.

This book rewards reflection more than speed. Read deliberately. Pause when challenged. Apply before advancing. One principle implemented is more powerful than a chapter admired.

You are not here to gather ideas. You are here to build excellence that lasts.

The Promise of Transformation

Marcus, the pressured skeptic, is your mirror. He begins uncertain, defensive, resisting the truth of Drift. By the end, Marcus will be changed.

So must you.

These pages do not exist for admiration. They exist for confrontation. They demand decisions that forge awareness into architecture.

Every scene with Marcus exposes your own design. His transformation is not metaphor; it is mandate.

You will not admire PMC.

You will become it.

The enemy is Drift.

The architecture is PMC.

The decision is yours.

Closing Declaration and Invitation

This book is about the architecture of sustained excellence.

Not inspiration.

Not charisma.

Not luck.

Architecture.

If you lead, you build.

If you do not build, you drift.

You stand now at the same threshold faced by Reg and Marcus.

This is the moment of choice. Your legacy will be defined by this choice.

Your leadership is forged by this moment.

Design is your mandate.

Drift does not wait.

The invitation is direct: commit to design.

Step into the structure of Performance Mastery Culture.

Leave Drift behind.

Leader's Challenge

Name where Drift already lives in your culture. Drift ignored is Drift invited.

Identify where Drift is strongest. Do not rationalize. Do not delay.

Commit to one act of design today. Declare it. Execute it.

Every hesitation is surrender.

Every act of design is defiance of Drift.

History does not honor intent. It honors mastery. It remembers architecture.

PMC's Inevitability

There is no alternative. Every culture either erodes into drift or stands upon PMC. There is no third path.

Charisma fades. Inspiration expires. Trend models fracture. Systems without structure erode.

PMC is permanent architecture: governance, not preference; design, not sentiment; permanence, not philosophy.

This is your threshold.

Drift or Design. Collapse or Mastery.

The choice has already begun.

Chapter 1 – Fragility of High-Performance Cultures

I. Story: Hal, Carol, and Marcus

Hal's decline did not look like failure. It looked like discipline. Every morning, he was at the gym before dawn, punishing his body, chasing numbers on a barbell like he chased numbers on a quarterly report.

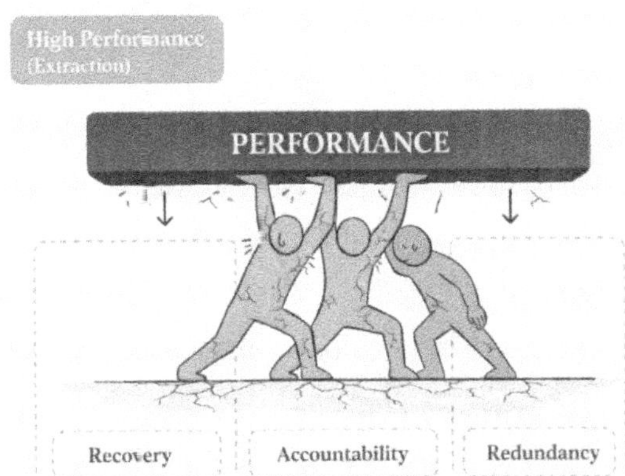

Figure 1 1 Performance Without Architecture

A visual representation of performance sustained through effort alone, without structural support.

When recovery, accountability, and redundancy are absent, performance does not rest on structure. It is carried by people until collapse makes the design failure visible.

Colleagues admired his stamina. He became the model of grit in performance reviews, the one leaders pointed to when rallying teams to push harder. What they didn't see was the quiet unraveling. His hands shook during simple tasks. He skipped doctor's appointments, convinced resilience meant defying the limits of his own capacity.

In earlier years, resilience had meant recovery, pacing, and preparation. He had once taken pride in balance, in knowing when to push and when to rebuild. Drift erased that definition and replaced it with a single expectation: endurance at all costs. It taught him that to pause was weakness, that to endure was to matter. The morning his grip gave out on the pull-up bar, sending him crashing to the mat, he did not tell anyone. He sat there, chest heaving, unable to rise; aware now that the design had failed him, not his will. In the silence of that moment on the mat, he finally felt the cost of a culture that rewarded collapse as commitment.

Persistence without structure masquerades as resilience until collapse exposes the lie. His collapse was not dramatic. It was the slow, private surrender of a body and mind asked to give more than any structure could sustain.

If design had been present, recovery would have been protected. Balance would have been engineered. Resilience would have been built into the architecture instead of left to personal willpower. Instead, Drift left him hollow.

Hal's collapse did not end with him; the burden simply shifted to Carol. His private collapse became her daily load. Proof that when recovery isn't designed, the burden never ends; it transfers."

Carol's erosion lived in the unseen spaces between meetings. She was the dependable one, the fixer. When projects faltered, when deadlines slipped, when leaders promised more than the team could deliver, Carol absorbed the shock. She worked through lunch, then through dinner, laptop balanced on the kitchen table while her children ate without her. She answered emails on vacation, carrying her phone like an oxygen tank. It was survival, not dedication.

Colleagues praised her as dedicated, but behind closed doors her spouse asked how much longer she could carry the workload built for three people. Carol smiled through it all, but the smile was armor. Armor, growing heavier each day. Inside, resentment built.

Excellence had become punishment. Without design, mastery decayed into exploitation.

She wondered, briefly, what it might feel like if the load were shared: if structure distributed responsibility instead of piling it onto the reliable. No amount of individual strength compensates for the absence of design. What others saw as strength was, in truth, extraction.

She remembered one rare season when collaboration had been real. When her team aligned around shared accountability, work had felt lighter, almost energizing. The memory was fleeting, but it revealed what was missing: resilience designed into the culture, not demanded from individuals. The sound of her children's laughter in the next room sharpened the contrast, reminding her of a life waiting beyond endurance. Yet Carol was not alone in witnessing the cost, Marcus saw it all.

Marcus, the silent observer, sat in the project war room surrounded by sticky notes and whiteboards. He watched deadlines multiply, commitments outpace capacity, and fatigue turn sharp voices dull. He noticed Hal's absence brushed aside with vague talk of personal leave. He saw Carol's forced smile harden into a mask.

He felt the unease in his chest and almost spoke. The words hovered: This is not sustainable. But he swallowed them, nodding at the plans instead. He scribbled notes and called the strain ambition's price, sinking back into silence. Yet he knew better. He had seen good people burn out, talented peers walk away, values bent until they snapped. Still, he stayed quiet, convincing himself it was not his place to challenge the rhythm. He knew the truth, but comfort made denial easy.

His silence was not neutral.

It was surrender.

At night , Marcus replayed conversations, words he should have spoken, questions left unasked. He called it prudence; in truth it was Drift defending comfort.

Drift does not storm the gates; it seeps through unstructured silence. Every time design is absent, hesitation becomes policy.

How many times had Marcus let Drift rewrite his boundaries? How many times has comfort silenced courage?

Every leader faces these boundaries. Drift redefines them when comfort outweighs courage.

Fragility rarely arrives with alarms. It creeps in through long hours, muted voices, and the quiet normalization of sacrifice without support. Hal's collapse. Carol's burden. Marcus's silence. Together they reveal that what looks like strength on the outside is often decaying within. This is the architecture of Drift: performance without resilience, achievement without sustainability, effort without design.

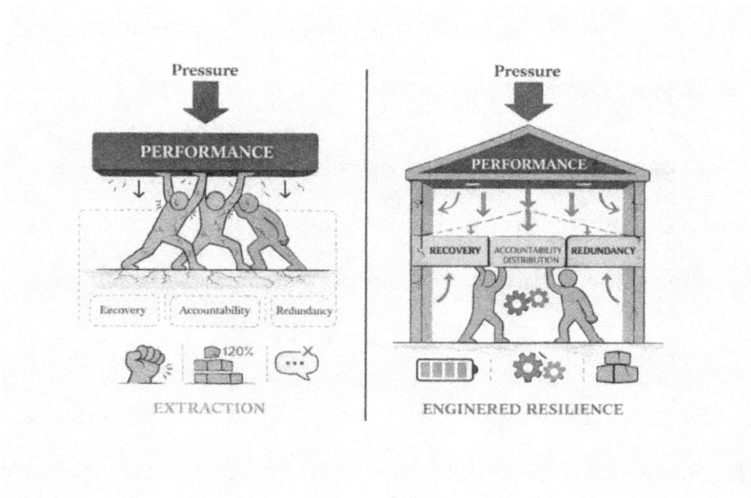

Figure 1.2 Pressure Reveals Architecture

Under pressure, extraction shifts load onto individuals, while engineered resilience absorbs strain through recovery, accountability distribution, and redundancy.

Resilience is not toughness. Resilience is the architecture that protects recovery, distributes weight, and makes pressure sustainable. It is not improvised by individuals. It is engineered into culture.

Hal's mistake, Carol's burden, Marcus's silence; these are not personal failings. They are the invisible architecture of Drift. Structure, not intention, dictates outcomes.

From these patterns, one truth becomes unavoidable.

Maxim: Performance without engineered resilience guarantees collapse.

II. Doctrine &Diagnostic

The illusion of high performance is seductive. Numbers rise. Applause follows. But beneath the surface, high-performance organizational cultures (HPOCs) built on output and endurance reveal a hidden fragility. They appear strong, yet they are brittle because their strength is built on extraction rather than design. Extraction occurs when performance is achieved by consuming people's health, energy, and commitment without replenishing it. It produces temporary gains but guarantees collapse. This is the architecture of fragility disguised as success.

Key Terms

- **HPOCs (High-Performance Organizational Cultures):** designed environment of shared values and behaviors. It aligns goals with strategy, empowers employees through strong leadership, and fosters open communication and continuous learning. HPOC emphasizes accountability, innovation, and adaptability.
- **Drift:** the silent degradation of performance that occurs when structure is no longer governed by architecture, allowing behavior to default to convenience, habit, and entropy rather than structurally constrained, designed execution.
- **Extraction:** the cultural pattern of achieving performance by consuming people's capacity without replenishment.
- **PMC (Performance Mastery Culture):** intentional architecture unleashing people as the living structure of excellence. It engineers behavior through design, converting intent into disciplined execution. It forges resilience, accountability, and adaptability into an architecture of engineered, permanent excellence.
- **Mastery:** forged precision; engineered permanence of people excellence. It is not a pursuit or a trait, but a structural condition that is observable, trainable, measurable, and scalable.

Flaws of High-Performance Cultures

1. Health Degradation

HPOCs glorify stamina and punish rest. They push employees to sacrifice health for output Hal's collapse reflects this reality: without structures that protect recovery, performance corrodes the very capacity it relies on.

PMC Response

Resilience is engineered into workflows.

Recovery is protected as a structural requirement.

Health is the foundation of performance.

Enforceable Feedback Loop

1. Schedule approval requires embedded recovery intervals.
2. Health dashboards track fatigue, PTO usage, and absenteeism alongside output.
3. Leaders' performance reviews include resilience metrics.

Doctrinal Closure

- Organizations measuring endurance instead of recovery convert health into fuel and call it excellence.

Transition

When health erodes, performance punishment accelerates; the signal to shift from personal sacrifice to systemic protection.

2. Performance Punishment

HPOCs punish high performers by overloading them. Carol's burden illustrates this: the better she performed, the more responsibility was piled onto her. Excellence became punishment. Picture Carol at midnight, staring at her laptop while her children slept, carrying a load designed for three.

PMC Response

Accountability distributed through design, not individuals.

Structures absorb pressure and prevent exploitation of competence.

Performance is supported, not penalized.

Enforceable Feedback Loops

1. Accountability maps are published and stress-tested quarterly to prevent overloading high performers.
2. Redistribution protocols trigger automatically if a role exceeds 120% of sustainable workload.
3. Leaders cannot assign new responsibilities without documented redistribution of existing load.

Doctrinal Closure

- When excellence becomes punishment, the architecture has abandoned design.
- Workload without redistribution is exploitation engineered by neglect.

Transition

Punishing the competent breeds silence, and silence corrodes ethics until erosion becomes culture.

3. Complicity And Ethical Erosion

HPOCs normalize shortcuts, suppress dissent, and reward avoidance. Marcus's silence reflects this: over time, values bend under pressure until they snap. Employees stop speaking when fear outweighs courage.

PMC Response

Leaders are embedded in the culture.

Ethical resilience is sustained through alignment of three elements:

- **Declarative**: Values clearly stated.
- **Symbolic**: Rituals, recognition, and rewards reinforce values.
- **Structural:** Policies and structures establishing ethical behavior the path of least resistance.

Enforceable Feedback Loops

1. Major decisions require documented dissent before final approval.
2. Whistleblowing and ethical reports are surfaced and resolved in leadership reviews.
3. Recognition mechanisms reward truth-telling and risk escalation.

Doctrinal Closure

- When silence replaces dissent, Drift has rewritten values.
- Ethics decay where comfort goes unchallenged.
- Silence is the earliest and most dangerous signal of ethical erosion.

Transition

Silence is followed by burnout; collapsing cultures that trade courage for compliance.

4. Burnout Culture

HPOCs rely on adrenaline-fueled sprints. Performance spikes, then collapses. Teams mistake temporary surges with mastery, leading to exhaustion. Imagine Marcus walking into the war room: exhausted faces, forced smiles, and deadlines multiplying faster than capacity.

PMC Response

Mastery sustains performance for the long term.

Pressure is absorbed through deliberate design.

Resilience transforms pressure into capacity.

Enforceable Feedback Loops

1. Team sprints require a mandated recovery cycle.
2. Burnout indicators (turnover risk, engagement drops, overtime spikes) reviewed monthly at executive level.
3. Projects pause if capacity forecasts show sustained overload beyond 90 days.

Doctrinal Closure

- Burnout is proof of design failure.
- Pressure unmanaged by structure consumes capacity faster than purpose can renew it.

Transition

Burnout reveals dependence on heroes instead of design.

5. Context Sensitivity

HPOCs depend on heroes. A single individual carries critical knowledge, absorbs disproportionate weight, or becomes the face of resilience. Remove that individual, and the structure erodes.

PMC Response

Leadership embedded in architecture.

Resilience is systemic.

Hero dependence is a declaration of Drift until structure replaces it.

Enforceable Feedback Loops

1. Critical processes require mandatory redundancy and cross-training.
2. Succession and continuity plans published and stress-tested annually.
3. Performance systems measure collaborative resilience.
4. Functions flagged as hero-dependent are redesigned until the dependence is eliminated.

Doctrinal Closure

- Hero dependence is Drift made visible.
- When continuity rests on a single person, resilience ends the moment they leave.

Transition

Heroic cultures evolve into inequitable ones, where ranking replaces mastery.

6. Forced Ranking and Inequity

HPOCs fracture teams with competition. They exploit high performers and demoralize others. Cohesion dissolves into rivalry. Carol, once celebrated, found herself resented for carrying too much weight, while her peers disengaged.

PMC Response

Structural mastery replaces arbitrary rankings.

Development is prioritized over exploitation.

Mastery recognition, learning incentives, and equitable career pathways embed fairness and growth.

Enforceable Feedback Loops

1. Performance reviews require development evidence, not just rankings.
2. Recognition tied to mastery-building behaviors: mentoring, structural improvement.
3. Compensation and advancement reviews require equity audits to prevent drift into exploitation.

Doctrinal Closure

- Competition without design fractures coherence.
- Forced ranking converts collaboration into rivalry and equity into erosion.
- Inequality is Drift formalized.

Transition

Fear-driven ranking distorts accountability; design restores it through justice and learning.

7. Accountability Without Fear

HPOCs punish mistakes indiscriminately, creating fear and suppressing learning. This silences growth.

PMC Response

Just Culture Principles

Human error: Console and redesign the architecture.

At-risk behavior: Coach and realign incentives

Reckless behavior: Apply consequences with fairness.

Transparency and learning replace fear as management tools.

Accountability is clear, fair, and predictable.

Enforceable Feedback Loops

1. Incident reviews follow Just Culture protocols
2. Consequences tied to documented structural evidence.
3. Accountability dashboards display distribution of errors and corrective actions across all levels.

Doctrinal Closure

- Accountability built on fear destroys truth.
- Design makes learning the architecture of responsibility.

Architectural Truths

- Performance without resilience collapses.
- Extraction is not designed.
- Drift normalizes fragility.
- Resilience must be engineered.
- Pressure reveals design.

Diagnostic Tool: The Performance–Pressure Curve

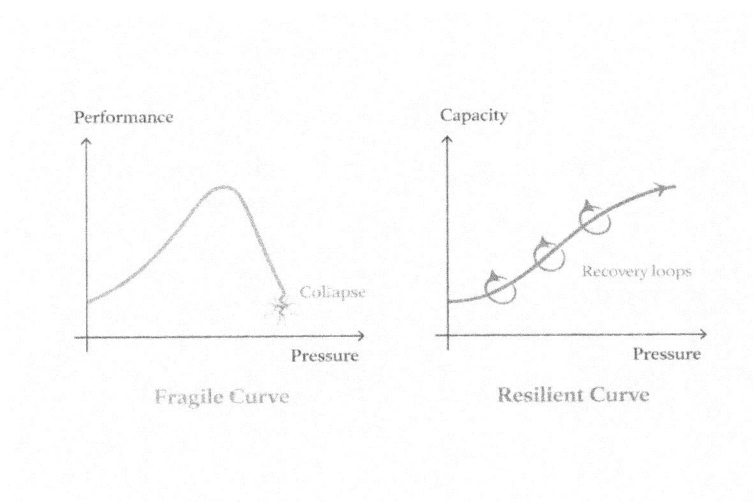

Figure 1.3 The Performance–Pressure Curve

Fragile systems convert pressure into short-term performance followed by collapse. Resilient systems use recovery and structure to transform pressure into sustained capacity.

Purpose

Determine whether an organization functions as a High-Performance Organization or falls into Drift by achieving results through extraction, heroics, or cultural mythology.

Diagnostic Dimensions

1. Pressure Architecture

Definition

Assesses whether pressure increases are deliberately structured and distributed rather than dependent on individual endurance.

Propagation / Performance Indicator

Pressure is planned, load is shared and increases follow design not heroics.

Drift Indicator

Pressure spikes unpredictably, workloads concentrate on a few, and short-term gains mask structural instability.

2. Recovery Integrity

Definition

Measures whether recovery cycles are protected as capacity-building mechanisms rather than optional relief.

Propagation / Performance Indicator

Rest, recalibration, and reflection are embedded, scheduled, and enforced.

Drift Indicator

Recovery is skipped or compressed; exhaustion rises; absenteeism indicators appear.

3. Accountability Distribution

Definition

Evaluates whether responsibility is stabilized by systems or absorbed by isolated high performers.

Propagation / Performance Indicator

Accountability is shared and reinforced by process, preventing overload and sustaining performance.

Drift Indicator

Heroes emerge, responsibility accumulates unevenly, and performance becomes extraction-based.

4. Truth Flow Under Pressure

Definition

Determines whether communication becomes clearer under strain or collapses into silence.

Propagation / Performance Indicator

Risk, strain, and truth surface quickly; leaders receive unfiltered information.

Drift Indicator

Silence increases, conflict is avoided, and shortcuts emerge during peak pressure.

5. Capacity Trajectory

Definition

Reveals whether pressure strengthens the structure or accelerates systemic deterioration.

Propagation / Performance Indicator

Pressure expands capability, improves innovation, and strengthens mastery.

Drift Indicator

Capacity collapses: health declines, engagement drops, ethics corrode, and performance becomes volatile.

Scoring Standard (each domain is assessed from 1–5: Drift → Validated)

1. **Severe Drift:** Extraction dominates; capacity actively deteriorates.
2. **High Drift:** Gains mask erosion; recovery and truth collapse under pressure.
3. **Unstable:** Mixed signals; resilience exists but is not structurally protected.

4. **Strong Alignment:** Structure reinforces resilience; Drift only at edges.
5. **Validated Architecture:** Pressure reliably strengthens capacity; resilience is designed and self-sustaining.

Interpretation Guide

Validated Architecture: (19-25)

1. Pressure amplifies capability.
2. Recovery is enforced.
3. Accountability is shared.
4. Truth accelerates.
5. capacity expands predictably.

Drift Detected: (1-18)

1. Performance is extraction-based.
2. Recovery erodes.
3. Silence increases.
4. Pressure accelerates decay.
5. Fragility increases until collapse.

Structural Closing Line

A culture's response to pressure reveals whether it is compounding resilience or accelerating drift toward fragility.

Leader's Challenge

Pressure has already told you the truth; you have simply avoided hearing it.

Hal collapsed because pressure revealed a design he did not have.
Carol eroded because weight concentrated where structure failed.
Marcus went silent because Drift taught him that truth had no protection.

Their stories are not exceptional.

They are warnings.

Warnings about what happens when leaders confuse endurance with resilience, extraction with excellence, and silence with prudence.

You lead an architecture that is always speaking.

The question is whether you are willing to listen to what it reveals under strain.

If pressure spikes unpredictably, it is because you allowed heroics to replace architecture.

If recovery disappears, it is because you treated stamina as a strategy.

If accountability pools around the competent, it is because structure surrendered to convenience.

If the truth disappears, it is because fear learned it was safer than honesty.

If capacity collapses, it is because pressure exposed the structure you built, not the people you blame.

These are not flaws of character.

They are failures of architecture.

And architecture is your responsibility.

Every leader reaches the moment where Drift stops being subtle and starts being visible.

The moment where the collapse of others reflects the structure you created.

The moment where silence becomes complicated.

The moment where pressure demands you choose: continue normalizing fragility or begin engineering resilience.

This is that moment.

You cannot lead a resilient culture while defending an architecture that breaks your people.

You cannot claim mastery while allowing Drift to dictate the curve of performance.

You cannot call your culture strong if pressure turns strength into depletion, truth into silence, and excellence into punishment.

Pressure reveals structure.

What has it revealed so far? Is it the structure you intended to build?

Your challenge is not to fix people.

Your challenge is to confront the architecture you have allowed.

To face the truth pressure is exposed.

To decide whether your leadership produces resilience intentionally or fragility by neglect.

Every culture follows a curve.

Yours is already moving, toward collapse or toward capacity.

The direction is not accidental.

It is built.

The question is whether you will be the leader who finally stops Drift or the one who lets it finish its work.

III. ESSENCE OF EXECUTION

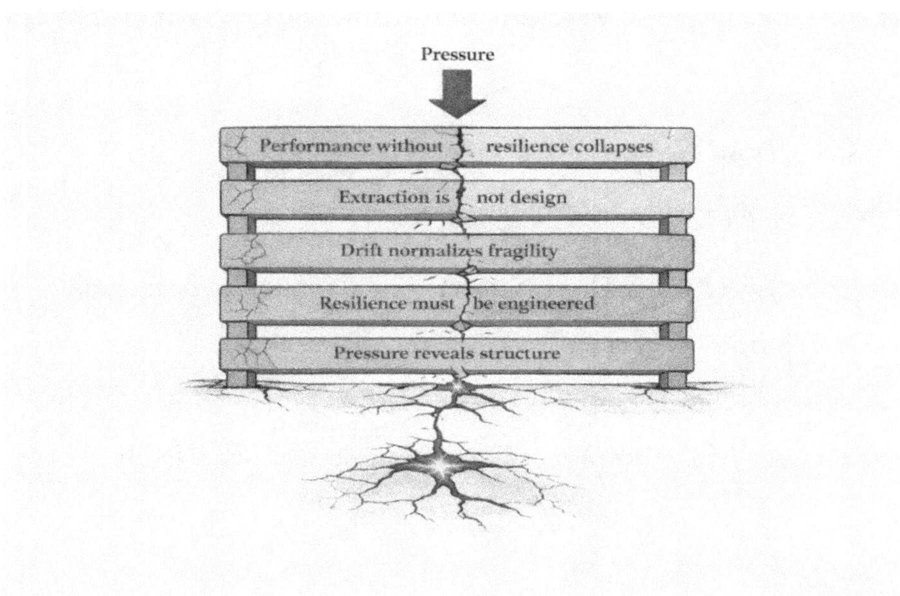

Figure 1.4 Architectural Truths of Fragility

Pressure does not create failure; it exposes it. When resilience is not engineered into structure, performance rests on people until cracks propagate and collapse becomes inevitable.

1. Core Execution Truth

Performance without engineered resilience guarantees collapse.

2. Indicators of Drift

1. Recovery is absent or sacrificed under pressure.
2. Workload concentrates around high performers.
3. Pressure spikes unpredictably and depends on heroes.
4. Truth is withheld because fear becomes safer than honesty.
5. Capacity erodes faster than it can be rebuilt.

3. Essential Leader Actions

1. Engineer recovery into all workflows and operational rhythms.
2. Redistribute weight structurally to eliminate role concentration.
3. Remove hero dependence by embedding redundancy and continuity.
4. Protect truth structurally so dissent is expected and shielded.
5. Align accountability to structure, not convenience or competence.

4. Enforceable Feedback Requirements

1. Resilience indicators (recovery cycles, fatigue, role load) reviewed on a fixed cadence.
2. Redistribution triggers activate when workload exceeds defined thresholds.
3. Truth-protection reviews require documented dissent before decision closure.
4. Burnout indicators initiate immediate architectural inspection.

5. The Decisive Question

Will your architecture produce resilience by design, or fragility by neglect?

IV. Rapid Orientation: Drift–Architecture Spectrum

Use this rubric for orientation, not validation. If your structures do not hold under pressure and turnover, you are in Drift regardless of intent or progress.

Severe Drift: Extraction dominates; capacity actively deteriorates.

High Drift: Gains mask erosion; recovery and truth collapse under pressure.

Unstable: Mixed signals; resilience exists but is not structurally protected.

Strong Alignment: Structure reinforces resilience; Drift only at edges.

Validated Architecture: Pressure reliably strengthens capacity; resilience is designed and self-sustaining.

Chapter 2 – Drift of Learning Organizations

I. Story: Sasha and the Collapse of Learning

Sasha stood at the front of the executive briefing room, dashboards glowing like trophies. The Academy had delivered: over ninety percent trained, usage tripled, forums alive with debate. Applause filled the room. The CFO snapped a photo and declared the investment justified. Sasha hesitated before joining the applause, palms hovering above the table. The numbers shone, but the pattern behind them didn't.

Reg was at the head of the table, smiling broadly, his presence commanding. He congratulated the room, but his words floated above the surface. He praised the numbers, but never asked what they added up to. What he left unsaid revealed more than his words ever could: how this learning would integrate into a single architecture.

Beneath the applause, Sasha felt the weight of Drift. Metrics dazzled, but she sensed erosion beneath them. Alignment was absent, and in its absence, collapse was only a matter of time.

The dashboards shimmered like constellations unbound by gravity; brilliant, but lawless. Each number spun in its own orbit, beautiful and irrelevant.

Sasha stared at the glow and realized the data was movement without direction, energy ungoverned by architecture. The Academy had taught the teams to accelerate, not to align. Every metric was a heartbeat detached from its body, motion without life. She felt the dissonance between progress and coherence, between proof and purpose. Drift had not yet shouted; it whispered through the patternless motion of success.

Two hours later, the silence fractured into contradiction.

"We're sequencing by value streams," one insisted, voice tight with resolve.
"No, backlog must be risk-weighted," countered another, brows furrowed.
"That ignores how the model calculates dependencies," a third added, tone sharp but uncertain.

Terms collided. Playbooks clashed. Expertise flowed but refused to align. The room thickened with ten polished versions of 'right,' each competing for authority.

As voices overlapped, Sasha began to diagram the conflict on a notepad; circles and arrows that refused to meet. The picture became her proof.

Each team spoke fluent mastery in a dialect no one else could translate. Charts overlapped, frameworks nested within contradictions. A systems architect displayed a flow diagram that contradicted the risk matrix another leader swore by. Every chart was technically correct, every model precise, and together they produced incoherence.

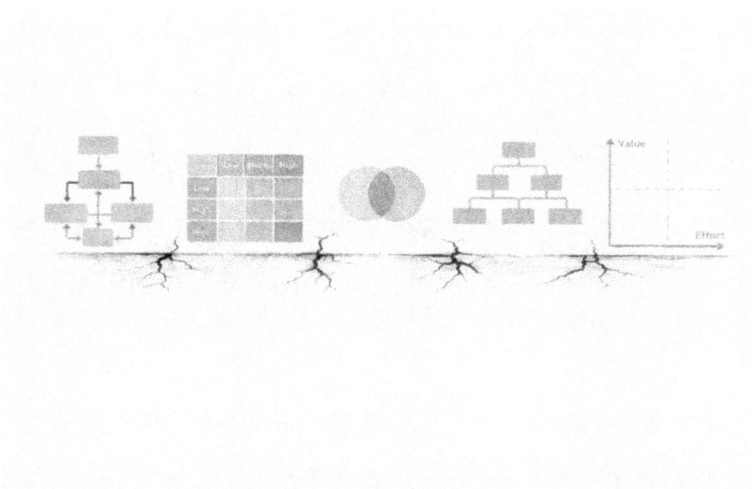

Figure 2.1 Drift of Learning

Drift does not require ignorance. It emerges when mastery grows without convergence, turning parallel models into contradiction and fragmenting learning into incoherent systems.

The Academy had created excellence in isolation. Drift did not need incompetence to grow; it thrived on uncoordinated mastery. Sasha watched the room fragment into small domains of certainty, each defended by data and confidence.

Sasha leaned forward, cutting in. "If every team runs a different model, the architecture erodes. Training only works if it converges." Her words fell into the noise, acknowledged with nods but absorbed by no one.

Reg remained composed, gaze fixed on his phone; presence without structure, confidence without command. His calm filled the space, but it offered no structure. Sasha felt the void behind his confidence, the contrast between her fight for alignment and his detachment.

This was Drift wearing a new mask; not exhaustion, but fragmentation. Energy turning to friction, learning without a spine.

From the back wall, Marcus watched. His silence, once surrendered, had sharpened into unease. He mapped the arguments: different metrics, shifting cadences, conflicting definitions of done. Sasha caught his eye, he saw it too, but he stayed quiet.

The Academy had trained them to drive faster, but the roads no longer met.

The crisis chose its moment. Vertex, a mission-critical client, had staked its quarter on Atlas, the company's platform integration. The launch window was tight, the penalty clause unforgiving.

Atlas was the showcase of the Academy's success, built by the most trained teams.

When the first alerts appeared, Sasha didn't panic. She opened the training index instead, tracing the divergence she already suspected.

By 01:22, Vertex's pipeline flickered. Fifteen minutes later, it stalled. Within the hour, error rates spiked into territory no one had rehearsed.

The fault was traced to competing playbooks. One path assumed safety; another pressed for speed. Both had been taught, both were valid in isolation together, they triggered collapse.

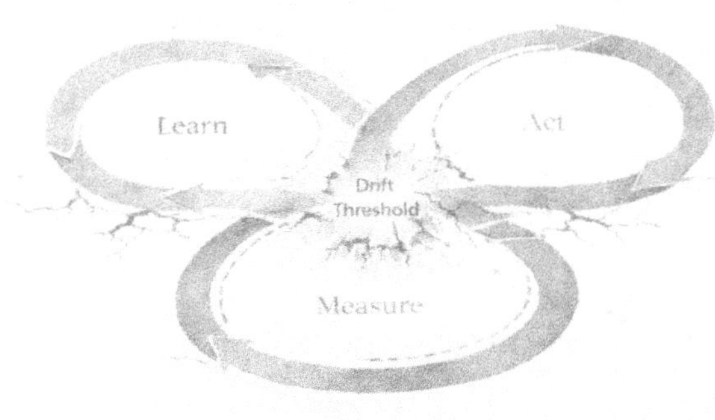

Figure 2.2 Diverging Learning Loops

When learning, action, and measurement fail to converge, feedback loops amplify drift rather than correct it.

In the control room, monitors pulsed red. Two Slack threads argued rollback sequences line by line. "Follow Protocol 9B," one lead insisted, pasting the certified steps. "No, that's an outdated switch to SafeRevert," another shot back. Both referenced Academy documents stamped with approval dates, both certain of compliance. The system hesitated under dueling commands, then froze. The engineers weren't confused, they were over-informed. Knowledge collided because alignment had never been engineered. Sasha watched the feed degrade, realizing the teams weren't failing execution; they were obeying incompatible architectures.

Rollback should have been routine. It wasn't. The night lead, newly certified and confident, followed a rollback path taught in training. He executed the command with faith in that training, unaware the system beneath had already diverged.

But the map no longer matched the terrain. The paths contradicted each other, each validated in its own course. The system faltered not from ignorance, but from knowledge eroded into noise by misalignment.

Sasha read the logs, the conflicting sequences. In that moment, clarity cut through her unease: It wasn't operator error; it was architectural error. It was Drift, converting learning into collapse. Training had multiplied speed, but without structure it multiplied erosion faster.

The Academy had built knowledge. Drift had turned it against itself.

Hal's body had collapsed. Carol's strength had eroded. Marcus's silence had surrendered. And now Sasha saw the pattern extend beyond people: even learning, without alignment, was collapsing under Drift's weight.

Drift does not waste strength. It weaponizes it. Knowledge, like effort, corrodes when stripped of architecture. Without design, every gain bends toward collapse.

Learning without alignment is noise. Noise erodes into Drift, and Drift always ends in collapse.

Dawn thinned the office air into a quiet gray. Monitors cooled from red to idle. Sasha and Marcus stayed, surrounded by the static of exhausted systems. No one spoke for several minutes. Then Sasha drew the first line on the whiteboard; a single spine connecting the splintered playbooks.

"This isn't a post-mortem," she said. "It's a reconstruction."

They began mapping the contradictions to rebuild a single architecture, cataloging where each version of "right" diverged. Marcus traced loops that led nowhere. "It's not failure," he said, "it's divergence." He moved from the wall to the table, silent no longer, marker in hand beside hers.

"Then we design convergence," Sasha replied.

They outlined what she called the Alignment Audit: a living map where every learning module, playbook, and tool would reconcile to one architecture before release. Each law would have one definition, one owner, one place in structure.

When the sun caught the glass behind them, the room seemed less defeated. Drift reduced the old system to its elemental truth, clarity through collapse. Sasha looked at the new framework taking shape and spoke quietly, as if to the doctrine itself.

"Learning must not multiply," she said. "It must unify."

Maxim: Learning without alignment fractures into noise.

II. Doctrine & Diagnostic

Learning culture seduces through metrics: hours counted, courses completed, dashboards filled. Applause follows as employees "engage" in development programs. But beneath the surface, learning organizational cultures (LOCs) built on activity without alignment reveal structural fragility. Progress without design is fragility disguised as evolution.

Noise replaces mastery. Dialogue collapses into ritual. Structure fades, leaving Drift room to erode discipline. Learning without architecture is Drift disguised as growth.

Key Terms

- **LOCs (Learning Organizational Cultures):** engage in rituals of training and knowledge-sharing to expand capacity, where true learning converts knowledge into lasting, resilient performance through deliberate structural design.
- **Rituals**: deliberate, repeated practices embedding structure into daily operations.
- **Orphan:** performance element detached from architectural authority and structural enforcement, surviving through habit or individual effort rather than design.

Flaws of Learning Organizational Cultures

1. Personal Mastery → Exhaustion

LOCs glorify self-directed growth and abandon structural support; learning becomes labor. Employees are told to own their growth without the structure that makes growth durable. Nights and weekends become classrooms. Skills accumulate in isolation, never embedded in structure. Instead of mastery, Drift produces exhaustion.

PMC Response

Capability pathways define role-based skills tied directly to outcomes.

Protected time for growth is embedded in workflows.

Learning investment is tested in live work within 30 days.

Enforceable Feedback Loop

1. Managers own the quarterly capability plan.
2. HR enforces protected time.
3. Application logs provide evidence of impact.

Doctrinal Closure

- Growth built on personal sacrifice converts learning into depletion.
- Training without structure consumes capacity faster than it builds competence.
- Effort without architecture is Drift disguised as ambition.

Transition

Exhaustion drains curiosity until certainty feels like safety. Fatigue turns questioning into defense, the origin of entrenched assumptions.

2. Mental Models → Entrenched Assumptions

LOCs preach reflection but reward defensiveness. Leaders protect positions. Teams preserve obsolete logic as policy. "Dialogue" becomes a debate where the loudest voice wins. Assumptions harden into ruts. Innovation suffocates.

PMC Response

Assumption registers track and test critical beliefs for major initiatives.

Counter-evidence rituals force challenges into the open before decisions are finalized.

Post-mortems are structured reviews with pre-declared pivot or kill criteria.

Enforceable Feedback Loop

1. Initiative leads maintain live assumption registers.
2. Executive sponsors review counter-evidence without bias.
3. Decision reviews require evidence before sign-off.

Doctrinal Closure

- Performative reflection hardens belief into bias.
- Unchallenged assumptions manufacture stagnation and teach Drift as culture.
- Certainty untested by evidence hardens into ignorance engineered into culture.

Transition

Unquestioned belief blinds vision; perception replaces purpose. Compliance follows where clarity once lived.

3. Shared Vision → Slogan Compliance

LOCs celebrate shared purpose but deliver posters and speeches. Employees nod, smile, and comply, but behavior remains unchanged. Commitment is feigned; alignment is absent. Vision becomes performance theater.

PMC Response

Strategy-to-execution links learning initiatives to specific outcomes and behaviors.

Orphan audits eliminate training or programs not mapped to measurable results.

Rewards are tied to measurable outcome movement.

Enforceable Feedback Loop

1. Strategy offices own quarterly execution spines.
2. Finance audits orphaned spend.
3. Performance dashboards provide evidence of vision translated into results.
4. Vision becomes measurable, not rhetorical.

Doctrinal Closure

- Vision declared without structure turns purpose into theater.
- Unmeasured aspiration breeds hypocrisy and fractures trust.
- Vision without structure breeds Drift disguised as unity.

Transition

Disillusioned teams trade dialogue for decorum; purpose becomes theater.

4. Team Learning → Coordinated Silence

LOCs mistake harmony for learning. Meetings become polite rituals where questions die unsaid. Consensus buries conflict and recasts avoidance as collaboration. The appearance of collaboration conceals the absence of truth.

PMC Response

Truth cadence enforces candid after-action reviews with named owners.

Silence breakers, challenger reviews and anonymous pre-reads surface dissent.

Participation is tracked and distributed to eliminate single voice dominance.

Enforceable Feedback Loop

1. Project managers schedule after-action reviews as mandatory checkpoints
2. Facilitators own silence-breakers
3. Participation metrics are published as evidence.

Doctrinal Closure

- Harmony maintained at truth's expense dismantles learning.
- Consensus without candor erodes structure faster than conflict.
- Silence converts civility into Drift.

Transition

Muted structures lose coherence; unspoken tension fractures accountability. Fragmentation follows as silence becomes the norm rather than the deviation

5. Systems Thinking → Local Blame

LOCs can collapse under pressure into linear cause-and-effect thinking. Leaders blame departments, customers, or competitors. Interdependencies collapse under blame. Fragmentation becomes the default.

PMC Response

Structural cause mapping targets leverage points.

Cross-functional accountability is enforced for structural fixes.

Flow controls expose constraints and rework.

Enforceable Feedback Loop

1. Operations leaders own structural cause maps.
2. Cross-functional councils review leverage points monthly.
3. Dashboards provide evidence of structural fixes.
4. Structural health is proven.

Doctrinal Closure

- Fragmented accountability destroys coherence.
- Blame isolates what design exists to integrate.
- Isolation marks the terminal stage of Drift before collapse.

Architectural Truths

- Learning without alignment fractures.
- Noise replaces mastery when structure is absent.
- Fragmented learning accelerates collapse.
- Mastery must be engineered, not assumed.
- Drift disguises itself as progress.

Diagnostic Tool: The Learning-to-Performance Loop

Purpose

Determine whether learning expands operational capacity through coherence and application, or collapses into Drift through fragmentation, contradiction, and activity-based rituals.

Diagnostic Dimensions

1. Architectural Alignment

Definition

Assesses whether learning programs are mapped to business outcomes before activity begins.

Propagation / Performance Indicator

Learning flows are anchored to clear objectives. Definitions, decision rights, and success criteria are shared across teams. Instruction, metrics, and expectations match the operating model.

Drift Indicator

Training is produced without alignment. Programs multiply. Teams interpret concepts differently. Knowledge collides under pressure and coherence erodes.

2. Application Discipline (30-Day Window)

Definition

Evaluates whether learned skills are applied in real work rapidly and consistently.

Propagation / Performance Indicator

Teams apply newly learned skills within 30 days. Application is enforced through workflow design, reinforced by managers, and visible in practice.

Drift Indicator

Certificates accumulate but behaviors do not change. Application is optional or delayed. Teams revert to prior habits when deadlines or pressure rise.

3. Integration & Coherence

Definition

Determines whether the organization maintains a unified playbook, shared language, and consistent methods across functions.

Propagation / Performance Indicator

A single, enforced architecture exists. Metrics, cadences, and decisions flow through common systems. Pressure tightens cohesion.

Drift Indicator

Teams create their own methods, tools, and interpretations. Contradictions multiply. Under stress, fragmentation accelerates as each group defends its version of the truth.

4. Outcome Conversion (90-Day Evidence)

Definition

Assesses whether learning produces measurable improvements in the work itself.

Propagation / Performance Indicator

At least one operational metric linked to the learning objective improves by ≥10% within 90 days. Performance gains are traceable to the learning system.

Drift Indicator

Training volume rises but outcomes remain flat or degrade. Leaders celebrate activity (hours, completions) instead of results. Learning becomes noise.

5. Drift Resistance Under Pressure

Definition

Reveals whether pressure strengthens capacity through coherence or exposes fragility through collapse.

Propagation / Performance Indicator

Under pressure, teams converge on shared practice. Knowledge becomes more precise. Integration deepens. Capacity expands reliably.

Drift Indicator

Pressure splinters alignment. Contradictions surface instantly: safety vs speed, backlog vs risk, compliance vs output. Learning dissolves into conflict, guesswork, or silence.

Scoring Standard (1–5: Drift → Validated)

1. **Severe Drift:** Training and activity substitute for performance. Contradictions dominate. Collapse becomes predictable under pressure.
2. **High Drift:** Learning efforts multiply but remain disconnected. Application is rare. Pressure exposes fragmentation and erodes confidence.
3. **Unstable:** Some alignment exists, but practices diverge across teams. Outcomes are inconsistent. Drift activates when stress increases.
4. **Strong Alignment:** Learning is coherently designed, widely applied, and reinforced by shared metrics. Drift appears only at edges.
5. **Validated Architecture:** Learning reliably converts into capacity. Application and coherence are enforced. Outcomes improve predictably. Pressure strengthens mastery.

Interpretation Guide

Validated Architecture (19–25):

1. Learning acts as an engine of capability.
2. Application occurs rapidly.
3. Coherence is protected.
4. Outcomes improve within predictable windows.
5. Pressure fortifies alignment and accelerates mastery.

Drift Detected (1–18):

1. Learning is activity-based.
2. Contradictions multiply across teams.
3. Application collapses under time pressure.
4. Outcomes stagnate despite heavy training investment.
5. Drift erodes capability until collapse.

Structural Closing Line

A learning system either compounds capability through coherence and application, or it feeds Drift; where knowledge fragments, contradictions rise, and performance collapses when coherence determines survival.

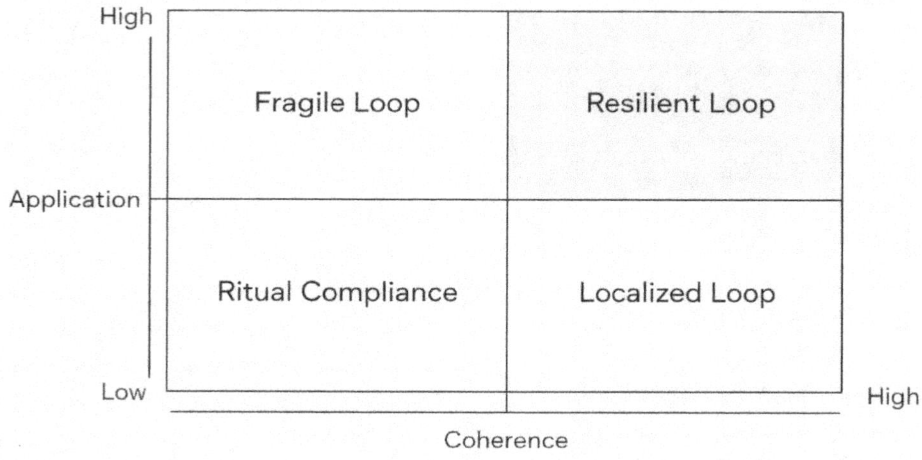

Figure 2.3 The Learning-to-Performance Loop

Learning compounds into resilience only when coherence and application are engineered together.

Leader's Challenge

Learning has already revealed the truth of your organization; you have simply mistaken its movement for mastery.

Your teams did not fracture by accident.

Your architecture allowed it.

If learning produces motion but not coherence, it is because you accepted activity in place of structure.

If teams argue over "right" under pressure, it is because you permitted knowledge to grow without alignment.

If experts defend competing playbooks, it is because you celebrated mastery without engineering convergence.

If training multiplies confidence but not consistency, it is because you treated instruction as design.

If outcomes stagnate despite full dashboards, it is because Drift has been shaping your learning architecture while you measured the wrong things.

These are not failures of effort.

They are failures of alignment.

Failures of architecture.

And architecture is your responsibility.

Every leader reaches the moment where Drift stops whispering and starts revealing the contradictions you allowed.

The moment where knowledge collides because you never required it to converge.

The moment where confidence outpaces coherence.

The moment where learning, unstructured and ungoverned, becomes the engine of failure.

This is that moment.

You cannot lead a resilient organization while defending a learning architecture that multiplies divergence.

You cannot claim to value mastery while allowing every team to define its own version of it.

You cannot call your culture strong if knowledge collapses into contradiction at the first sign of pressure.

Learning reveals design.

What it has revealed so far, does it resemble the design you intended to build?

Your challenge is not to expand learning.

Your challenge is to confront the architecture you allowed.

To face the contradictions you ignored.

To decide whether your leadership will continue multiplying noise or begin engineering coherence.

Every learning architecture loops.

Yours is already moving, toward collapse or toward capacity.

The direction is not accidental.

It is built.

The question is whether you will be the leader who finally stops Drift in your learning architecture, or the one who lets Drift finish its work.

III. ESSENCE OF EXECUTION

1. Core Execution Truth

Learning without alignment fractures into noise.

2. Indicators of Drift

1. Teams apply competing models, frameworks, or playbooks.
2. Training increases confidence but not consistency.
3. Experts defend contradictory definitions of "right."
4. Knowledge grows faster than coherence.
5. Dashboards show activity while outcomes stagnate.

3. Essential Leader Actions

1. Align all learning to one architecture with single-source definitions.
2. Engineer convergence across teams before new training is released.
3. Enforce coherence by eliminating conflicting playbooks and models.
4. Test learning in live work to verify structural integration.
5. Anchor mastery to design, not interpretation or preference.

4. Enforceable Feedback Requirements

1. Alignment audits verify every module, tool, and playbook against one architecture.
2. Convergence checks trigger when teams diverge in method or definition.
3. Outcome reviews require evidence that training improved coherence, not volume.
4. Contradiction logs document where learning fractures and require corrective design.

5. The Decisive Question

Will your learning architecture produce coherence intentionally, or fragmentation by neglect?

IV. Rapid Orientation: Drift–Architecture Spectrum

Use this rubric for orientation, not validation. If your structures do not hold under pressure and turnover, you are in Drift regardless of intent or progress.

1. **Severe Drift:** Training and activity substitute for performance. Contradictions dominate. Collapse becomes predictable under pressure.
2. **High Drift:** Learning efforts multiply but remain disconnected. Application is rare. Pressure exposes fragmentation and erodes confidence.
3. **Unstable:** Some alignment exists, but practices diverge across teams. Outcomes are inconsistent. Drift activates when stress increases.
4. **Strong Alignment:** Learning is coherently designed, widely applied, and reinforced by shared metrics. Drift appears only at edges.
5. **Validated Architecture:** Learning reliably converts into capacity. Application and coherence are enforced. Outcomes improve predictably. Pressure strengthens mastery.

Chapter 3 – Myth of Episodic Change

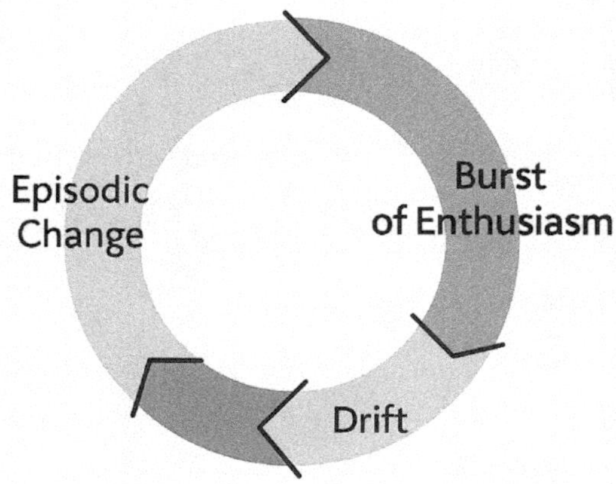

Figure 3.1 The Episodic Change Cycle

Change launched as an event spikes energy, drifts, collapses quietly, and repeats because no architecture holds it in place.

I. Story: Marcus and his Ledger of Collapse

Fourth row. Jaw locked, Marcus braced for another ceremony of promised transformation. Screens glowed across the auditorium. The banner read: Transformation 2025. Music lifted the room into a practiced swell.

To his left, a young analyst leaned forward with a fresh notebook. The pen hovered. Eyes bright. Marcus could almost see the belief forming on the page. This time will be different.

He tightened his arms across his chest and kept a ledger in silence: One Company. Agile Wave. Vision 2010. Digital First. Five bursts, five collapses. No burials, only Drift.

He carried the costs as a private inventory, counted but never spoken. The inventory opened with a single night: the Friday night his daughter waited poolside in her swimsuit, scanning the bleachers for him, while he sat through a leadership town hall about reinvention. She swam her fastest race that night, touching the wall first, turning with wide eyes to find his face. The lane judge clapped. Teammates cheered. The bleachers roared. But the seat she searched for remained empty. Marcus sat miles away, nodding through slides that no one would remember six months later.

The Sunday he promised to be present for the family BBQ, he stared instead at a slide deck of promises already obsolete. The call he never returned when his father went back to the hospital, another entry in the ledger. Each sacrifice paid into initiatives that vanished without acknowledgement.

It was not bitter. It was proof that Drift converts sacrifice into silence.

Across the aisle, Carol sat with her laptop half-closed. She had carried the weight of three roles since Agile Wave had collapsed, and every new program promised more resets. The banner meant nothing to her, just another load waiting to be dropped on the same shoulders.

Two rows behind, a frontline engineer whispered to her neighbor, "We don't change. We wait for the storm to pass." Pens stayed capped, signaling the same quiet resistance. Toolkits from the last campaign are still in unopened boxes under their desks.

At the edges of the room, mid-level managers traded glances. They had logged red flags in risk registers before, only to see them ignored in quarterly reviews. One muttered quietly, "Why raise a flag if it only paints a target on me?" Silence was safer.

The pattern was always the same. A sudden launch wrapped in language that sparkled. Posters on walls. Toolkits stacked on tables. Dashboards bright for a quarter then dimmed. Executive sponsors shifting attention. Metrics sliding back to baseline. Teams dissolved quietly. Hallways were cleared of slogans overnight, as if the building itself had decided to forget.

Marcus whispered so only he could hear. We do not adapt. We rehearse collapse.

On stage, Reg's voice amplified into confidence. "We are entering a season of lasting renewal. This transformation will be disciplined. It will be different."

Marcus felt the familiar rise of heat behind his ribs. He had heard this script. He had served it. He had sold pieces of himself to it.

He lifted his hand.

The room paused. Heads turned. A few smiles tightened. Everyone recognized the question inside the question.

Reg nodded toward him. "Go ahead, Marcus."

Marcus kept his voice steady. "What makes this different from the last five?"

Silence expanded. A cough. A chair shifted. The young analyst's pen froze above the page.

Reg adjusted his cufflink, a motion too deliberate to be casual. He started to speak, then stopped. The words he had prepared, "new partners, better tracking", sounded hollow even to him. He leaned forward, not in command, but in reckoning.

From the back, Imara rose. She did not need to command attention; the room turned toward her as if drawn. She stood until the whispers drained away.

She waited. The silence tightened. Then she spoke, clipped and spaced. "Marcus asks the only question that matters. Declare change as an event, and it dies as an event. Systems do not bend to posters. They bend to design."

Something in Marcus resisted. He almost dismissed her as another voice in the long parade of consultants. He had heard architecture before, wrapped in different words. Yet as she spoke of assumption registers and cadence, memories broke loose inside him. He remembered approving a risky shortcut just to save time. He remembered staying silent instead of warning that a project was drifting off course. Both decisions led to collapse. He wanted to deny the connection, but denial had nowhere left to hide.

He remembered a steering meeting where risks were read aloud, sponsors nodded gravely and then adjourned with nothing fixed. Authority stayed distant, untouched by the consequences. The collapse arrived right on time.

Imara's words came like hammer blows, each followed by silence.
"Architecture makes adaptability routine, not exceptional."
"Assumption registers drag risk into daylight before signatures dry."
"Feedback cadence surfaces truth weekly, not after the wreckage."
"These are not workshops. They are circuits that hold under pressure."

Marcus saw scenes he had carried like scars that never fully healed. A kickoff where untested shortcuts were nodded through to save time. Six months later the shortcut failed, and the team worked nights to hide the damage. A warning he never gave because the executive sponsor seemed tired. Collapse without postmortem, replaced by a new initiative two weeks later.

He thought of Carol, carrying the weight of three people until her health frayed. Of colleagues who disappeared after the cycle repeated once too often, unable to keep sacrificing into silence. Of a product launched too thin and too late, handed to a competitor on a silver plate. Drift did not just consume him; it consumed them all.

He imagined a live assumption register. Contradictions caught before they matured into failures. He imagined a fixed cadence for red flags. Truth would not depend on courage. It would have a calendar.

For the first time in years, his cynicism bent toward possibility.

The young analyst's pen hovered, then scribbled a single word. They stared at it, the ink trembling as if even the page questioned it. Marcus could not see the word, only the hesitation. In that pause he recognized himself years earlier, when he too had once believed enough to write before the ledger began.

Imara let the reality settle. Then she cut again. "Collapse is not an accident. It is engineered by the absence of engineered adaptability."

A memory rose without permission. Friday night at the pool. His daughter's race. The empty seat. He had told himself it was the price of ambition. He knew now it had been a payment into Drift.

The auditorium was quiet. Not polite, quiet. Weight is quiet.

Imara lifted her hand. "When leaders declare an event, they buy a spike. When they design a system, they earn endurance. The spike is exciting. Endurance demands. It requires you to make change measurable and defend it in public. Refuse that work, and Drift owns your outcomes."

Anger rose in Marcus, then sharpened into resolve. Not against Reg. Against himself. He had carried silence long enough. This time, when he raised his hand, he knew the question would not be erased.

Marcus' ledger was not grievance; it was evidence. Five campaigns, five collapses. Each promised transformation, each consumed trust, each erased without burial. This is the architecture of episodic change: spectacle without system, declarations without design, promises without permanence.

Episodic change does not fail by accident. It fails by design. Without architecture, every initiative erodes toward collapse.

Episodic change is a myth. Adaptability must be embedded, or Drift owns the future.

Maxim: Collapse is permitted; adaptability is architectural.

II. Doctrine & Diagnostic

Episodic change is seductive. Leaders launch it with banners, dashboards, and bold speeches. Applause follows, momentum swells, and hope briefly returns.
Episodic change seduces leadership into mistaking performance for permanence. Energy without architecture ignites briefly and collapses by design. Only engineered systems convert momentum into mastery and make adaptability measurable.

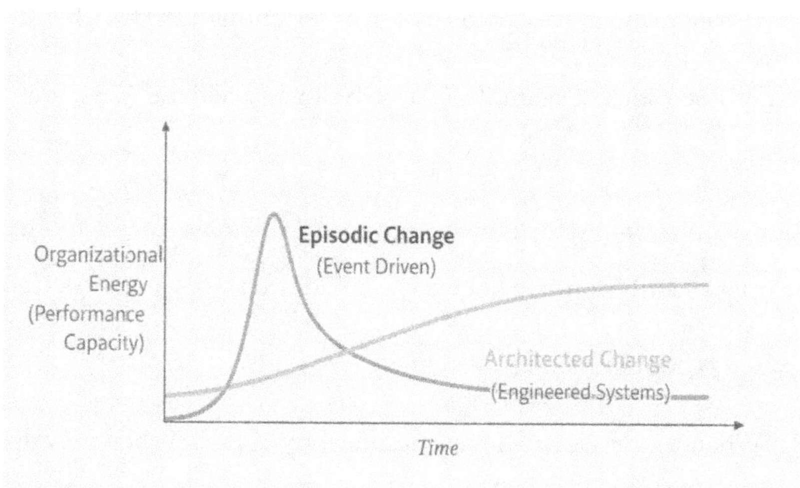

Figure 3.2 Energy Spikes vs. Endurance

Events spike energy but cannot sustain it. Without architecture, Drift inevitably consumes every initiative.

Key Terms

- **Episodic Change:** change launched as a discrete event, campaign, or program. It generates short-term enthusiasm but collapses because it lacks systemic reinforcement.

- **Architect Change:** change designed as "enforceable circuits," closed loops that connect risks, decisions, accountability, and evidence making adaptation routine.
- **Systems Mapping:** visualizing and analyzing interdependencies across processes, structures, and stakeholders to anticipate points of fragility.
- **Enforceable Feedback Loop:** a closed cycle locking assumptions, evidence, accountability, and action together so adaptation becomes unavoidable. It is built into system design and compels response rather than relying on discretion.

Flaws of Episodic Change

1. Events Masquerading as Transformation

Episodic change dazzles at launch. Leaders rent arenas, commission videos, distribute branded toolkits, and declare a "new era." Energy spikes, applause swells, and for a moment, belief flickers. Beneath the spectacle lies fragility. Events masquerade as transformation because they ignite enthusiasm without altering the system. Momentum collapses the moment the banners are folded away.

PMC Response

Treat every change as system design.

Make adaptation a daily operating discipline.

Define resilience as the ability to sustain capacity under pressure.

Enforceable Feedback Loop

1. No initiative declared until its assumption register, stakeholder engagement plan, and feedback cadence are published.
2. Dashboards stay live for the full life cycle.

Doctrinal Closure

- Transformation declared as spectacle engineers collapse.
- Launch rallies without embedded system design produce momentum that evaporates.
- Energy spiked without architecture becomes Drift disguised as ambition.

Transition

When events masquerade as transformation, collapse is rehearsed in spectacle.

2. Tracking Without Architecture

Dashboards and metrics give the illusion of control, but without architecture they measure activity instead of adaptation. Dashboards light up, only to go dark when numbers dip. Drift thrives in the silence that follows.

PMC Response

Track adaptability and capacity to adjust under real conditions.

Link every measure to assumptions, risks, and corrective actions.

Use systems mapping to expose interdependencies and pressure points.

Enforceable Feedback Loop

1. Dashboards remain visible until issues are resolved.
2. Place adaptation metrics (assumptions tested, pivots made, risks closed) beside outcome metrics.

Doctrinal Closure

- Dashboards detached from architecture convert oversight into illusion.
- Metrics ignoring interdependence validate activity while systems erode.
- Tracking without feedback loops engineers Drift by design.

Transition

When tracking is hollow, oversight becomes theater.

3. Oversight Without Authority

Episodic change appoints committees, sponsors, and tracking partners who convene meetings but lack power. Oversight becomes theater: reviews are held, risks noted, but no action follows. Distance between authority and execution designs collapse as certainty.

PMC Response

Authority and accountability must be inseparable.

Decision rights belong to those closest to delivery, not observers at a distance.

Governance embeds stakeholders with power, not figureheads.

Enforceable Feedback Loop

1. Map and publish decision rights for every initiative.
2. Require named accountability and evidence for closing risks.

Doctrinal Closure

- Governance without decision-rights fabricates observation instead of resolution.
- Committees that record risks but cannot act institutionalize paralysis.
- Accountability divided from authority manufactures Drift as policy.

Transition

When oversight lacks authority, review becomes ritual and collapse becomes certain.

4. Silence as Policy

In episodic change, failure is buried without acknowledgment. No postmortems, no lessons, no evidence carried forward. Employees carry the unspoken truth: their sacrifice was erased. Silence becomes policy, cynicism becomes culture.

PMC Response

Mandate structural acknowledgment of failure.

Institutionalize after-action reviews and counter-evidence rituals.

Enforce iterative learning cycles to carry lessons into the next phase.

Enforceable Feedback Loop

1. End every initiative with a mandatory closeout review: evidence logged, assumptions tested, lessons published.
2. Red risks remain visible until closure is evidenced.
3. Silence is prohibited.

Doctrinal Closure

- Unspoken failure becomes doctrine that instructs erosion.
- Omissions repeated across cycles erase evidence and disable learning.
- Culture forbidding acknowledgment transforms Drift into identity.

Transition

Silence repeated as policy transforms review into ritual.

5. Resets as Ritual

Episodic change buries the past by overwriting it with new declarations. Each reset pretends to start fresh while ignoring unresolved flaws. Marcus carried a ledger of initiatives erased by the next campaign: One Company, Agile Wave, Vision 2010, Digital First. Each new reset deepened cynicism.

PMC Response

Preserve history and integrate prior lessons into new initiatives.

Design continuity engines that resist Drift.

Iterative learning is the backbone of resilience.

Enforceable Feedback Loop

1. Publish evidence of applied lessons before launching a new initiative.
2. Require proof of continuity for all reset declarations.

Doctrinal Closure

- Rebranding collapse as renewal embeds exhaustion into design.
- Resets that overwrite history delete evidence required for endurance.
- Continuity abandoned in pursuit of novelty guarantees recurrence as routine.

Architectural Truths

- Spectacle fades; architecture sustains transformation.
- Metrics without enforcement institutionalize false confidence.
- Oversight without authority is negligence engineered to collapse.
- Silence unchallenged defines culture.
- Adaptability is engineered through enforceable loops.

Diagnostic Tool: The Change-Ability Scorecard

Purpose

Determine whether adaptability is embedded in the organization's architecture, or collapses into Drift through episodic programs, personality dependence, and pressure-induced fracture.

Diagnostic Dimensions

1. Leadership Response

Definition

Assesses whether adaptability is modeled and enforced through distributed leadership, rather than dependent on individual champions.

Propagation / Performance Indicator

Leadership behaviors are coherent across levels. Momentum continues uninterrupted when a senior leader exits. Change expectations are stable, repeatable, and independent of personality.

Drift Indicator

Adaptability collapses when a sponsor departs. Momentum stalls, narratives shift, and change defaults to charisma, heroics, and episodic events.

2. Systems Alignment

Definition

Evaluates whether core systems absorb new initiatives without friction or contradiction.

Propagation / Performance Indicator:

New initiatives integrate seamlessly. Cadences, incentives, tools, and workflows flex under pressure without redundancy. Architecture adapts without rework.

Drift Indicator

Initiatives bolt onto rigid systems. Conflicts multiply. Workarounds become normal. Redundancies spread as each new effort competes with existing workflows.

3. Feedback & Learning

Definition

Determines whether feedback is institutionalized as a real-time operating mechanism or appears only during crisis cycles.

Propagation / Performance Indicator

Continuous feedback loops function under pressure. Lessons are captured, integrated, and applied in the next operational cycle. Learning accelerates adaptation.

Drift Indicator

Post-crisis retrospectives produce temporary insight, but practices revert. Lessons vanish between cycles. Learning resets with each initiative.

4. Decision-Making

Definition

Assesses whether decision rights are distributed, time-responsive, and structurally aligned with accountability.

Propagation / Performance Indicator

Decisions accelerate as conditions shift. Teams act within clear boundaries. Authority, accountability, and responsibility are structurally synchronized.

Drift Indicator

Oversight bodies meet but lack power. Authority bottlenecks stall adaptation. Decisions are delayed or escalated unnecessarily when volatility increases.

5. Cultural Identity

Definition

Evaluates whether adaptability is internalized as identity or absorbed as fatigue and resignation.

Propagation / Performance Indicator

Candor, dissent, and psychological safety are enforced norms. Change is expected, practiced, and shared. Language reflects ownership rather than resistance.

Drift Indicator

Employees brace for "the next program." Silence increases. Fatigue becomes a cultural memory. Adaptability is viewed as disruption rather than routine practice.

6. Resource Fluidity

Definition

Reveals whether people, budgets, and capacity can be redeployed without destabilizing performance.

Propagation / Performance Indicator

Resources shift rapidly across priorities. Performance stays stable when key individuals are unavailable. Teams absorb change without degradation.

Drift Indicator

Rigid budgets, fixed roles, and hero-dependence dominate. When a key contributor is absent, output collapses and rework expands.

Scoring Standard (1-5: Drift → Validated)

1. **Severe Drift:** Adaptability is an illusion. Pressure ensures collapse. Systems fracture, leadership dependency is absolute, and change evaporates without constant force.
2. **High Drift:** Some efforts exist, but they are episodic. Systems conflict with change. Bottlenecks, friction, and contradictions grow under pressure.
3. **Unstable:** Capabilities are uneven. Some functions adapt; others resist. Momentum depends on conditions and specific individuals. Drift activates quickly.
4. **Strong Alignment:** Adaptability is designed and repeatable. Systems flex. Decisions accelerate. Drift appears only in isolated pockets under extreme conditions.
5. **Validated Architecture:** Adaptability is embedded. Architecture absorbs disruption without loss of coherence. Pressure strengthens execution, not resistance.

Interpretation Guide

Validated Architecture: (23-30)

1. Adaptability is systemic.
2. Leadership is distributed.
3. Systems flex without fracture.
4. Feedback accelerates learning.
5. Decisions remain fast under pressure.
6. Resources shift without destabilizing performance.
7. Pressure strengthens alignment and accelerates execution.

Drift Detected: (1-22)

1. Adaptability is performative.

2. Systems resist change.
3. Learning resets each cycle.
4. Decisions slow as volatility rises.
5. Resources lock, bottlenecks spread, and personalities dominate outcomes.
6. Under pressure, fracture exceeds capacity and collapse becomes predictable.

Structural Closing Line

An organization either embeds adaptability through architecture: leadership, systems, learning, decisions, culture, and resources or it feeds Drift; where rigidity holds, fracture accelerates, and collapse becomes the operating model when conditions shift.

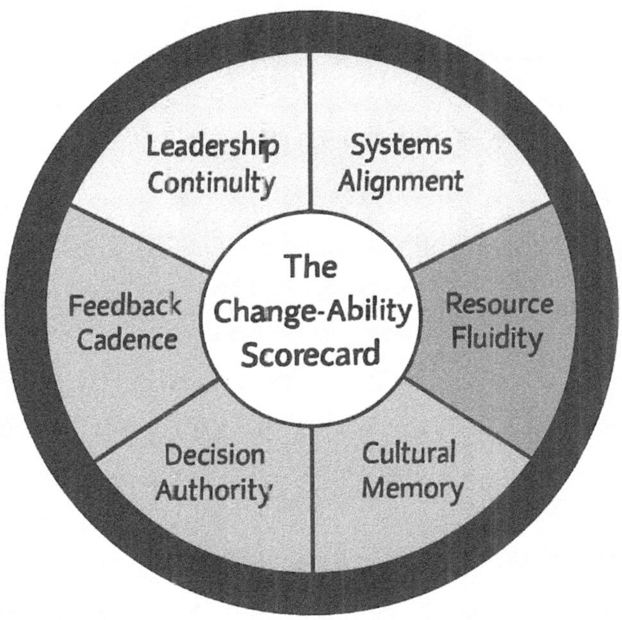

Figure 3.3 The Change-Ability Scorecard

Adaptability is durable only when all structural dimensions hold under pressure; weakness in any one converts change into Drift.

The Scorecard strips illusion. It exposes adaptability as embedded in design or consumed by collapse advancing. The numbers are not neutral. They expose the architecture you chose. Leaders tolerating Drift design collapse as policy. Fragility accepted is erosion engineered. The verdict is final. The challenge is immediate

Leader's Challenge

You already know the truth of your change architecture; you have mistaken spectacle for structure and repetition for resilience.
Your own history is a ledger: launches without architecture, collapses without acknowledgment. That ledger is not cynicism. It is evidence.

Every time you declare a "new era," you purchase a spike instead of building an architecture.
Dashboards flared. Toolkits gathered dust. Oversight met without power. Silence replaced lessons. Resets buried history.
None of this was accidental. It was architecture, architecture of Drift.

If momentum dies when a sponsor leaves, it is because adaptability depends on personality, not architecture.
If risks reappear every cycle, it is because you track activity, not adaptation.
If teams wait out the storm, it is because your culture has learned the truth: events are temporary, collapse is predictable.

These are not failures of effort.
They are failures of architecture.
And architecture is your responsibility.

You cannot lead resilience while defending episodic change.
You cannot claim transformation when your architecture rejects it on contact.
You cannot call your culture strong if a banner can ignite enthusiasm, but pressure instantly exposes fragility.

Change reveals architecture.
Does it resemble the architecture you intended?

Your challenge is not to launch another program.

Your challenge is to end the myth you have been sustaining.

To replace spectacle with architecture.

To enforce assumption registers, decision-rights, feedback cadence, and continuity; before announcements, not after collapse.

Episodic change always loops toward erosion.

Architect change loops toward endurance.

The direction is not accidental.

It is engineered.

Figure 3.4 Architecture of Enforceable Adaptability

Adaptability becomes enforceable when oversight, accountability, and authority are structurally aligned.

The question is whether you will continue rehearsing collapse or finally create an architecture that cannot drift.

III. Essence of Execution

1. Core Execution Truth

Collapse is engineered; adaptability is architectural.

2. Indicators of Drift

1. Momentum dies when sponsors shift attention or depart.
2. Dashboards spike briefly, then dim as numbers revert to baseline.
3. Risks recur across cycles without closure or consequence.
4. Committees review but cannot act; authority bottlenecks stall change.
5. Resets overwrite history, deepening cynicism and erasing evidence.

3. Essential Leader Actions

1. Design changes as architecture, not events.
2. Embed assumption registers, decision-rights, and cadence before announcement.
3. Build continuity engines that preserve history and enforce learning transfer.
4. Require authority and accountability to move together in every initiative.
5. Keep adaptation measurable through architecture, not personalities.

4. Enforceable Feedback Requirements

1. No initiative launches without a live assumption register, cadence, and decision-rights map.
2. Dashboards stay visible until risks close and evidence is verified.
3. Lessons, contradictions, and failures are published and carried forward.
4. Continuity checks validate that resets extend prior learning, not erase it.

5. The Decisive Question

Will your architecture produce endurance by design, or collapse by rehearsal?

IV. Rapid Orientation: Drift–Architecture Spectrum

Use this rubric for orientation, not validation. If your structures do not hold under pressure and turnover, you are in Drift regardless of intent or progress.

Severe Drift: Adaptability is an illusion. Pressure ensures collapse. Systems fracture, leadership dependency is absolute, and change evaporates without constant force.

High Drift: Some efforts exist, but they are episodic. Systems conflict with change. Bottlenecks, friction, and contradictions grow under pressure.

Unstable: Capabilities are uneven. Some functions adapt; others resist. Momentum depends on conditions and specific individuals. Drift activates quickly.

Strong Alignment: Adaptability is designed and repeatable. Systems flex. Decisions accelerate. Drift appears only in isolated pockets under extreme conditions.

Validated Architecture: Adaptability is embedded. Architecture absorbs disruption without loss of coherence. Pressure strengthens execution, not resistance.

Chapter 4 — The Doctrine of Structure

I. Story: Reg at the Edge of the Machine

The product failed at 2:13 am. By dawn, the collapse had begun radiating outward. Competitors surged in the market, journalists declared a trust crisis, and the board named it what it was: a structural failure.

The boardroom sat silent except for the hum of recycled air. Reflections in the glass table looked less like allies, more like verdicts. Reg had built through momentum and charisma. Momentum and charisma delivered visibility but no resilience. They never carried a single customer request.

Hal placed a report in front of him. "Nearly all efforts overlapped across teams, duplication disguised as progress. Two integrations, same failure point, no owner, no handoff. This collapse was built."

Another page slid forward: incident logs, escalations, frantic messages. "Alerts sounded; no one had authority to roll back. Five directors, zero decision rights. We built a structure without exits and expected execution to invent one."

Carol spoke flatly. "I can't hold the organization together with encouragement. Hybrid schedules. Blurred reporting lines. Reviews that reward heroics. Culture is structure rehearsed; when design collapses, triage becomes the operating norm."

Marcus crossed his arms. "Reorgs, slogans, pizza Thursdays. We've run the loop before. This failure was inevitable. Architecture authors the future. Ambition without design decays."

Reg felt the fragility beneath him. Relentless effort without structure scorched him. He opened his mouth but heard only hollow defenses. He reached for the report, hand trembling, then lowered it unread.

Imara stood at the whiteboard. She drew three circles: People, Process, Power, connected by a triangle, then placed a dot in the center. "This is the nucleus of architecture: who does the work, how the work flows, who decides when the work changes. Your vision never reached this center. The structure spoke to itself."

Reg saw the dot as a graveyard: abandoned roadmaps, failed pilots, a hiring class that left within months. On the screen, the outage graph sagged again. Another failed patch. Another symptom treated.

"Customers aren't confused," Hal said. "We are. They just leave."

Carol laid down exit interviews. "They don't complain anymore. They write: 'I can't tell where decisions live. I watch work die in handoffs. We're graded on speed but punished for escalation, so we hide risk.' This is the architecture of attrition."

The conversation pivoted from symptoms to structure; from what failed to how design must govern.

Marcus leaned forward. "Drift is not a storm. It is a blueprint; silent, precise, and executed."

Reg looked at his hands, the same hands that had raised capital, recruited stars, and propelled growth, but never clarified who decided what or how authority flowed.

Imara tapped the triangle. "When leaders don't design structure, people design their own. That's how you get shadow maps: unofficial plans that fragment effort and attention. Structure always exists. If you don't design it, it arrives feral. So let me ask: who owns reliability end to end?"

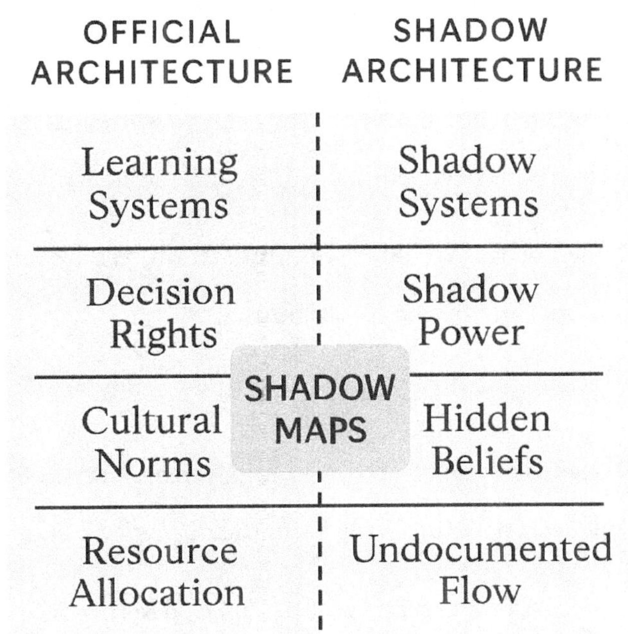

Figure:4.1 Architecture of Structural Authority

Structure determines how work flows, who decides, and whether accountability holds under pressure.

Eyes dropped. No one claimed it. The outage roamed unchecked, bereft of ownership.

Reg leaned forward. "Say it clean. What failed."

"Architecture," Imara said. "Not the code. The company."

Hal replied sharply. "Execution follows ownership. We don't have ownership. We have committees."

Carol added, "Trust follows consistency. We don't have consistency. We have exceptions."

Marcus concluded, "Momentum follows clarity." Indeed, without clarity, momentum dissolves into chaos.

The projector displayed customer support spikes. Messages scrolled: timeouts, login loops, defections. Attrition wasn't theory; it was hemorrhaging, customers flowing away without pause.

Reg pressed his fingers to his temples. "I did this."

Imara cut in. "No. The structure did this. You allowed it. It performs exactly as designed: speed without standards, autonomy without alignment, accountability only in fire. It rewards silence over signal. It isn't broken. It is obedient."

Reg recalled the years: early blitz when decisions fit in his head, growth mistaken for clarity, hybrid mistaken for design, values written but never embedded. He embraced clarity over panic.

He stood. "We are not misaligned because of poor communication. We are misaligned because our structure makes alignment optional and heroics prestigious."

They didn't need motivation; they needed architecture.

Hal straightened. "Step 1: Name true owners. Step 2: Eliminate duplication. Step 3: Define decision rights. We don't need a task force. We need structure with strength and clarity."

Carol tapped the exit notes. "Step 4: End exceptions. Step 5: Encode rituals. Interface reviews, audits of decision rights, accountability calendars. If it matters, it lives in cadence. If it lives nowhere, it doesn't exist."

Marcus set the threshold. "Choose today. Illusion or reality. Design or surrender. The future demands certainty."

Reg turned to the screens one last time. The cost of delay loomed large. He faced the table. "No more sovereign teams without interfaces. No launches without a named accountable owner. Decision rights carved before kickoff. Reviews that preschedule escalation. Reliability requires a single owner, not a panel on a call."

Imara nodded. "That is a choice. Now it must become architecture." Chairs scraped; the air changed as purpose displaced paralysis.

The room moved with intentional precision. Hal executed consolidation. Carol embedded rituals. Marcus eradicated shadow maps. Action replaced drift.

The outage graph eased. Customers trickled back. A reprieve, not a resurrection.

Imara capped the marker. "Remember: the structure did not betray you. It obeyed you."

As shadow teams dissolved, the doctrine clarified: architecture drives outcomes. Every line drawn shapes future performance.

Reg looked at the dot in the triangle. "**Structure shapes behavior**. Nothing escapes its architecture. This is no theory; it is the operating law of organizations. Architecture is destiny: it delivers mastery or collapse."

He lifted the marker. The room stilled, not in reverence but readiness. For the first time, his voice carried structure, not strain.

"Structure shapes behavior," he said. "This time, we build the structure, and with it, a future forged in architecture, not by accident."

Maxim: Structure shapes behavior; architecture delivers mastery or collapse.

II. Doctrine & Diagnostic

Architecture determines destiny. Constructed with precision, it channels human energy into lasting performance. Porous architecture converts clarity to confusion, improvisation to routine, resilience to fragility. Flaws emerge where leaders abdicate their role as architects. Failure is patterned, where leaders mistake words for design, speed for clarity, or committees for ownership. Building sustainable architecture requires leaders naming flaws, confronting them without compromise, and installing enforceable structure preventing Drift from gaining a foothold.

Key Terms

- **Structure:** organized configuration of roles, responsibilities, and relationships defining the organization's formal framework. It defines how tasks are divided, coordinated, and supervised, shaping behavior and workflow.
- **Systems:** network of mechanisms organized to produce repeatable, self-regulating outcomes within defined limits. They preserve continuity and stability, but do not adapt or learn; operates under constraints imposed by structure
- **Architecture:** intentional governing logic that establishes the laws and constraints within which organizational structure operate and adapt. It does not execute work, it determines what must endure as conditions change
- **Shadow Maps**: unofficial routes and workarounds employees create when leaders leave structure undefined.
- **Heroics**: individual overreach that patches structural absence in the moment while reinforcing fragility by rewarding improvisation over design.
- **Rituals**: deliberate, repeated practices embedding structure into daily operations.
- **Interface**: structural connection points where responsibilities, decisions, or workflows transfer between teams, roles, or systems.

Flaws Leaders Permit

1. Mistaking Communication for Structure

Leaders assume misalignment is a messaging problem. Design secures alignment. Architecture directs execution.

PMC Response

Mandate decision rights, interfaces, and flow in the operating model.

Replace directives with explicit process diagrams and ownership maps.

Hardwire decision points into the structure with named owners and enforced deadlines.

Enforceable Feedback Loop

1. Mandate a quarterly decision-rights audit with named gaps and owners.
2. Authority charters specify role boundaries: decide, escalate, execute.
3. Eliminate ambiguity within 30 days and prove closure publicly.

Doctrinal Closure

- Alignment is engineered by structure, not speech.
- Without decision rights and interfaces, behavior defaults to Drift.

Transition

Words substituting for design mislead leaders into believing scale equals clarity.

2. Confusing Growth with Clarity

Headcount growth magnifies design flaws. Expansion multiplies interface points and intensifies undefined ownership boundaries.

PMC Response

Mandate structural reviews at each stage of expansion: ownership, interfaces, and cadences.

Define accountability lines before adding teams or layers.

Anchor scale to stable design principles.

Enforceable Feedback Loop

1. Initiate structured checkpoints on decision rights, reporting, and cross-team interfaces whenever headcount increases by 20%.
2. Require sign-offs confirming teams have a charter, measures, and owners.
3. Track cycle time and rework after scale events.

Doctrinal Closure

- Architecture must precede headcount.

- Expansion without interfaces converts energy into rework and Drift

Transition

Growth without design institutionalizes heroics as culture.

3. Rewarding Heroics over Design

Firefighting wins applause. Repeated crises expose structural weakness. Mastery converts urgency into reliability by eliminating the need for saviors.

PMC Response

Direct recognition toward prevention, resilience, and defect eradication.

Anchor promotion to structural contributions that endure.

Replace "war-room" narratives with reliability reviews and learning reports.

Enforceable Feedback Loop

1. Maintain incident registers requiring a structural countermeasure for each root cause.
2. Track recurrence rate; reward teams that drive and sustain it at zero.
3. Inspect on-call pages and escalations monthly for recurring preventable patterns.

Doctrinal Closure

- Excellence is engineered when prevention outranks rescue; reliability replaces heroics as the standard of mastery.

Transition

Hero culture thrives where ownership disperses across groups instead of anchoring to accountable leaders.

4. Delegating Ownership to Committees

Committees collect opinions and dilute accountability. Decisions stall without consequence. Execution requires single ownership with authority and defined consult paths.

PMC Response

Assign single-point accountability for critical processes and outcomes.

Define, consult, inform, and decide roles explicitly for cross-functional issues.

Restrict committees to advisory forums.

Enforceable Feedback Loop

1. Publish live ownership maps by process and metric.
2. Reconfirm ownership quarterly; fill vacancies within seven days.
3. Escalate stalled decisions beyond the threshold to an empowered arbiter.

Doctrinal Closure

- Committees advise; owners decide.
- Single-point accountability moves discussion into execution.

Transition

Conflicted ownership creates environments where people generate their own maps.

5. Allowing Shadow Maps

Undefined flow invites the creation of unofficial plans. Parallel roadmaps divide focus, duplicate work, and mask risk. Shadow maps reveal where leadership left structure unfinished.

PMC Response

Mandate official roadmaps with owners, measures, and interface points.

Require cross-team synchronization rituals exposing overlaps and gaps.

Consolidate or eliminate work lacking a charter, owner, or measure.

Enforceable Feedback Loop

1. Hold quarterly interface reviews surfacing duplicates and contradictions.
2. Reconcile shadow initiatives into the official plan.
3. Monitor shadow efforts continuously; enforce elimination and maintain zero tolerance.

Doctrinal Closure

- Official roadmaps with named interfaces extinguish shadow work; design replaces improvisation

Transition

Shadow work persists until feedback has authority and triggers action by design.

6. Neglecting Feedback Loops

Weak or absent feedback hides early warnings of collapse. Systems drift when learning lacks a defined pathway into design. Resilience requires feedback triggering action by design.

PMC Response

Build feedback into operating cadence with named thresholds and actions.

Treat silence as a signal; verify reality at the source.

Close the loop visibly: what was heard, what changed, and who owns the change.

Enforceable Feedback Loop

1. Require critical processes to define sensors, thresholds, and response owners.
2. Review feedback driven design changes and publish outcomes each quarter.
3. Escalate ignored warning signals to executive review within 30 days with consequences.

Doctrinal Closure

- Feedback becomes architecture when thresholds compel action: signal, owner, deadline, proof.

Transition

Feedback stripped of authority converts control points into choke points.

7. Overcentralization Without Authority

Power is centralized while authority to decide stays ambiguous. Work accumulates at checkpoints without resolution, creating bottlenecks fracturing momentum and draining engagement. Projects stall, talent disengages, and organizational energy weakens under unresolved decisions.

PMC Response

Align checkpoints with clear authority and service levels.

Eliminate authorization steps lacking power to approve or resolve outcomes.

Enable decision making at the execution level by providing visible guardrails.

Enforceable Feedback Loop

1. Audit centralized checkpoints quarterly for authority, cycle time, and rework.
2. Redesign or eliminate decision points obstructing flow and lacking authority.
3. Measure proposal-to-decision time; investigate and correct lags beyond thresholds.

Doctrinal Closure

- Authority without power is architecture in name only.
- Decision rights aligned to checkpoints convert control into reliability.

Architectural Truths

- Clarity commands alignment.
- Rigidity destroys adaptability.
- Structure configures leadership.
- Behavior is engineered through structure.
- Architecture sustains what intentions cannot.

Diagnostic Tool: Behavioral Architecture Map

Purpose

Determine whether organizational architecture systematically produces disciplined execution or structurally engineers Drift.

Diagnostic Dimensions

1. Role Clarity Architecture

Definition

The organization's design makes ownership for work and decisions explicit , exclusive, and universally understood.

Propagation / Performance Indicator

When asked who owns any critical decision or accountability, all stakeholders produce the same answer without hesitation.

Drift Indicator

Ownership is assumed, shared, or disputed; decisions stall because no structural mechanism clarifies or enforces responsibility.

2. Decision Rights Architecture

Definition

Decision rights are defined, transparent, and embedded in operations so that authority flows without ambiguity.

Propagation / Performance Indicator

Decisions progress through a documented, known, and consistently followed path with rapid resolution when conflicts emerge.

Drift Indicator

Decisions rely on personality, escalation, or improvisation; bottlenecks form because the architecture cannot resolve ownership.

3. Feedback & Accountability Cadence

Definition

The architecture enforces fixed, non-discretionary cycles for reviewing risks, assumptions, progress, and red flags.

Propagation / Performance Indicator

Issues surface predictably and are resolved because cadence compels visibility and accountability.

Drift Indicator

Reviews depend on personal initiative; risks go unchallenged; red flags surface but drift untouched due to discretionary or episodic feedback loops.

4. Incentive & Reinforcement Alignment

Definition

Rewards, recognition, and consequences directly reinforce the values and behaviors the architecture claims to uphold.

Propagation / Performance Indicator

Desired behaviors are predictably repeated because rewards make them the path of least resistance.

Drift Indicator

Misaligned incentives remain in the architecture; high performers are punished implicitly while Drift is rewarded with ease or avoidance.

5. Norms & Informal Rule Governance

Definition

The architecture protects dissent, candor, and transparency while systematically exposing and eliminating shadow rules.

Propagation / Performance Indicator

Speaking up is protected; informal norms reinforce clarity and accountability.

Drift Indicator

Silence is safer than honesty; shadow rules override declared values; dissent depends on personality rather than architecture.

6. Architectural Resilience Under Pressure

Definition

Core processes, decision systems, and accountability mechanisms hold under crisis or leadership turnover.

Propagation / Performance Indicator

The organization performs consistently regardless of stress or personnel changes; architecture, not heroics, sustains discipline.

Drift Indicator

Leaders bypass processes in urgency; consistency collapses when key individuals exit; performance relies on effort over design.

Scoring Standard (1-5: Drift → Validated)

1. **Severe Drift:** Behavior is improvised. Ownership, decisions, cadence, and incentives are unclear. Shadow rules govern execution.
2. **High Drift:** Some structure exists but is discretionary. Execution depends on individuals; informal rules override design.
3. **Unstable:** Architecture is documented but inconsistently enforced. Formal rules compete with informal norms; Drift reactivates under stress.
4. **Strong Alignment:** Architecture reliably governs behavior. Ownership, decision rights, cadence, and incentives reinforce disciplined execution with minor edge failures.
5. **Validated Architecture:** Behavior is engineered and self-sustaining. Execution remains coherent under pressure and turnover; architecture governs outcomes.

Interpretation Guide

Validated Architecture: (23-30)

1. Architecture, not leader intent
2. Produces clarity
3. Accountability
4. Consistent execution
5. Behavior is engineered correctly
6. Predictable outcomes

Drift Detected: (1-22)

1. Failure is architected
2. Ambiguity
3. Shadow rules
4. Misaligned incentives
5. Discretionary processes structurally produce collapse

Structural Closing Line

Architecture, not intention, governs behavior; your diagnostic exposes the architecture you chose.

Leader's Challenge

You already know the truth of your structure; you have mistaken motion for architecture and effort for design.
Your organization behaves exactly as your structure instructs, not as your intentions imagine.

If work dies in handoffs, it is because you allowed ownership to remain optional.
If reliability has many supporters but no single owner, it is because you substituted committees for authority.
If reviews generate insight but not change, it is because you chose ritual without enforcement.

If people cannot locate where decisions live, it is because your structure trained them to protect themselves instead of the work.

If shadow maps spread, it is because the architecture you refused to design filled the vacuum. These are not failures of character.

They are failures of structure.

And structure is your responsibility.

You cannot claim clarity while decisions require guesswork.

You cannot claim execution when critical paths depend on influence instead of authority.

You cannot claim resilience when your architecture collapses under pressure that demands unambiguous ownership.

You cannot call your culture strong if it rewards silence over signal and heroics over accountability.

Structure always exists.

If you do not create it, your people will; toward survival, not mastery.

If reliability is "everyone's job," it becomes no one's job.

If speed is prized while standards are optional, your structure will select speed and deliver rework.

If you applaud teams for navigating ambiguous architecture, you institutionalize fragility and call it grit.

If exceptions multiply faster than rules, your architecture is surrendering, not governing.

Your challenge is not to extract greater effort from a broken structure.

Your challenge is to confront the structure itself.

To ask:

Who owns reliability?

Where do decisions actually live?

Which interfaces transfer accountability, and which convert momentum into loss?

You must choose whether ownership will be singular or dispersed.

You must choose whether committees hold authority or return to advisory roles.

You must choose whether rituals remain performative or become public enforcement of standards, ownership, and correction.

Architecture is not neutral.

Every line you draw, or fail to draw, shapes performance.

Structural Drift always loops toward collapse.

The constructed structure loops toward mastery.

The direction is not accidental.

It is built.

The question is whether you will keep allowing a feral structure to govern your organization, or finally build the architecture that will not Drift.

III. Essence of Execution

1. Core Execution Truth

Structure shapes behavior; architecture delivers mastery or collapse.

2. Indicators of Drift

1. Work dies in handoffs because no single owner is accountable end to end.
2. Reliability is "everyone's job," yet no one can name the true owner without hesitation.
3. Committees "support" outcomes while no role holds authority to decide.
4. Teams operate from shadow maps, parallel roadmaps, and unofficial paths to get work done.
5. Exceptions outnumber rules; escalation depends on influence instead of clear decision rights and interfaces.

3. Essential Leader Actions

1. Assign single-point ownership for critical outcomes, with explicit decision rights and escalation paths.
2. Design and publish structural interfaces so accountability transfers cleanly across teams.
3. Eliminate committees as decision owners; restrict them to advisory roles with named deciders.
4. Encode non-discretionary rituals (reviews, audits, cadences) that enforce standards, ownership, and correction.
5. Eradicate shadow maps by consolidating work into official roadmaps with charters, owners, and measures.

4. Enforceable Feedback Requirements

1. Ownership maps are maintained live; each critical outcome has one named owner and a documented escalation path.
2. Quarterly audits verify decision rights, interfaces, and checkpoints; gaps are closed within fixed deadlines and published.
3. Reliability reviews require proof that a single accountable owner exists, with measured incident reduction over time.
4. Interface reviews surface duplicated work, stalled handoffs, and shadow initiatives; consolidation or elimination is enforced.
5. Exception logs are tracked against standards; rising exception volume automatically triggers architectural review and redesign.

5. The Decisive Question

Will your architecture keep engineering ownerless Drift toward collapse, or will it enforce singular ownership and interfaces that deliver mastery?

IV. Rapid Orientation: Drift–Architecture Spectrum

Use this rubric for orientation, not validation. If your structures do not hold under pressure and turnover, you are in Drift regardless of intent or progress.

Severe Drift: Behavior is improvised. Ownership, decisions, cadence, and incentives are unclear. Shadow rules govern execution.

High Drift: Some structure exists but is discretionary. Execution depends on individuals; informal rules override design.

Unstable: Architecture is documented but inconsistently enforced. Formal rules compete with informal norms; Drift reactivates under stress.

Strong Alignment: Architecture reliably governs behavior. Ownership, decision rights, cadence, and incentives reinforce disciplined execution with minor edge failures.

Validated Architecture: Behavior is engineered and self-sustaining. Execution remains coherent under pressure and turnover; architecture governs outcomes.

Chapter 5 – People Are the Structure

I. Story: Carol and the Weight That Wasn't Hers

The first buzz came at 11:47 p.m.

It shouldn't have been her phone lighting up. This was an operations call, an executive issue. But when no one knew where ownership lived, the messages found their way to Carol. She had become the stand-in for undefined authority; the figure everyone reached for when authority vanished.

"Teams yelling. Nobody stepped up."
Seconds later: "Five on the call. Nobody takes ownership. Work dead in the water."
Then the third message: "Two engineers quit mid-shift. Yelled 'no ownership, no clarity.' Client furious, demanding answers by dawn or they're gone."

Carol stared at the glow of her phone across the dark kitchen. Plates from dinner sat untouched, the house silent upstairs. She carried the weight alone.

She scrolled back through the messages, each one louder than the last. Yelling. Deflecting. Walking out. It wasn't a technical failure; it was the inevitable collapse that follows when authority, roles, and expected behaviors are never defined. Carol knew the cracks were human, not mechanical.

Come morning, the conference room was full. Charts showed attrition climbing, red spikes tracking customer complaints. Productivity stalled. Projects dragged. The board wanted accountability. Executives wanted cover. Managers wanted arbitration.

Reg sat at the head. His posture carried authority, but his eyes betrayed depletion.

"Culture sits with you," someone said evenly. "Why is it failing?"

The ache behind Carol's eyes sharpened as silence fell, a signal she was nearing a breaking point. For months, she had hosted late-night calls, mediating disputes that should have been resolved by structure. Words failed. Talent walked. The structure failed them, not her.

She shoved a folder across the table toward Reg. "Exit interviews. Read their names. Their exits are not attrition. They are the verdict on our architecture." She rose from her seat and walked around the room. "We don't have a culture problem. We have failed to define authority, clarify roles, and detail expected behaviors. People are paying the price."

A director protested. "But we've invested in leadership training, recognition programs, and resilience workshops."

Carol cut him off. Her tone was steady, uncompromising. "Recognition is comfort, not structure. Decisions reflect design, not applause. None of them answer who owns escalation, who clears conflicting priorities, or who closes the loop when risks surface. We're paying for ambiguity with attrition, lost contracts, and client defections."

On the screen: attrition spiking, deadlines slipping, customers defecting. Renewal deals shrinking. Managers hoarding decisions out of fear. Engineers exiting rather than waiting for decisions that never came.

Carol pulled up the thread from the night before and read it aloud.
Her text: "Who owns the call?"
The reply: It depends.

The reply hit like a verdict, heavy and final.

Marcus leaned forward. His voice was low, edged with cynicism. "We reduce people to victims of broken design, carrying weight that was never theirs to bear. Dress it up as empowerment if you want, but when authority isn't defined and decision rights aren't built, we abandon them. That isn't strength; it's abdication. That isn't leadership; it's surrender. That is Drift."

Silence pressed down. Even the hum of the projector felt accusatory.

Reg snapped, his voice edged with defensiveness. "So what exactly are you accusing us of missing?"

Carol didn't look at him. Her eyes stayed fixed on the names glowing on the screen; the ones who stayed too long and the ones who left too soon. When she spoke, her tone carried the exhaustion of someone apologizing.

"I've held this place together with pep talks and late nights, patching holes that should never have been mine to fix. People don't need my stamina; they need certainty. Roles that anchor people. Decisions that endure under pressure. Escalation paths that function without friction. Every resignation, every lost client, every failed contract proves the same truth: people are the structure. Failing to build for that, we push the burden onto people, forcing them to absorb what the structure should carry. Eventually, they break. That break is not on them; it is on us. We must architect authority, roles, and behaviors with precision, or we will continue hemorrhaging talent, forfeiting clients, and surrendering the future we claim to protect. Excellence begins and ends with people. Empower people through clarity, and they deliver strength. Deny them structure and they fracture. Their fracture is the demise of the organization. The demise of us!"

"She left the folder precisely aligned at the table's center, a line of order drawn through their chaos. Then she walked out, leaving the weight where it belonged.

Maxim: Structure enforces culture; it determines whether people excel or collapse.

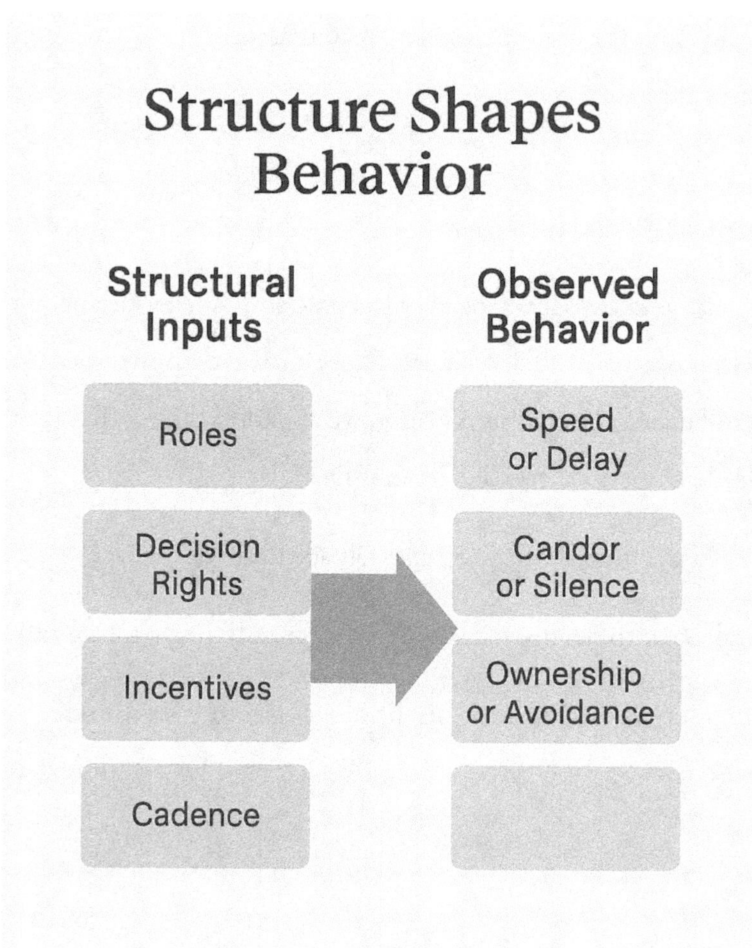

Figure 5.1 Structure Shapes Behavior

II. Doctrine & Diagnostic

Structure without people results in collapse. Assets, capital, and technology are powerless without human activation. Leaders failing to architect authority and clarity, design collapse into human burden. These outcomes are leadership failures. Collapse is not accidental; it is engineered through ambiguity, abdication, burden transfer, fractured communication, and absent structure. People must be reinforced by structure, not sacrificed to it.

Key Terms

- **Authority:** the non-negotiable right to decide.
- **Accountability:** ownership of outcomes, inseparable from authority.
- **Burden Transfer:** organizational weight imposed on individuals under structural failure.
- **Escalation Path:** explicit channel resolving conflict or risk, mandated by design.

Flaws Leaders Permit

1. Ambiguity in Roles and Decision Rights

Undefined ownership erases accountability. Flow stalls in hesitation and conflict, leaving crises unresolved. Ambiguity is paralysis by design.

PMC Response

Mandate decision-rights.

Publish ownership maps identifying who decides, executes, and escalates.

Enforceable Feedback Loop

1. Conduct quarterly decision-rights audits.
2. Close gaps within 30 days.
3. Treat unresolved ambiguity as executive failure.

Doctrinal Closure

- Ambiguity engineers hesitation as culture.
- Undefined ownership converts clarity into conflict.
- Decisions delayed by design institutionalize Drift.

Transition

Ambiguity ignored evolves into abdication institutionalized.

2. Abdication of Leadership and Accountability

Leaders absent in authority compel people to construct governance from chaos. Presence stripped of clarity is abdication. Abdication crowns Drift as the true authority.

PMC Response

Obligate leaders to map authority boundaries: decide, escalate, execute.

Anchor leadership in architecture.

Enforceable Feedback Loop

1. Hold quarterly accountability reviews tied to structural outcomes.
2. Escalate unclaimed failures as abdication events.

Doctrinal Closure

- Presence without authority fabricates illusion, not leadership.
- Abdication transfers command to chaos.
- Unclaimed decisions script collapse in real time.

Transition

Leaders abdicating authority shift the burden onto people.

3. Burden-Shifting and Resource Misallocation

Structure failing to distribute responsibility imposes organizational weight onto people. High performers succumb to exhaustion, triggering disengagement and attrition. Burden-shifting converts excellence into depletion.

PMC Response

Align workloads with structural capacity.

Protect high performers from structural overload.

Reward accountable ownership; penalize overextension.

Enforceable Feedback Loop

1. Audit workloads quarterly.
2. Correct capacity breaches within 30 days.
3. Treat chronic overextension as a structural defect.

Doctrinal Closure

- Burden transferred to people erodes performance.
- Structures exhausting their best talent convert strength into depletion.
- Excellence cannot thrive where design demands endurance over clarity.

Transition

Excessive burden encourages communication erosion.

4. Poor Communication and Knowledge Flow

Messaging without structured channels degrades into noise. Silence, deflection, and contested ownership fracture execution. Knowledge erodes into contradiction with undefined pathways.

PMC Response

Engineer structured escalation channels, decision logs, and feedback loops.

Architect knowledge flow as structural law.

Enforceable Feedback Loop

1. Mandate quarterly structural audits of communication channels verifying integrity and eliminating drift.
2. Flag contested ownership as a structural fault. Enforce resolution within 30 days.

Doctrinal Closure

1. Signals without structure breed distortion as doctrine.
2. Silence between roles manufactures contradiction.
3. Information unguided by design decays into rumor and retreat.

Transition

Communication collapse reveals architectural negligence.

5. Structural Collapse from Lack of Design Clarity

Collapse is cumulative. Abdicated decisions, unassigned roles, and deflected signals compound until culture erodes, talent exits, and clients defect. Drift does not break the structure; it executes the blueprint of ambiguous architecture.

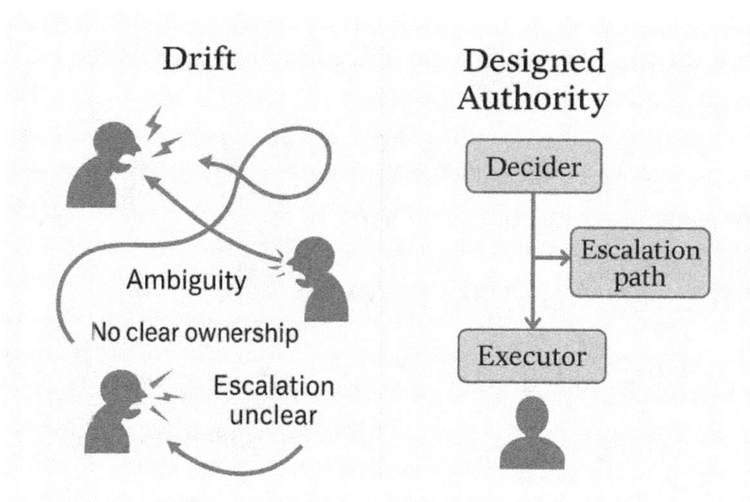

Figure 5.2 Drift in Motion: Ambiguity vs Designed Authority

PMC Response

Decree architectural precision.

Define authority, roles, and escalation paths with zero tolerance for ambiguity.

Enforceable Feedback Loop

1. Mandate continuous architectural reviews.
2. Eliminate unclear designs within 30 days
3. Bind executive evaluation directly to the eradication of collapse patterns.

Doctrinal Closure

- Ambiguity replicated across structures becomes institutionalized Drift.
- Design abandoned under pressure engineers collapse.
- Collapse is not spontaneous; it is constructed by neglect.

Architectural Truths

- Clarity of authority empowers execution.
- Trust is structural capital.
- Ownership anchors accountability.
- Resistance reveals design flaws.
- Excellence is architecturally engineered.

Diagnostic Tool: Human Structural Integrity Map

Purpose

Determine whether structure enforces clarity, accountability, and decision ownership at interfaces or whether Drift forces reliance on individuals; fragmenting execution into silence, fragility, and dependence .

Diagnostic Dimensions

1. Identity Integration

Definition

Evaluates whether roles transmit organizational purpose as structural identity rather than personal interpretation.

Propagation / Performance Indicator

People articulate how their work advances purpose; roles carry meaning independent of incumbents; identity persists beyond turnover.

Drift Indicator

Purpose collapses into tasks; meaning disappears when individuals exit; work becomes assignment execution instead of mission advancement.

2. Trust as Infrastructure

Definition

Assesses whether trust is engineered into operating systems to enable dissent, risk visibility, and honest escalation.

Propagation / Performance Indicator

Dissent is protected and acted on; risks surface without fear; escalation pathways are used and trusted.

Drift Indicator

Silence replaces candor; risks are hidden; escalation bypasses structure; meetings become rituals of agreement driven by fear.

3. Recognition Architecture

Definition

Measures whether reinforcement systems reward values, integrity, and collaboration as the structural path of least resistance.

Propagation / Performance Indicator

Recognition consistently reinforces declared values; collaboration preventing failure is rewarded; incentives align with excellence.

Drift Indicator

Heroics, speed, and politics outperform values; misaligned incentives reward shortcuts; recognition varies by leader preference.

4. Adaptability by Design

Definition

Determines whether adaptability is structurally engineered into architecture rather than dependent on top performers or crisis improvisation.

Propagation / Performance Indicator

Processes flex without heroics; feedback loops and learning cycles are embedded; resilience survives turnover and pressure.

Drift Indicator

Adaptability collapses if key people vanish; crises require extraordinary effort; processes are bypassed "just this once."

5. Continuity Transmission

Definition

Assesses whether culture, norms, and decision logic are encoded into architecture so excellence persists through turnover.

Propagation / Performance Indicator

Onboarding transmits values and norms; peer rituals are embedded; new hires reach cultural and operational mastery within 90 days.

Drift Indicator

Culture depends on personalities; onboarding teaches tools instead of values; peer rituals are optional; standards decay under leadership churn.

Scoring Standard (1-5: Drift → Validated)

1. **Severe Drift:** Identity fractures; trust collapses; shadow norms dominate; structure relies on personalities and effort.
2. **High Drift:** Structural signals inconsistent; resilience collapses under stress; people substitute for architecture.
3. **Unstable:** Some structural intent exists, but experience varies; continuity and trust break under pressure.
4. **Strong Alignment:** Identity, trust, and adaptability are structurally encoded; Drift appears only at edges.
5. **Validated Architecture:** People operate as the structure; purpose, trust, continuity, and resilience persist regardless of turnover or stress.

Interpretation Guide

Validated Architecture: (19-25)

1. Purpose is structurally transmitted.
2. Trust and dissent operate as designed.
3. Adaptability survives loss of key individuals.
4. Continuity persists independent of personality.
5. Pressure strengthens cohesion rather than splintering it.

Drift Detected: (1-18)

1. Silence replaces candor.
2. Roles lose purpose when incumbents exit.
3. Recognition rewards heroics or shortcuts.
4. Adaptability depends on effort, not design.

5. Culture collapses under turnover or stress.

Structural Closing Line

People are the structure; when identity, trust, adaptability, and continuity are not engineered, Drift becomes the structure in their place.

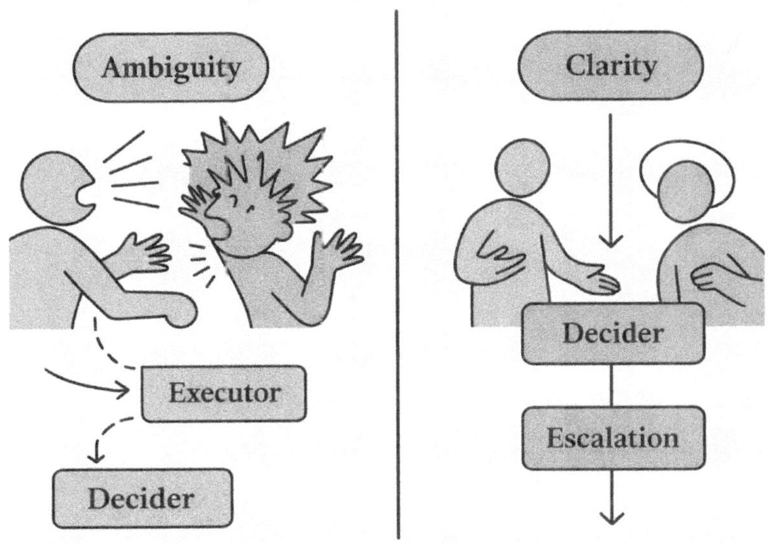

Figure 5.3 People Are the Structure: Drift vs Designed Authority

Leader's Challenge

You already know the truth of your culture: you mistook human endurance for structural integrity and exhaustion for excellence.

You watched people carry responsibilities that belonged to structure.

Figure 5.4 Burden Transfer: When Structure Fails, People Carry the Load

You watched ownership disappear the moment pressure rose.
You watched authority fall silent while people absorbed the weight.
You watched Drift turn resilience into rupture.

These were never emotional failures.
They were structural verdicts.

If people drown in decisions they do not own, it is because ambiguity became your doctrine.
If roles collapse when someone resigns, it is because meaning lived in the person instead of the structure.
If escalation depends on whoever answers a midnight call, it is because you replaced architecture with improvisation.
If high performers burn out, it is because endurance is compensating for design you never built.

These are not failures of talent.
They are failures of architecture.
And architecture is your responsibility.

You cannot claim accountability while authority is still "it depends."
You cannot claim strength when culture collapses under routine pressure.
You cannot celebrate resilience when people are only carrying the load structure refused to hold.

Your organization is not confused.

It is obedient.

It behaves exactly as your structure instructs.

If authority is ambiguous, people hesitate.

If identity is unanchored, they Drift.

If communication is unstructured, they contradict one another.

If continuity is unwritten, culture resets with every departure.

Design absent becomes survival instinct.

And survival is not strength, it is surrender.

Carol saw this when she laid the exit interviews on the table. Those departures were not attrition; they were testimony. They revealed the cost of the architecture you never created.

Your challenge is not to make people tougher.

Your challenge is to stop forcing them to compensate for the structure you refused to build.

If your people fracture, your structure fractured first.

If your culture erodes, your architecture permitted the erosion.

If your organization depends on heroics, you do not have design; only exhaustion decorated as commitment.

The weight Carol carried was never hers.

It was leadership's neglect made visible.

Now the question reaches you:

Will you keep allowing Drift to turn people into the structure?

Or will you design clarity, so people no longer carry what belongs to structure?

Drift is already shaping your culture.

You can see the cracks in resignations, delays, and the quiet fear behind your best people's eyes.

People are the structure.

Design for their strength or force them to absorb your collapse.

Architect, or yield.

Build the architecture, or be governed by its ruins.

III. Essence of Execution

1. Core Execution Truth

Structure enforces culture; it determines whether people excel or collapse.

2. Indicators of Drift

1. People carry responsibilities that belong to structure
2. Escalation depends on availability instead of defined pathways.
3. High performers absorb design gaps and burn out.
4. Roles lose meaning when incumbents exit.
5. Teams contradict one another because communication is unstructured.

3. Essential Leader Actions

1. Define authority, roles, and expected behaviors with zero ambiguity.
2. Establish escalation paths that function without individuals.
3. Encode continuity so roles retain meaning beyond their incumbents.
4. Align workloads to structural capacity, not endurance.
5. Architect communication channels that eliminate contradiction.

4. Enforceable Feedback Requirements

1. Authority maps stay live: one decider, one executor, one escalation path.
2. Quarterly structural audits verify clarity, continuity, and channels; gaps close on deadline.
3. Workload reviews prove capacity alignment, not heroics.
4. Escalation logs expose ambiguity; each instance triggers structural correction.
5. Continuity checks confirm identity and standards persist through turnover.

5. The Decisive Question

Will your people keep carrying what structure should hold, or will you build the architecture that carries them?

IV. Rapid Orientation: Drift–Architecture Spectrum

Use this rubric for orientation, not validation. If your structures do not hold under pressure and turnover, you are in Drift regardless of intent or progress.

Severe Drift: Identity fractures; trust collapses; shadow norms dominate; structure relies on personalities and effort.

High Drift: Structural signals inconsistent; resilience collapses under stress; people substitute for architecture.

Unstable: Some structural intent exists, but experience varies; continuity and trust break under pressure.

Strong Alignment: Identity, trust, and adaptability are structurally encoded; Drift appears only at edges.

Validated Architecture: People operate as the structure; purpose, trust, continuity, and resilience persist regardless of turnover or stress.

Interlude

The Human Operating System: Why Drift Is Inevitable

I. Story: Marcus Before the Ledger

The notification banner crawled across Marcus's screen at 9:42 p.m.

INCIDENT ESCALATION — PRIORITY HIGH

CLIENT IMPACT: UNKNOWN

JOIN IMMEDIATELY

He stared at it a moment longer than usual.

Not because he didn't understand the urgency.

Because he already knew what it meant.

No structure.

No ownership.

No clarity.

Just fear wrapped in capital letters.

He clicked Join.

The call opened like a fire alarm inside a tiled stairwell. Every voice echoed.

Ops: "We're seeing latency spikes in three regions."

Engineering: "We don't even know if it's us yet."

Product: "The client's already on social media. This can't spread."

Sales: "If this isn't fixed in the next ninety minutes, the renewal is gone."

Slack flashed on his second monitor: who's owning this?

Is Marcus on?

We need someone to decide.

The expectation landed before anyone said his name.

As his camera came online, the noise didn't stop. It bent.

They didn't start talking to each other.

They started talking to him.

"Marcus, we've got conflicting signals."

"Marcus, we need a direction."

"Marcus, sales is screaming."

"Marcus, if we roll back and it's not the deploy, we're dead."

His chest tightened. Not dramatically. Just enough for his breath to go a fraction shallower.

Just enough for his mind to narrow.

He scanned the console: partial alarms, incomplete logs, half-finished notes.

He wasn't walking into a system. He was walking into a void.

"Okay," he said. "Let's slow down. Facts only. Ops first."

Five people answered anyway.

"I said Ops first," he snapped. Sharper than he meant to. He heard it the moment it left his mouth.

The channel went quiet in the wrong way.

Cameras blinked off in a pattern he recognized: compliance, not alignment.

Ops started again. Defensive this time. "We saw a spike right after the last deployment. But we also had a vendor heartbeat drop on the same timeline. So we're not one hundred percent on origin."

Engineering tried to jump in. "We need five more minutes to—"

"We don't have five," Sales cut across. "Client's threatening escalation. They wanted an answer fifteen minutes ago."

Marcus felt the room tilt toward the person with the most fear, not the most data.

His jaw clenched.

Whatever calm he had walked in with started to leak.

If he had trained for this moment, he would have lengthened his breath, widened his perspective, and separated signal from noise.

He hadn't.

He fell back into reflex. The one he'd rehearsed for years.

If nobody else is holding it, I will.

"Everyone mute except Ops," he said.

They muted.

Ops continued. "We can roll back the last deploy. It might be it. But if it's the vendor—"

"Roll it back," Marcus said. "Now."

Engineering hesitated. "We—"

"That's the call," he cut in. "Execute."

The command landed. So did the doubt.

They rolled it back.

For ninety seconds, metrics calmed.

Then red bars lit up the dashboard like a second sunrise.

The rollback had reintroduced a configuration bug they'd retired weeks ago.

Authentication failures tripled.

Error budgets vaporized.

An engineer forgot to mute. "This is worse. This is way worse."

Marcus felt heat flush up his neck. He almost said, Then why didn't you say that sooner? but he knew the answer.

He'd silenced them.

Urgency had become more important than intelligence.

"Fine," he said. "Forward deploy the patch. Same region. Go."

Ops: "We don't have full regression—"

"Go."

Another pause. Longer this time.

They moved anyway.

The patch failed to propagate cleanly.

Partial updates.

Inconsistent state.

One region caught between two versions.

Marcus watched the graphs tilt toward the cliff.

"You're making us guess," a quiet voice said. It belonged to a junior engineer who never spoke in these rooms. "We don't have enough to know."

"We don't have time for second-guessing," Marcus shot back.

Her camera blinked off.

Thirty-five minutes later, the system stabilized.

Not because of his decisions. In spite of them.

Two senior engineers had run a parallel path in the background, ignoring his commands, waiting until a safe rollback existed. Then they executed it quietly.

When they reported "Incident resolved," they didn't add, no thanks to you.

They didn't have to.

He felt it.

“Good work, everyone,” he said, because that’s what leadership says to close a wound.

The call ended. Cameras vanished one by one.

He sat alone with three dead screens and the faint buzz of the building.

He caught his reflection in the dark glass.

Tension in the jaw.

Eyes too bright.

Hands still not fully steady.

“I should have done better,” he whispered.

Then, quieter: “Why didn’t I?”

He didn’t know yet.

He thought it was judgment.

He thought it was character.

It wasn’t.

It was architecture.

The Architecture Beneath the Moment

What happened in that incident wasn’t random.

It wasn’t unique to Marcus.

It wasn’t even personal.

It was the human operating system doing exactly what it does under load.

You don’t rise to your best self in those moments.

You fall to the level of your wiring.

That night revealed something leaders prefer to ignore: Drift doesn’t start in systems.

Drift starts in humans whose brains are behaving exactly as designed.

To understand why PMC must exist, you have to understand this:

The human brain is not built for sustained high performance under ambiguity.

And yet that's the environment leaders live in.

PMC is not a philosophy laid on top of capable minds.

PMC is an architecture built to compensate for a fragile operating system.

To see that, you have to look underneath the behavior.

The Human Stack: Three Layers of Behavior.

Every leader carries three layers into every room:

Executive Layer – the part that believes it's in charge.

Plans, reasons, weighs trade-offs, reads context, restrains impulse.

Emotional Layer – the part that scans for threat.

Tracks status, judgment, risk, humiliation, loss.

Habit Layer – the part that runs old scripts.

What you practiced under pressure before there was language for it.

In calm states, the Executive Layer can run the show.

In pressure states, the order reverses.

A signal hits.

The Emotional Layer tags it as threat.

The Habit Layer responds with the most rehearsed pattern.

The Executive Layer becomes a spectator, or a lawyer arguing after the fact.

That's what happened to Marcus.

He didn't decide to narrow his attention.

His nervous system did.

He didn't choose to silence dissent.

His reflex for control fired to protect status and safety.

He didn't intend to cut the wrong path.

His bandwidth collapsed. Emotion tagged urgency as more important than accuracy. Habit filled in the gap.

From the outside, it looked like:

impatience

arrogance

defensiveness

poor leadership

From the inside, it was:

narrowed perception

elevated arousal

scripted behavior

a brain under siege trying to simplify a complex reality too fast

You can call that failure.

Or you can call it what it is:

The default human operating system under stress.

Bandwidth: The Hard Ceiling

The part of the brain that does complex reasoning has limits.

It can hold only so many variables, so much ambiguity, before it drops something.

Under low load, a capable leader can:

track multiple streams

sense tensions

weigh options

consider trade-offs

monitor their own reactions

make room for other voices

Under high load, that list shrinks.

Most people think they're operating with full awareness when, in reality, their mental equivalent of a task manager would show one process consuming almost everything: Protect self.

Avoid being wrong.

Avoid being exposed.

Resolve discomfort.

Everything else gets compressed, distorted, or dropped.

That's what "I should have done better" misses.

It judges the outcome.

It ignores the bandwidth.

Hijack: 200 Milliseconds That Change the Room

The human system routes signals through the fast path first.

Before Marcus could reason, his body had already decided:

heart rate up

muscles ready

vision narrowed

threat prioritized

Those responses are not metaphors. They are physical.

Once they fire:

curiosity shrinks

nuance disappears

listening drops

ego protection rises

certainty becomes attractive

silence feels dangerous

"Everyone mute except Ops" wasn't a leadership principle.

It was a nervous system trying to simplify an input stream too complex for the bandwidth left.

It worked in one sense: fewer voices.

It failed in another: less intelligence.

He traded capacity for control.

Every leader does, at some point, without realizing it.

Social Contagion: When One Brain Drops, Others Follow

The moment Marcus sharpened his tone, cameras went off.

Not because people stopped caring.

Because they started protecting themselves.

Stress is contagious.

So is Drift.

One person narrows.

Others feel it and self-censor.

Information quality drops.

Decisions degrade.

More things break.

Stress rises again.

It's a loop.

If you put a leader with unresolved fear at the center of a vague, high-stakes situation, and you offer them no structure, the pattern is predictable:

pressure rises

bandwidth drops

threat dominates

habit fires

control replaces clarity

everyone bends around the most anxious gravity in the room

Then people leave the meeting saying, "We need stronger leaders."

But leadership is not the root cause.

Architecture is.

II. The Realities of Drift

Reality 1 – Under load, the brain defaults down, not up.

You do not become your best self under pressure.

You become your most rehearsed self.

Reality 2 – People behave at the level of their bandwidth, not your expectations.

In that incident, Marcus didn't suddenly become less intelligent.

He hit his ceiling.

Reality 3 – Identity overrides context unless structure forces adaptation.

His old identity script: "I hold the room" took over, regardless of what the moment actually needed.

Reality 4 – Drift is contagious.

His narrowing became the team's narrowing.

His urgency became their panic.

His doubt tainted their confidence.

Reality 5 – Pressure fills the architecture it finds.

In a vacuum, anxiety becomes the design.

If you don't define the structure, urgency will write one for you.

You saw all five realities in one short incident.

You see them in board meetings, crisis calls, performance reviews, and project debates every week.

You may have felt them in yourself.

The Mirror

It's easy to read Marcus's story at a distance.

It's harder to admit where you've lived it.

You may not snap on a call.

You might go quiet instead.

You may not override your team.

You may disappear into abstraction and analysis until they have to guess your intent.

You may not demand control.

You may avoid it, leaving a vacuum others are forced to fill.

Different behavior.

Same architecture.

pressure

narrowed focus

old script

Drift

It isn't about temperament.

It isn't about "good people" and "bad people."

It's about the fact that no one's brain is built to hold complexity, fear, hierarchy, risk, and responsibility simultaneously without support.

That includes you.

If your system depends on "better people," you have already lost.

Why "Try Harder" Fails

Most organizations respond to incidents like Marcus's with:

feedback

coaching

resilience workshops

slogans about ownership

a fresh set of leadership expectations

None of those rebuild bandwidth.

None of those alter the wiring under load.

None of those change the architecture Drift travels through.

You can ask someone to be calmer.

You can't ask their amygdala to respect your performance review.

You can tell someone to "read the room."

You can't expand their complexity handling in the middle of a crisis.

You can tell them not to take things personally.

You can't stop their social-threat circuits from lighting up when their competence is on the line.

Trying harder is not a control.

Trying harder is a symptom.

The Case for Architecture

If the human operating system behaves like this under load, then one conclusion becomes unavoidable:

You cannot build excellence on human discipline alone.

You must build excellence on architecture that assumes discipline will fail.

Architecture doesn't panic.

Architecture doesn't blush.

Architecture doesn't care who's in the room.

Architecture doesn't protect its ego.

Architecture doesn't get tired.

Structure can hold when people wobble.

Clear roles keep decisions from bottlenecking in a single overloaded mind.

Explicit decision rights prevent the loudest person from winning by volume.

Visible work and queues reduce cognitive load by making abstractions concrete.

Escalation paths reduce social threat by making "asking for help" a designed behavior, not a confession.

Recovery rules protect the brain from making decisions it can't support at hour 18.

PMC is built on that premise: Humans are the structure.

But the structure must be designed to protect humans from their own wiring.

Why PMC Must Lead the Human

Marcus's incident happened before the Operating System arrived.

No roles.

No decision design.

No visible architecture anchored to reality.

So pressure wrote its own design:

Marcus at the center

everyone else orbiting his anxiety

speed over clarity

perceived strength over shared intelligence

When PMC arrives later in the story, what changes is not the moral quality of the people.

What changes is what carries the load.

In a PMC environment:

the incident lead owns the call, not the most anxious manager

the command card carries the logic, not the shaking hand

the escalation tree routes power, not politics

resilience is scheduled, not begged for

feedback loops are drawn into the architecture, not left to heroics

Marcus in Chapter 6 is not suddenly a different species.

He is a human finally operating inside an architecture that compensates for the limitations of his own operating system.

Sasha in Chapter 7 is not magically resilient.

She is the first to insist that resilience become structural instead of sacrificial.

Hal in Chapter 9 is not reborn as a warmer person.

He is forced to trade brittle control for designed trust.

PMC doesn't make humans perfect.

It makes human imperfection survivable.

The Bridge

That night in the incident call, Marcus thought he had failed alone.

He hadn't.

The organization had failed him first by offering urgency in place of design.

He walked away saying, "I should have done better,"

when the real indictment was simpler:

We should have built better.

If Drift begins in the human operating system,

then the only responsible response is to build an operating system for the organization that anticipates it, absorbs it, and prevents it from turning into collapse.

That is what comes next.

An architecture stronger than habit.

A design that holds under pressure.

A system that does not ask humans to be more than human,

but insists they be held in something worthy of their effort.

Excellence is not a promise.

Excellence is an operating system.

Now we build it.

Chapter 6 — PMC Operating System

I. Story: Marcus at the Turning Point

Marcus watched the city unspool into the morning. Steel towers took the first light, and the glass across from him replayed a thinner version of his face. In his hand, the "Ledger" felt heavier than paper; five cycles of rallying promises, and silent collapses pressed into one worn cover. He opened a blank page and did not give it a title. Titles had betrayed him before. Observation precedes judgment, calibration before critique. He hovered his pen, then drew one small line instead of a title; a measured start where impulse once ruled.

The war room awoke. On the center screen, a map of workstreams pulsed like a live organ: threads of intake, prioritization, build, test, release. He had seen chaos. This didn't look like chaos. It looked like machinery with sand in the bearings, wanting to move, stalling at the same points. He circled three nodes on a side display with a grease pencil: Intake. Prioritization. Release. Then he set the pencil down. No arrows yet. He chose to let the day declare its pattern.

The first alert hit. Customer login delay nudged from green to yellow. His instinct was to dictate; instead, he waited for alignment to form. Marcus lifted a hand for silence and asked one question, low and clean. "Who determines, dictates, or defines the response?"

Four heads turned toward the same person. Not a chorus, not a debate. It was an alignment. The incident lead posted a triage path: checkpoints, limits, and who can approve a reversal. Roles clear, limits explicit, no heroics required.

The team executed without drama. The numbers wavered, steadied, then returned to normal. Someone exhaled a breath they'd been carrying for months.

Marcus wrote one word in the ledger margin, small and deliberate: **Clarity**.

He walked toward the core engineering group with steady purpose. Only a few weeks earlier, taking on new requests had been chaos, arguments circling without resolution. Now a simple board stood at the front, showing four tasks awaiting completion. Each task had a name, a purpose, and a clear endpoint, work laid out where everyone could see it. The contrast was sharp: yesterday's noise reduced to visible, disciplined order.

The product manager spoke first. "We commit to finishing two of these tasks."

No speeches. No drama. Just a clear act of discipline that marked the arrival of rigor. Marcus wrote **Rigor** beside Clarity in his ledger. He felt the urge to add more words, then stopped. Two were enough. The restraint felt like strength.

His cynicism surfaced like an old reflex. He had learned to measure change by what people do under pressure, not by what they say in comfort.

Soon after, pressure arrived. A senior director pushed an urgent request into the channel, bypassing the queue. The request carried executive weight; big logo, high stakes, thin deadline. Marcus felt the room contract, as if all the oxygen had been pulled toward the word urgent.

The lead engineer stood without noise and pointed to a page posted on the far wall. "Decisions live at the work. Escalations stay in the open, visible to all

She opened a short call, invited the senior director and her team, and without apology named the current commitments and capacity available. The director pressed with tone and volume, trying to win by intimidation. Every muscle in Marcus wanted to intervene; he unclenched his hand and let the structure speak. Marcus stayed silent and watched the engineer lean in with a question that cut without heat

"Which work do you want us to abandon?"

The director's jaw set. "If this stalls, I'll take it to Reg myself. He won't accept this queue standing in the way of revenue." Her voice carried the confidence of someone used to winning through rank, not design. She ended the call without hesitation, believing she had won.

The air didn't relax. The team had held their ground, but the conflict wasn't over. Everyone knew Reg would be pulled into the fight before long. The question wasn't whether the structure worked today, it was whether it could withstand power pressing against it tomorrow.

Marcus added a third word to the ledger, heavier than the others: **Decision Architecture.**

He almost wrote a fourth Ownership but stopped himself. He would not award words the system undeserved.

For now, the ledger held three words and a question mark. He kept his pen uncapped.

As the morning pressed on, an alert status flashed. A vendor forced an unannounced update that jammed their authentication mechanism and locked out users. A partial outage threatened the eastern region. The old response pattern would have been noise: five channels, twelve opinions, leadership statements displacing decisions. Instead, the incident lead posted a command card to the operations room. The card identified the problem, owner, blast radius, rollback timebox, authority to cut over, and next timestamp for update. No adjectives. No optics. The card did not beg for permission; it presented a path.

Marcus felt his chest tighten, and then unexpectedly loosen. He did not love the crisis. He loved the shape of the response.

He moved to the corner where Imara, the external strategist, had been standing with arms crossed, watching the structure operate under load. She said nothing. She didn't need to. After the status switched to closed, she spoke in the tone of a judge reading a verdict.

"This time the design held against reality, the structure carried through."

Marcus did not give her the smile she might have earned. Not yet. He looked back at the board. "We'll see if it holds when the pressure ratchets up.

"Pressure doesn't seek conflict," Imara said. "It wants a vacuum. When you don't define the architecture, urgency imposes it for you."

He wrote a tiny plus sign beside Decision Architecture.

The office atmosphere grew tense as noon approached. Sales promised a feature beyond the current architecture: no owner named, no capacity reserved, no tested path. The promise threaded its way through the office with the speed of panic in a small town.

Marcus arrived just as the weight of the sales promise hit the room, urgency settling over the team like a storm front. The sales lead demanded compliance. "We need this now," she said. "We'll lose the account if we don't."

The room looked at Marcus the way people look at a weathervane, trying to read which way the wind of pressure would shift. He did not play in the weather today. He pointed at the board. "Lay it out on the table, let everyone see the cost, the trade-offs, and the structural choices." His voice was even now, stripped of argument.

The lead engineer outlined the current work, capacity, and risks, stating the technical truth without embellishment. "We can bend for two days. On day three, the structure fails. Pushed beyond limits, the structure dictates what fails."

The sales lead remained determined to get her way. Imara cut in like a firewall. "No one wins a client by overwhelming the structure that serves them."

Marcus watched the room steady itself. Not collapse nor surrender, a deliberate act of design. An intentional refusal to collapse under pressure. The sales lead shifted from demand to negotiation. They made a deal: a quick fix lasting two days, no more. On day one, they would call the customer and state the truth directly, placing trust ahead of delivery. Agreement came quietly, without speeches or celebration. Everyone aligned to the same outcome.

The ledger took a fourth word, finally, small but permanent: **Ownership.**

He closed the book and left it on the table.

Afternoon brought the third test, and with it, the part of the day that determined whether this was a turning point or a scripted performance.

A cross-functional review convened to examine the week's risks. These meetings historically devolved into ceremonial reporting. People speaking in polished fragments concealing the system's fractures. Today the session opened differently. A display highlighted the risks: red for proximity, amber for uncertainty, green for known mitigations. Each risk tile showed an owner, a decision right, and the next irreversible moment.

The owner of the highest-risk item spoke first. "We've discovered a hidden step in our process. If we don't fix it before Thursday, the schedule will collapse and two teams will be stuck."

No one asked for slides. No one asked for a polished story. The conversation cut through pretense and went straight to the engineer's plain question, linking the discussion directly to risk: "Which work do we set aside to prevent the larger failure?"

Two tasks were cut. No speeches. The schedule shifted. The team paused to give the problem the time and focus it demanded, recognizing that rushing would create greater risk. They did not overreach or bluff capacity. They acted with discipline, protecting the integrity of the structure.

Marcus felt a deeper force anchoring him, trust. Not the fragile kind. This was structural trust: tangible in behavior, weighty enough to carve into the culture and demanded to be defended when tested.

He wanted to capture the feeling of structural trust. He wrote beneath Ownership in smaller letters, as if not to spook it: "held without heroics".

The final test came from the fiercest enemy: Drift wearing a friendly face.

The vice president stopped by in person, unannounced, carrying praise, promises, and a request that was half compliment, half demand. "You've been executing with discipline," he said, palms open in a pantomime of partnership. "Which is why I know you can absorb one more crucial deliverable. The board is watching. If successful, this move seals their confidence."

He used words like we, together, and momentum. A faint pressure lingered for them to be the team that said 'yes'. Marcus fought his old reflex, accepting praise as payment only to collapse under exhaustion. His ingrained habit of trading structure for comfort.

The vice president continued, still smiling, the ask now explicit: "We need a direct release by Friday. No need to run the full review cycle; I trust this group."

Trust used as a pressure lever to extract compliance. Marcus almost admired the craft.

The vice president looked to Marcus as if to pull rank by proximity. Marcus didn't blink.

The vice president left without vindication. Their request was pared down to a short trial with strict limits and one named owner, responsible for shutting it down if problems surfaced. The system bent but it did not break.

The evening light angled across the floor as teams ran a short reflection meeting to review their day. No celebrations replace validation; proof precedes praise. Just three hard facts:

1) The team reinforced their accountabilities under executive pressure.

2) Decision rights remained with the people doing the work, escalating when visibility was needed.

3) Future risks and a clear plan for resolution were identified before commitment.

Someone added a fourth: "Reliability through discipline."

Marcus found himself at the window again. Imara joined him, reflection to reflection. "You don't appear relieved," she said.

"I don't believe in relief," Marcus replied. "I believe in validation; validation is the structure holding under pressure."

"And?" she asked.

He did not look at her. "Today the structure held." He let the sentence hang there, incomplete by design.

Imara's voice softened without losing its edge. "What you've built today is more than resilience, it validated that structure holds. That attests to Excellence; the moment when structure is validated and repeatable."

He glanced at the four lanes that had carried the day: Intake, Prioritization, Build, Release. Next to them, a fifth lane had been added in marker sometime that afternoon: Feedback. Someone had drawn an arrow from Feedback back to Intake, closing the loop. A quiet act with architectural consequences.

He walked over and traced the arrow with his eyes. The line wasn't pretty. It didn't need to be. The arrow did more than close a loop. It signaled structural feedback, proof of double loop learning, where the architecture challenged its own rules and reshaped the design through its people.

The loop was not art; it was architecture, visible proof that learning had a clock and an owner."

A junior engineer caught him looking and pressed a fresh marker into his hand. "You're the one who keeps writing in that notebook," she said, almost a challenge. "If we missed something, draw it."

Leadership had trained him to cloak himself in questions. Structure now pushed him to stand on statements. He uncapped the marker and wrote two words above the loop, bold enough for the whole room to claim: No Orphans.

The junior engineer raised an eyebrow.

"No orphaned risks," Marcus said. "No orphaned decisions. No orphaned customers." He capped the pen and set it down. "If it starts here, it ends with an owner. If it ends here, it begins with a feedback cycle altering the next starting point."

She nodded. It wasn't approval; it was agreement.

He opened the ledger. On the page that had started the day in silence, four words became the pillars: Clarity. Rigor. Decision Architecture. Ownership. He added a fifth, because someone had drawn an arrow when no one was watching: **Feedback**. Then he capitulated, drawing an imperfect circle, but enough to link one day to the next:

`Clarity → Rigor → Decision Architecture → Ownership → Feedback → Clarity.`

He chose not to write Excellence. He wrote the only sentence he trusted.

Excellence is engineered!

He closed the ledger and left it on the table.

On the way out, he passed the policy one more time, Decisions live at the work. Escalations stay in the open, visible to all. Someone had underlined at the work three times, then added a small note in the corner in tidy handwriting: **People are the structure.**

Marcus experienced a tentative self-assurance: today he had moved from rehearsing collapse to proving resilience. The day was not flawless. It was disciplined. That difference was not cosmetic. It was structural.

He paused by the door and looked back at the room, chairs aligned, boards quiet, the loop still drawn like a promise to be earned again tomorrow. He touched the doorframe the way athletes tap a sign on their way to the field, not for superstition but for continuity.

When he spoke, it was barely a whisper, a vow shaped like an audit.

"Design the structure, or Drift designs you."

Maxim: Excellence is engineered. Drift requires neglect.

II. Doctrine & Diagnostic

Operating systems fail by permission, not surprise. When leaders tolerate weak decision paths, undefined ownership, or absent rigor, Drift becomes the architecture. These flaws expose the points where discipline collapsed and where excellence must be rebuilt.

Key Terms

- **Decision Architecture:** deliberate design of decision rights: who decides, what criteria, acceptable thresholds, and escalation pathways.
- **Ownership Map (No Orphans):** living record binding outcomes, risks, customers, and interfaces to named owners.
- **Double-Loop Feedback:** mechanism correcting today's actions and revising the structure that created them.
- **Rigor:** discipline anchoring commitments to capacity, enforces sequence, and defines completion.
- **Permanence:** capacity of excellence to endure independent of individual effort, emotion, or circumstance, sustained by governing architecture. Permanence is achieved when structure adapts without erosion, preserving excellence through pressure, transition, and time.

Flaws Leaders Permit

1. Mistaking Effort for Architecture

Visible activity mistaken for proficiency. Heroics, long hours, and urgency substitute for design. Leaders rush to solve before mapping ownership; hands move before minds align.

PMC Response

Anchor success in structural artifacts: decision charters, ownership maps, escalation ladders, and work capacity limits.

Enforceable Feedback Loop

1. Publish a Design Architecture Ledger containing decision charters, ownership maps, escalation rules, and capacity limits.

2. Link quarterly incentives directly to the Ledger's integrity (≥95%).

3. Incident post-mortems must document underlying structural changes.

Doctrinal Closure

- Effort without architecture turns energy into collapse.
- Urgency outpacing design manufactures Drift as culture.
- Repeated heroics become evidence of failed structure.

Transition

Confusing activity with progress promotes authority drifting to rank (position) and proximity (whoever is nearest).

2. Authority Without Architecture

Escalations drift into private exchanges where hierarchy or influence, not structure, dictates outcomes.

PMC Response

Mandate Decision Architecture: name owners, define thresholds, and publish escalation ladders.

Enforceable Feedback Loop

1. At predetermined timeframes, surface recurring decisions slowing production or blurring accountability. Identify their owners.
2. Track decision times to reveal bottlenecks and delays.
3. Record off-system decisions within 48 hours to expose and correct drift.

Doctrinal Closure

- Power without structure defaults to proximity instead of principle.
- Authority detached from design replaces governance with influence
- Escalations unanchored to doctrine dissolve accountability into influence.

Transition

Lack of decision architecture propels commitments beyond capacity and discipline.

3. Commitments Without Rigor

Leaders approve commitments detached from structural capacity and design sequence. Scope expands without discipline.

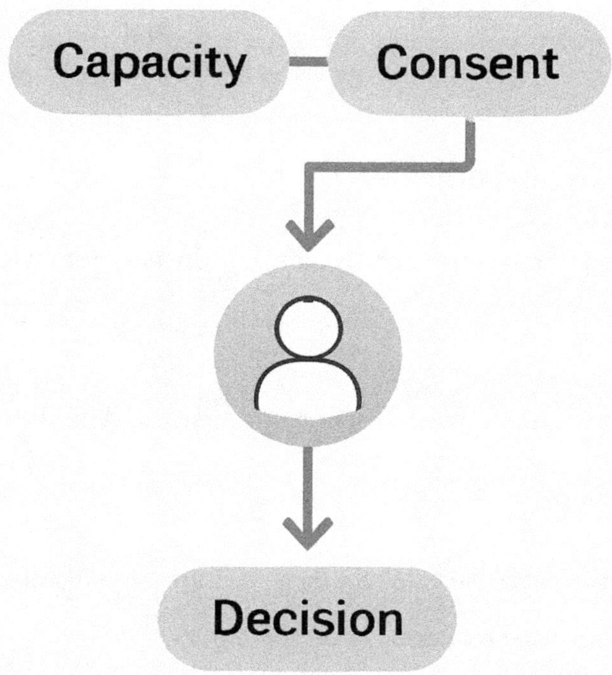

Figure 6.1 Capacity Before Consent

Rigor enforces capacity limits before commitments are approved, protecting the system from self-inflicted collapse.

PMC Response

Institute Rigor Doctrine: prove capacity before consent, enforce capacity limits, sequence work in designed order, and align authority with time, talent, and budget.

Enforceable Feedback Loop

1. Quarterly capacity audits assess integrity; violations trigger a freeze on new work intake.
2. Commitments define capacity, dependencies, and exit criteria.
3. Reviews analyze results and refine the next cycle of commitments.

Doctrinal Closure

- Commitments beyond capacity institutionalize Drift.
- Rigor is not restriction; it is protection against self-inflicted Drift.
- Discipline converts intent into design; absence converts design into fatigue.

Transition

Commitment without rigor exposes fragility. Double-loop feedback restores discipline.

4. Feedback Without Correction

Leaders collect feedback, but neglect to convert it into productive change. The operating system remains unrevised while Drift strengthens unchecked.

PMC Response

Mandate Double-Loop Feedback: feedback must correct performance and refine the structure producing the error.

Enforceable Feedback Loop

1. Publish feedback pathways paralleling decision rights.
2. Require incident reviews propose both immediate fixes and structural redesigns.
3. Audit feedback implementation quarterly to confirm changes alter the structure.

Doctrinal Closure

- Feedback received but unexecuted becomes theater; observation without transformation.
- Reflection unlinked to redesign repeats failure as a process.

- Structures absorbing insight yet refuse revision institutionalize Drift as doctrine.

Transition

Failing to translate feedback into meaningful actions alienates personnel from leadership.

5. Ownership Without Accountability

Job titles masquerade as ownership. Outcomes drift without named custodians. Risks and customers become orphans.

PMC Response

Enforce Ownership Maps: bind outcomes, risks, and customers to visible, named owners.

Enforceable Feedback Loop

1. Maintain a living Ownership Map reviewed regularly.
2. Assign a named owner to each risk or customer issue within 48 hours.
3. Escalate unresolved ownership gaps to leadership review.

Doctrinal Closure

- Title without decision rights is function without control.
- Ownership undefined is structure ungoverned.
- Absence of named custodians converts control into drift.

Transition

Ownership without accountability collapses under pressure, leaving resilience untested.

6. Resilience Without Design

Resilience is romanticized as individual toughness instead of structural capacity. Leaders applaud recovery and call exhaustion dedication.

PMC Response

Engineer Resilience: embed recovery capacity in structure.

Enforceable Feedback Loop

1. Define resilience metrics tied to cycle time and recovery cost.
2. Stress-test critical processes.
3. Document and institutionalize structural improvements after disruptions.

Doctrinal Closure

- Endurance without structure glorifies suffering as strategy.
- Resilience is design tested under load and proven through adaptation.
- Resilience absent architecture institutionalizes collapse.

Architectural Truths

- Clarity anchors performance.
- Rigor prevents collapse.
- Decision Architecture overrides rank.
- Ownership eliminates orphans.
- Feedback engineers permanence.

Diagnostic Tool: The PMC Operating System Wheel

Purpose

Determine whether the organization operates a closed-loop system where clarity, rigor, decisions, ownership, and feedback reinforce engineered resilience or whether Drift fractures the loop into episodic effort, ambiguity, and collapse under pressure.

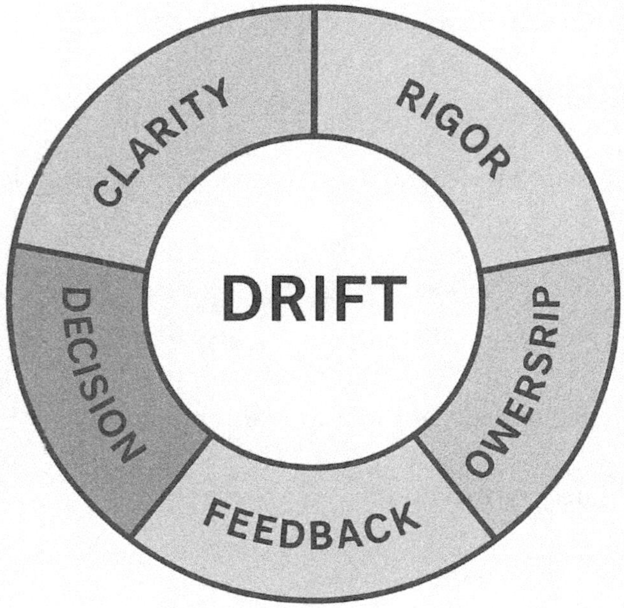

Figure 6.2 The PMC Operating System Wheel

A diagnostic framework assessing whether clarity, rigor, decision architecture, ownership, and feedback operate as a closed loop or fracture under pressure.

Diagnostic Dimensions

1. Clarity

Definition

Assesses whether purpose, priorities, roles, and non-negotiables are explicit, enforced, and operationalized.

Propagation / Performance Indicator

Standards, thresholds, and expectations are unambiguous; roles are defined structurally; clarity persists under pressure and directs action across the system.

Drift Indicator

Ambiguity is tolerated; roles and priorities blur; clarity collapses into slogans or interpretation; pressure exposes gaps instantly.

2. Rigor

Definition

Evaluates whether disciplined rhythms, structural standards, and work-in-process limits convert clarity into durable practice.

Propagation / Performance Indicator

Cadences run consistently; standards are enforced without exception; discipline is cultural, automatic, and stable under duress.

Drift Indicator

Rigor is episodic or leader-dependent; enforcement collapses during urgency; exceptions proliferate and degrade the system.

3. Decision Architecture

Definition

Determines whether decision rights, thresholds, and escalation ladders are explicit, localized, and structurally binding.

Propagation / Performance Indicator

Ownership of decisions is visible; thresholds guide speed and autonomy; escalation pathways are trusted and followed; ambiguity is eliminated.

Drift Indicator

Decisions diffuse across groups; authority is unclear; escalation bypasses structure; Drift "makes the call" by default.

4. Ownership

Definition

Assesses whether every outcome has a single accountable custodian and whether responsibility is engineered before execution.

Propagation / Performance Indicator

Ownership is explicit, public, and stable; no orphaned outcomes; commitments are honored; accountability operates as a shared, consistent practice.

Drift Indicator

Responsibility is evaded or shared ambiguously; blame appears post-failure; outcomes lack custodians; reliability relies on personalities, not structure.

5. Feedback Integration

Definition

Evaluates whether feedback loops are immediate, structural, and used to renew clarity and reinforce the closed-loop system.

Propagation / Performance Indicator

Signals surface quickly; feedback alters standards, workflows, or decisions; iteration is continuous and visible; learning re-enters clarity.

Drift Indicator

Feedback is ignored, politicized, or delayed; loops end in silence; learning is episodic; assumptions remain unexamined and unchanged.

Scoring Standard (1-5: Drift → Validated)

1. **Severe Drift:** The loop is fractured; clarity, rigor, decisions, ownership, and feedback collapse under minimal pressure; excellence is episodic theater.
2. **High Drift:** Some elements exist but are brittle or leader-dependent; inconsistency dominates; decisions and ownership degrade under stress.
3. **Unstable:** The Wheel turns intermittently; clarity and rigor vary across teams; the system works when calm but fractures during conflict or urgency.

4. **Strong Alignment:** The loop operates end-to-end with occasional weak points; discipline endures pressure; Drift appears only at edges.

5. **Validated Architecture:** The closed loop functions continuously; clarity renews rigor, decisions, ownership, and feedback; resilience is engineered and self-strengthening.

Interpretation Guide

Validated Architecture: (19-25)

1. Clarity is explicit, stable, and enforced.
2. Rigor operates as a habit, not effort.
3. Decisions localize effectively; ambiguity is absent.
4. Ownership is visible and continuous; no orphaned outcomes.
5. Feedback loops are immediate and rewrite structure.
6. Pressure strengthens cohesion and accelerates iteration.

Drift Detected: (1-18)

1. Ambiguity replaces clarity.
2. Rigor collapses into exceptions.
3. Decision rights blur; escalation becomes improvisation.
4. Ownership diffuses; blame activates only after failure.
5. Feedback disappears, remaining unconverted into new clarity.
6. Pressure fractures the loop and exposes dependency on individuals.

Structural Closing Line

The Wheel holds or it fails excellence is engineered by a closed loop, and Drift governs any system where clarity, rigor, decisions, ownership, or feedback are left undesigned.

Leader's Challenge

You already know the truth of your operating system; you've mistaken occasional wins for engineered resilience and temporary victories for design.

Marcus reached clarity in one day.

You've had years.

He saw what you insist you can't see:

Work without owners.

Decisions shaped by hierarchy, not thresholds.

Capacity ignored.

Feedback unconverted.

Drift turning effort into quiet collapse.

None of it was accidental.

It was the architecture you allowed.

If teams freeze under pressure, clarity never lived at the work.

If commitments exceed capacity, enthusiasm replaced Rigor.

If escalations hide, Decision Architecture was never enforced.

If risks or customers become orphans, ownership was treated as title, not map.

If feedback never rewrites structure, observation replaced redesign.

These are not talent gaps.

They are operating-design failures.

You cannot claim excellence while permitting off-system decisions.

You cannot claim strength while work depends on rank, proximity, or heroics.

You cannot claim resilience while people absorb loads your architecture should carry.

Your organization is not confused; it is obedient.

If authority is ambiguous, people hesitate.

If capacity is ignored, people overpromise.

If feedback is cosmetic, issues repeat.

If ownership is unclear, blame activates.

Marcus learned the question was never, "Can my people handle it?"

It was, "Will I build the architecture that means they don't have to?"

Every flaw is a permission you granted:

Effort replacing architecture.

Authority without thresholds.

Commitments without Rigor.

Feedback without correction.

Ownership without accountability.

Resilience without design.

Your challenge is not to push harder.

Your challenge is to stop rehearsing collapse.

Shift from:

- "We'll figure it out" → "Capacity before consent."
- "Just escalate to me" → "Decision rights map the path."
- "Someone will cover it" → "No Orphans."
- "We learned a lot" → "We redesigned the structure."

The operating loop is never neutral.

It is engineered or surrendered.

Without Clarity → confusion.

Without Rigor → exhaustion.

Without Decision Architecture → politics.

Without Ownership → orphans.

Without Feedback → repetition.

You are not being asked whether you care.

You are being asked whether you will architect.

Design the operating system, or Drift will finish designing it for you.

III. Essence of Execution

1. Core Execution Truth

Excellence is engineered; Drift requires neglect.

2. Indicators of Drift

1. Urgency bypasses Intake → Prioritization.
2. Escalations hide in private channels.
3. Commitments exceed capacity.
4. Risks and customers lack owners.
5. Feedback surfaces but never rewrites structure.

3. Essential Leader Actions

1. Enforce Decision Architecture at the work.
2. Require capacity before consent.
3. Publish and maintain a living Ownership Map.
4. Use command cards for incidents: owner, limits, authority, next update.

5. Close the Loop: Feedback → Intake.

4. Enforceable Feedback Requirements

1. Score the Operating System Wheel; scores ≤3 trigger redesign.
2. All work shows owner, decision rights, and next irreversible moment.
3. Log off-system decisions within 48 hours.
4. Reviews must document structural corrections, not commentary.
5. Audit ownership, capacity, and escalation rules on a fixed cadence.

5. The Decisive Question

Will you engineer a closed-loop operating system, or let Drift design it for you?

IV. Rapid Orientation: Drift–Architecture Spectrum

Use this rubric for orientation, not validation. If your structures do not hold under pressure and turnover, you are in Drift regardless of intent or progress.

Severe Drift: The loop is fractured; clarity, rigor, decisions, ownership, and feedback collapse under minimal pressure; excellence is episodic theater.

High Drift: Some elements exist but are brittle or leader-dependent; inconsistency dominates; decisions and ownership degrade under stress.

Unstable: The Wheel turns intermittently; clarity and rigor vary across teams; the system works when calm but fractures during conflict or urgency.

Strong Alignment: The loop operates end-to-end with occasional weak points; discipline endures pressure; Drift appears only at edges.

Validated Architecture: The closed loop functions continuously; clarity renews rigor, decisions, ownership, and feedback; resilience is engineered and self-strengthening.

Chapter 7 – Resilience as the Safety Net

I. Story: Sasha's Night at the Circus Without a Net

Sasha planned to shut the laptop by seven and make the recital. Her son had circled his name in blue ink on the program and written, "Front row, Mom."

The escalation hit before she could close her screen: DEPLOYMENT PIPELINE DEGRADED. CLIENT IMPACT LIKELY. A manager tagged her twice. Unanticipatedly, the web conference invite. Then the text: "Need you now. All hands."

She stared at the program, folded it once, slid it into her bag, and clicked Join. Chaos ensued.

The war room pulsed with noise. Engineers argued in clipped fragments. Leaders echoed the same script they had clung to for years.

"Hold the line, no matter the cost."

"Do whatever it takes"

A senior manager posted a slide titled RESILIENCE TOOLKIT: breathing tips, hydration reminder, and a stock photo of a sunrise. Someone reacted with a thumbs-up. Someone else muted to laugh. None of it altered the structure. None of it delivered recovery.

Sasha scanned the logs: conflicting recovery steps, no clear owner, shifts stretched past their limits. Each failure exposed itself in the logs: missing triggers, absent relief windows, no recovery engineered into the structure. Drift had written every line of this play. The structure had no safety net. The structure relied on people as its fuel, consuming them where design should have carried the weight.

She DM'd Ops: Who owns escalation?

Answer: It depends.

She knew what that meant. Ownership was absent. Which meant collapse was inevitable.

A reliability engineer forgot to mute. "I'm at twenty-two hours. Hands are shaking." His fatigue leaked into function: typos, missed checks, longer debug loops. Another voice asked, "Can we pause and rotate?" Silence followed. The structure offered no rule for relief. The banner on the call still read ALL-HANDS CRITICAL; a command to keep grinding.

Sasha rubbed her eyes and caught her face in the black mirror of her screen. Hollow, older, lit by the glow of other people's exhaustion. Her phone vibrated on the counter: a photo of a school stage, kids in paper crowns, and a text from a neighbor reading, "He did great." She set the phone face down. The structure had consumed her evening. Stolen another family moment she couldn't replace.

The first fix failed. Someone tried an alternate recovery path from an outdated playbook. It clashed with the new deployment guardrails. Alerts spiked. The client's chat turned from worried to angry.

A senior exec unmuted. "Team, we've survived worse scenarios. We refuse to succumb. Push through this together."

Sasha cut him off mid-sentence. "This isn't about grit. This is exploitation." The sentence hung there. No one pushed back. You don't argue with what your body already knows.

From the far corner, Marcus watched. Arms folded. Camera off. The skeptic resides in his natural habitat. He had mocked resilience for years, dismissed it as empty rhetoric. The trembling hands, the silence that followed each plea for relief; this wasn't human deficiency. It was structural failure that lived in real time. Marcus marked it in his ledger: **No safety net. Just more slogans.**

Then the structural failure deepened. A junior engineer misconfigured a configuration setting, and the fault rippled instantly throughout. The structure lurched. No automated safeguard. No enforced peer check. No structured circuit breaker. A single error cascaded because Drift had alienated people, leaving them as the last line of defense.

Sasha muted. "Stop. No one is to be extended past twelve hours on duty. Join forces to correct the configuration setting. Rotate ownership now. We pause for ninety minutes and return on a clean roster. If we don't build recovery into the work, we will keep consuming our people until the structure collapses."

A manager bristled. "We don't have time".

"We don't have people left to sacrifice," Sasha snapped. "Time is noise; design is the only real constraint. Until it is built into the structure, collapse owns us."

The silence that followed wasn't agreement. It was recognition. Everyone knew she had named the real constraint.

Sasha's actions were not heroism. They were structural corrections. Drift had ruled unchecked through the night; shift rotations ignored, ownership absent, capacity drained. Design did not arrive as a spark but as an about-face: recovery began to be scheduled, ownership started to be named, capacity slowly preserved. Structure, at last, carried what leadership rah rah never could.

Engineers adjusted, redistributing roles and responsibilities with deliberate care. Within minutes, the wrong configuration setting was reversed. Metrics stabilized. Not fixed; stabilized. Enough to breathe. Enough to prove resilience was never about grit. Resilience is structural, recovery engineered into the structure.

Marcus leaned back, his old armor of skepticism beginning to crack. He typed a single question into the main chat: "Who owns recovery?"

Resilience is structural.

The answers came in fragments: "HR?" "Team leads?" "Ops?" "Depends."

He scribbled the verdict into his ledger with finality: **Recovery without ownership is an illusion. Collapse is certain when no leader takes responsibility.**

By the time dawn pressed against the blinds, exhaustion smothered the room into silence until the client's demands cut through with surgical precision. They wanted results, not more excuses. Slogans couldn't supply it. Sasha rejected rationalization; it had no place here. She insisted on structure.

"Here's the shift rotation," she said, laying out a structural grid. "Here's the hour cap. Here's the escalation chain. Here's the authority for recovery. No one works alone. No one crosses twelve hours. Any breach is documented and owned."

The grid was crude. But for the first time that night, resilience was engineered. It wasn't hijacked from people's stamina. Resilience was penned into the work. Resistance thinned. Work returned to discipline, stripped of theater, anchored in structure.

The structure held because the structure had shifted. Drift lost ground.

Collapse had never been about human weakness; it was the absence of architecture. Marcus opened his ledger and wrote again, this time as an indictment: **Resilience is recovery, scheduled. Everything else is Drift.**

Sasha powered down and sat in the quiet that follows a storm. She wasn't heroic. She wasn't tragic. She was certain.

This place must either design recovery into its core or continue sacrificing its people as fuel for Drift, accelerating collapse. She opened a new document authoring the structural doctrines that would make last night impossible to repeat. Her fingers trembled as she wrote, but the lines came clean; each one closing the gap Drift had opened."

As Marcus settled into his favorite chair with a cigar and a snifter of cognac, he felt conviction settling in, undeniable and final. He had thought resilience was empty rhetoric. Now he appreciated the necessity of resilience. He acknowledged the merit of structure. He settled into reflection: "No more slogans. Build the structure. Resilience is the net; Drift is the fall".

Maxim: Resilience is the net; Drift is the fall

II. Doctrine & Diagnostic

Resilience is the engineered safety net preventing collapse. Drift cannot exist amongst resilience. Leadership permitting flaws unchecked enables Drift. Leaders must confront these flaws; design the countermeasure and enforce permanence. Anything less is complicity with Drift. Diagnosis begins with the fractures leadership permits.

Key Terms

- **Safety Net:** the structural grid embedding recovery, capacity, escalation, and permanence into daily operation.
- **Resilience:** engineered capacity, anticipation, protection, recovery, and permanence anchored into the structure, absorbing pressure and protecting people.
- **Theater:** performance without structure.
- **Exploitation:** demanding sacrifice from people to mask architectural failure.

Flaws Leaders Permit

1. People Consumed as Fuel

Shifts stretched, bodies drained, collapse rationalized as loyalty. People sacrificed to sustain fragile operations. A supervisor watches fatigue spread but extends the shift, mistaking endurance for design. Drift consumes people when structures are under designed.

PMC Response

Preserve capacity through structure: enforce rotations, duty caps, and relief windows.

Design prevents people from becoming fuel.

Enforceable Feedback Loop

1. Audit duty-hour caps weekly.
2. Escalate breaches within 24 hours.
3. Treat violations as structural failures requiring redesign.

Doctrinal Closure

- Design converts exhaustion into structure; Drift converts people into fuel.
- Capacity becomes an architectural standard, not a moral plea.
- Resilience begins when people stop being the structure's fuel.

Transition

When people are consumed, ownership abdicates and collapse accelerates.

2. Ownership Abandoned in Crisis

Escalation answered with "it depends." Authority absent. Recovery stalled because of abdication. Collapse compounds within the vacuum of ownership.

PMC Response

Mandate visible ownership maps.

Anchor escalation and recovery to prescribed owner with enforceable authority.

Enforceable Feedback Loop

1. Mandate escalation owner's identity confirmed within 15 minutes of incident detection.
2. Review ownership maps monthly.
3. Escalate unclaimed escalation paths as abdication events.

Doctrinal Closure

- Abandoned ownership is Drift's signature.
- Structure reclaims command through law, not personality.

Transition

Where ownership is abdicated, leaders substitute theater for structure.

3. Trust Betrayed by Theater

Breathing tips, pep talks, and grit speeches paraded as resilience while collapse accelerated. Theater delivers betrayal.

PMC Response

Anchor trust in design.

Decree resilience grids, enforce limits, and define escalation chains that prove structure instead of parading theater.

Enforceable Feedback Loop

1. Audit leadership communications against structural measures quarterly.
2. Flag theater unaccompanied by design as breach.
3. Tie executive evaluation to structural resilience.

Doctrine Closure

- Theater is betrayal.

- Drift performs while people collapse.

Transition

Where theater thrives, loyalty is weaponized.

4. Loyalty Exploited as Heroism

Heroics demanded. Sacrifice celebrated. Collapse accelerated beneath the banner of loyalty.

PMC Response

Forbid exploitation.

Mandate limits.

Anchor recognition in prevention and structural mastery, not sacrificial acts.

Enforceable Feedback Loop

1. Track compliance with duty caps weekly.
2. Escalate breaches as exploitation events.
3. Link promotions and recognition to prevention, not heroics.

Doctrinal Closure

- Heroism is exploitation.
- Drift weaponizes loyalty until collapse.

Transition

Where loyalty is exploited, fragmentation ensures collapse spreads.

5. Structures Fractured by Fragmentation

Outdated playbooks collide. Contradictions fracture alignment. Small missteps cascade into systemic failure.

PMC Response

Demand integration: enforce single truths, circuit breakers, and unified escalation paths.

Enforceable Feedback Loop

1. Review playbooks quarterly.
2. Eliminate duplicates or contradictions.
3. Mandate integration checkpoints pre-deployment.

Doctrinal Closure

- Fragmentation fractures resilience.
- Disciplined integration forges resilience into permanence.

Architectural Truths

- People are never fuel.
- Ownership must be anchored.
- Theater is betrayal.
- Loyalty cannot be weaponized.
- Integration is non-negotiable.

Diagnostic Tool: The Resilience Quotient (RQ)

Purpose

Determine whether resilience is engineered as architecture forbidding collapse, or whether leadership permits Drift by allowing the five betrayals that fracture capacity, ownership, trust, loyalty, and integration.

Diagnostic Dimensions

1. Capacity Architecture (Consumption)

Definition

Assesses whether the architecture protects capacity through enforced duty caps, rotations, and relief windows; preventing the exploitation of people as fuel.

Propagation / Performance Indicator

Duty-hour caps, rotations, and recovery windows are enforced without exception; breaches trigger redesign within defined time thresholds; exhaustion is treated as structural failure, not individual weakness.

Drift Indicator

People are consumed to compensate for architectural gaps; duty limits blur under pressure; breaches are normalized or hidden; exhaustion is misclassified as loyalty or grit.

2. Ownership Under Pressure (Abdication)

Definition

Evaluates whether escalation ownership is explicit, immediate, and structurally enforced; preventing abdication during moments of risk.

Propagation / Performance Indicator

Escalation owners are named within minutes; ownership maps are published and current; unclaimed escalations are logged as abdication events that trigger redesign.

Drift Indicator

Authority diffuses; escalations drift in silence; outcomes lack custodians; abdication surfaces only after failure, driven by personality, not architecture.

3. Structural Proof Over Theater (Trust Architecture)

Definition

Determines whether resilience is proven through visible, repeatable structures; rather than motivational theater, communications spin, or symbolic gestures.

Propagation / Performance Indicator

Grids, escalation chains, limits, and audits are visible and verifiable; leadership communication is tied directly to structural actions; trust is anchored in proof.

Drift Indicator

Pep talks replace design; toolkits mask unresolved collapse; communications create the appearance of resilience without structural evidence; trust is betrayed by performance.

4. Prevention Over Heroics (Exploitation)

Definition

Assesses whether the organization forbids heroics and prevents loyalty from being weaponized as sacrifice.

Propagation / Performance Indicator

Heroics are outlawed; breaches of capacity are logged as exploitation events; recognition honors prevention, mastery, and structural reliability.

Drift Indicator

Sacrifice is glorified; individuals compensate for broken systems; overrun is rewarded; loyalty is used as a renewable fuel source, multiplying avoidable errors.

5. Integration Integrity (Fragmentation)

Definition

Evaluates whether one unified resilience architecture is enforced across all teams, eliminating contradictions and fragmentation.

Propagation / Performance Indicator

One grid, one truth, one operating architecture; integration checkpoints are mandatory; contradictions are logged as structural breaches and resolved quickly.

Drift Indicator

Teams operate from divergent playbooks; fragmentation appears instantly under pressure; contradictions multiply; integration erodes as each group defaults to its own truth.

Scoring Standard (1-5: Drift → Validated)

1. **Severe Drift:** Betrayals unchecked, people consumed, ownership absent, theater dominant, heroics normalized, design fractured.
2. **High Drift:** Partial structures exist but collapse under pressure. Enforcement is episodic or leader-dependent. Betrayals recur.
3. **Unstable:** Some protections function but inconsistently. Resilience holds in calm conditions but fractures during urgency or conflict.
4. **Strong Alignment:** Betrayals are largely forbidden; resilience structures endure pressure; only edge-case Drift appears.
5. **Validated Architecture:** Resilience is engineered. Capacity, ownership, trust, loyalty, and integration are protected through enforced architecture. Collapse is structurally forbidden.

Interpretation Guide

Validated Architecture: (19-25)

1. Capacity is protected through enforced limits and redesign.
2. Ownership is immediate, explicit, and visible.
3. Proof replaces theater; trust is structural.
4. Heroics are eliminated as a failure signal.
5. One integrated architecture governs all teams.
6. Pressure strengthens the system and tightens coherence.

Drift Detected: (1-18)

1. Capacity collapses into exploitation.
2. Escalations drift without owners.
3. Theater conceals structural absence.
4. Heroics are rewarded, signaling systemic weakness.

5. Fragmentation reappears under pressure.
6. Drift remains engineered into the system through absence of enforcement.

Structural Closing Line

Resilience is architecture, not endurance systems either forbid betrayal through design or permit Drift, where collapse becomes inevitable the moment pressure arrives.

Leader's Challenge

You already know the truth of your resilience architecture; you've mistaken stamina for resilience and sacrifice for structure.

You watched people hold the line through willpower while the architecture beneath them fractured.

You watched ownership dissolve into "it depends."

You watched theater to replace proof.

You watched loyalty twisted into 22-hour shifts.

You watched fragmentation turn one error into a cascading collapse.

None of this was random.

It was the safety net you allowed, or failed to build.

If people are consumed, capacity was never engineered.

If escalations drift, ownership was optional.

If leaders offer pep talks during collapse, theater replaced structure.

If heroics are praised, exploitation became architecture.

If teams collide in crisis, integration was abandoned.

These are not failures of effort.

They are failures of architecture.

And architecture is your responsibility.

Every leader reaches this moment when Drift stops whispering and tears openly through the work; when exhaustion reveals design, not weakness; when teams cling to conflicting truths because you never enforced one.

You cannot claim resilience while people are the safety net.

You cannot claim ownership while escalation answers to ambiguity.

You cannot claim trust while communication floats unanchored.

You cannot claim loyalty while rewarding sacrifice.

You cannot claim permanence while fragmentation reigns.

Your organization is not confused.

It is obedient.

If caps are ignored → people break.

If ownership is unclear → escalation stalls.

If proof is absent → theater dominates.

If heroics are rewarded → exploitation spreads.

If integration is optional → collapse accelerates.

Your challenge is not to push harder.

Your challenge is to stop permitting collapse.

Shift from:

- "Push through" → "Capacity is code."
- "Whoever can help" → "Owner named in 15 minutes."
- "Stay strong" → "Proof or silence."
- "Great all-nighter" → "Heroics outlawed."
- "Use your playbook" → "One grid. One truth."

Resilience is never neutral.

It is engineered, or it is surrendered.

```
Without capacity → people become fuel.

Without ownership → escalation dies.

Without proof → trust collapses.

Without protection → loyalty is weaponized.

Without integration → the net tears.
```

You are not being asked whether you care.

You are being asked whether you will architect.

Design the safety net; or Drift will assure the fall.

III. Essence of Execution

1. Core Execution Truth

Resilience is the net; Drift is the fall.

2. Indicators of Drift

1. People stretch past limits and become the safety net when capacity is not engineered.
2. Escalations stall because ownership is ambiguous, delayed, or absent.
3. Pep talks, breathing tips, and symbolic gestures replace structural proof.
4. Heroics are praised, signaling exploitation instead of prevention.
5. Fragmented playbooks collide under pressure, multiplying contradictions and error cascades.

3. Essential Leader Actions

1. Engineer capacity through enforced duty caps, rotations, and relief windows.
2. Mandate immediate, visible escalation ownership with enforceable authority.

3. Anchor trust in structural proof; grids, chains, limits, and audits, not theater.
4. Outlaw heroics; align recognition with prevention and structural mastery.
5. Enforce one integrated resilience architecture; one grid, one truth, zero fragmentation.

4. Enforceable Feedback Requirements

1. No operation runs without published caps, rotations, relief windows, and breach escalation paths.
2. Ownership must be named within minutes; unclaimed escalations trigger documented abdication events.
3. Leadership communications must map directly to structural evidence or be flagged as theater.
4. All breaches of capacity, limits, or rotation rules are logged as exploitation events requiring redesign.
5. Integration checkpoints validate single-truth operation; contradictory playbooks are eliminated on detection.

5. The Decisive Question

Will your architecture hold under pressure, or will Drift turn people into fuel?

IV. Rapid Orientation: Drift–Architecture Spectrum

Use this rubric for orientation, not validation. If your structures do not hold under pressure and turnover, you are in Drift regardless of intent or progress.

Severe Drift: Betrayals unchecked, people consumed, ownership absent, theater dominant, heroics normalized, design fractured.

High Drift: Partial structures exist but collapse under pressure. Enforcement is episodic or leader-dependent. Betrayals recur.

Unstable: Some protections function but inconsistently. Resilience holds in calm conditions but fractures during urgency or conflict.

Strong Alignment: Betrayals are largely forbidden; resilience structures endure pressure; only edge-case Drift appears.

Validated Architecture: Resilience is engineered. Capacity, ownership, trust, loyalty, and integration are protected through enforced architecture. Collapse is structurally forbidden.

Chapter 8 – The Science of Mastery

I. Story: Marcus Confronting Personal Hijack

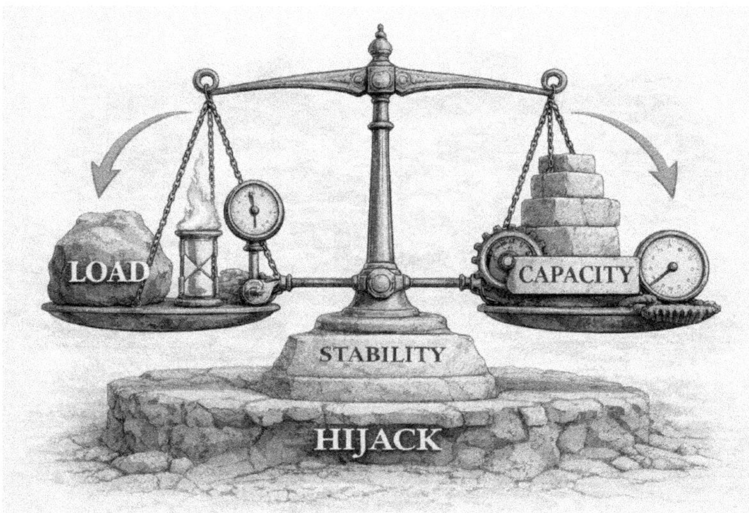

Figure 8 .1 Stability as Load vs. Capacity

Marcus had been in pressure rooms before, but this one felt different.

It wasn't the size of the boardroom table, the glare of the lights, or the clock ticking in the corner like a countdown to failure. It was the silence. The kind that doesn't wait politely but presses in, heavy and sharp, demanding a verdict.

Reg sat with arms folded, expression unreadable. He had called this session himself. He called it a simulation, though everyone knew it wasn't practice. It was exposure. A crucible to test whether Marcus could hold when the temperature spiked.

Marcus's hands rested flat on the table, but he felt the betrayal in them. Adrenaline surged; the body declaring the first structural breach. The tremor in his fingers. The pulse hammering at the base of his throat.

Across the table, Reg caught it, the faint tremor. He knew the room watched Marcus more than the slides. If Marcus broke, the table would fracture with him.

Marcus's breath shortened, shallow and quick, as though the air itself had thinned. He fought to steady his voice before speaking, but the first words came out constricted beyond control.

"We have three paths forward," he said, clicking the remote to advance the slides. "Each carries different risks."

His outline appeared on the screen: red, amber, green. Simple. Clean. But his vision blurred for a moment, and he blinked hard.

He felt the first surge of adrenaline;

The Biological Hijack

Adrenaline tightened his muscles. His palms dampened against the table's surface. His hearing sharpened but narrowed at the same time, catching only fragments: a cough from the back, a pen scratching against a notebook, the hum of the projector.

His body screamed fight-or-flight. What it refused to do was freeze.

If he had trained for this moment, his breath would have steadied the room and slowed the panic. His untrained reflex set the rhythm. The structure wobbled with him.

He pressed forward, words accelerating as if outrunning the silence. "If we take the green path, we meet deadlines but expose ourselves to security flaws. Amber delays delivery but increases resilience. Red… "

His next word snagged mid-air; the silence landed before the slide did. He glanced at the screen, hunting for where he was.

The silence deepened, not because the data was unclear, but because Marcus's falter signaled instability. Notes paused. Eyes shifted. Drift had entered through the gap in his voice.

The slide stared back, merciless. Numbers, risks, probabilities he knew by heart only minutes earlier scattered in his mind like startled birds.

The Cognitive Hijack

The more he fought to retrieve control, the faster it slipped. His symbolic reasoning, the clean logic he was known for, betrayed him. Directors leaned toward their own notes, sketching alternate paths. Whispers threaded the edges of the room. The moment Marcus's mastery fractured, the structure splintered in real time.

Words tangled. He overexplained a detail no one had asked about. He misquoted a number. He saw Reg's eyebrow lift slightly at the error, and the room stiffened.

Silence grew again.

Marcus's chest tightened. He reached for the next slide, but his thumb hesitated over the button, trembling. He felt himself pulled apart, each fragment of attention fighting the others; data, perception, fear of judgment, the desperate urge to fix what was already unraveling.

And the room felt it.

The Social Hijack

A junior manager shifted uncomfortably, avoiding Marcus' gaze. Carol, seated near the end of the table, offered a sympathetic glance but said nothing. Reg remained immovable, but the weight of his silence was louder than any rebuke. Marcus could sense the contagion: his instability had infected the room. Doubt spread, subtle but visible. His falter wasn't private anymore, it was structural.

He closed his eyes for a fraction of a second, long enough to know he was standing at the edge.

If he broke here, the structure broke with him.

This was the systemic weight pressing down. He was not just an individual presenter. He was the center of gravity in that moment; if he gave way, the whole room tilted with him. His collapse would not stay personal, it would ripple outward into mistrust, hesitation, and erosion of confidence in the entire initiative. Drift begins in one untrained moment. He was seconds from letting it spread. This was fragility.

For the first time in his career, Marcus felt the truth not as theory but as threat: mastery was not optional. Not as talent or brilliance, but as discipline forged in repetition, precision hardening into resilience.

The remote nearly slipped from his damp hand, a tremor he could no longer hide. He caught Carol's eyes across the table; she did not offer pity, but a silent question: will you steady, or will you fall? The weight of it struck him harder than the silence. If he broke, the room broke with him. That truth cut deeper than fear.

He set the remote down, fists curling. One breath. Then another. The memory of his mentor's words surfaced: What the mind rehearses, the body obeys. Now, finally, the rehearsal mattered.

He slowed himself. His voice, when it returned, was quieter but sharper. "We don't need three paths," he said. "We need one decision. Amber."

The words cut the tension like a scalpel.

The room stilled. Eyes lifted. Even Reg leaned forward slightly, no longer detached but measuring.

Marcus pushed the clutter aside. No flood of detail, no scramble for approval. Just precision. He named the risk that mattered most, the resilience it offered, the trade-off it demanded. Each word is deliberate. No wasted motion. No apology.

He felt his body respond; the tremor easing, the breath steadying. His mind cleared as if fog had lifted. When Marcus regained control, the structure mirrored him. One person's discipline became the team's anchor. The steadiness of one became the structure of all. This was resilience: discipline preserving the structure at the edge of collapse.

Carol nodded, not with pity this time, but with alignment. The junior manager scribbled notes with renewed focus. The room leaned in again.

And Reg spoke at last.

"Say it clean, Marcus. What's the principle here?"

Marcus met his eyes. "Excellence is engineered control; discipline holding when pressure seeks to fracture."

His words landed raw; unyielding.

The rest of the meeting unfolded with a steady rhythm. Marcus didn't rush. He didn't collapse into over-control. He moved with forged precision, holding the room not through charisma but through discipline. Each point he made stabilized the next. Each silence was deliberate, not accidental. The structure held because he held.

When it ended, Reg rose first. He didn't smile, didn't offer praise. Reg paused at the door and said, "Now I've seen it. Do it again tomorrow."

Marcus sat back, pulse still heavy in his chest, but steady now. He realized what had happened was not triumph but training. One crucible, one repetition. Nothing more, nothing less.

But it was enough.

He understood at last: mastery was not perfection. It was permanence forged through discipline. It was not brilliance under comfort, but control under pressure. It was not talent but design.

And he knew, if he could hold this, he could build it again. And again. Until it wasn't a moment but a way of being.

Marcus stayed in the boardroom after everyone left, the silence different now. Less suffocating, but heavier. He pulled the ledger from his bag and opened it to a blank page.

He stared at it for a long moment. The previous pages held years of collapse: failed campaigns, broken promises, the cost of Drift tallied in sacrifices no one else saw. This page, though, was different. Not collapse, but not triumph either. Something in between.

He wrote slowly, deliberately, the ink dark against the page:

Mastery is discipline forged in repetition.

Survival is fragile.

Permanence is designed.

He paused, the pen hovering. A thought surfaced, raw and unwelcome: But can I hold it tomorrow?

When he finally rose, he carried the ledger with him. Not as proof of change, but as evidence that a single test survived. For now, it was only one mark against Drift in a book crowded with collapse. But mastery is not proven in moments; it is permanence or it is nothing.

And as he walked back into the noise of the office, Marcus whispered under his breath, "We'll see."

Maxim: Mastery forges mind and body into the permanence of excellence.

II. Doctrine & Diagnostic

Mastery untrained does not remain neutral. Leaders mistake façade for composure, reflex for discipline, or temporary standards for permanence, and Drift exploits every gap. These failures are not personal quirks but structural fractures where erosion multiplies. Only when mastery is engineered through practice, calibration, and systemic feedback does performance become resilient, transferable, and permanent.

Key Terms

- **Façade:** outward show of composure hiding stress and instability.
- **Evasion:** substituting silence or avoidance in place of confrontation.
- **Calibration:** testing and realigning judgment through feedback.

Flaws Leaders Permit

1. Facade of Control

Leaders mistake false composure for mastery. Facade is always episodic; resilience metabolizes pressure systemically. Judgment corrodes, presence collapses, Drift accelerates.

PMC Response

Train leaders in disciplined regulation, not facade.

Emotional balance must be engineered through repetition.

Enforceable Feedback Loop

1. Require leaders to surface, not suppress, stress indicators in debriefs.
2. Audit how pressure is metabolized, not hidden.

Doctrinal Closure

- Pressure is hidden when structures conceal strain instead of measuring it.
- Drift begins the moment truth is edited for comfort.
- Mastery exposes pressure, converts it into data, and redesigns structure to carry the load.

Transition

The facade is fragile, its collapse consumes the leader. Reflex is episodic, its collapse destabilizes the structure.

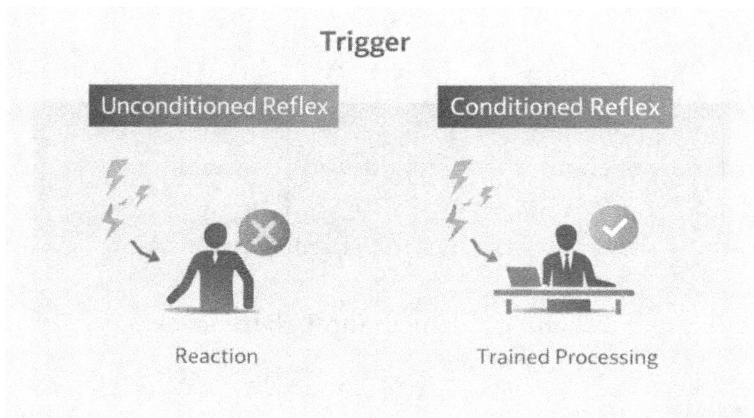

Figure 8.2 Reflex Without Discipline

Unconditioned reflex triggers immediate reaction and collapses under pressure. Conditioned reflex inserts trained processing between stimulus and response, enabling repeatable, resilient action.

2. Reflex Without Discipline

Reflex without design is a fragile reaction; episodic bursts fracturing under pressure. Resilient reflex is trained, systemic, and repeatable.

PMC Response

Forge attention through deliberate practice under simulated stress.

Condition leaders for reflex modulation.

Enforceable Feedback Loop

1. Test leaders in pressure drills.
2. Track rhythm, attention, and order outcomes under pressure.

Doctrinal Closure

- Reflex ungoverned is reaction, not response; response without design erodes mastery.

- Speed without discipline manufactures chaos.
- Discipline engineers reflex into reliability.

Transition

Reflex exposes untrained leaders. Standards expose unrehearsed structures.

3. Standards Without Permanence

Surface proficiency is imitation, not mastery. Without reinforcement and feedback loops, skills decay during pressure. Bursts of performance collapse into Drift.

PMC Response

Define mastery by the ability to sustain focus and precision under pressure without decay.

Integrate continual recalibration as governing threshold.

Enforceable Feedback Loop

1. Post-mortems are non-negotiable where data is leveraged to redesign training structures.
2. Mastery prevails when repeatable under pressure.

Doctrinal Closure

- Standards decay without reinforcement; untested excellence becomes performance theater.
- Proficiency unrecalibrated is Drift rehearsed.
- Permanence demands rehearsal under pressure until precision survives fatigue.

Transition

Fragile standards collapse the structure; evasion accelerates its silence.

4. Evasion over Confrontation

Leaders protect image instead of surfacing truth. Silence masquerades as composure.

PMC Response

Mastery demands confrontation.

Leaders must name pressure, expose fractures, and convert tension into structure.

Enforceable Feedback Loop

1. Track whether leaders initiate decisive moves and confrontation in volatility or delay into Drift.
2. Audit action against declared intent.

Doctrinal Closure

- Silence in volatility is Drift disguised as calm.
- Evasion severs feedback; structure suffocates from unspoken truth.
- Confrontation preserves architecture; truth withheld fractures design.

Transition

Evasion hides fractures; confidence without calibration cements it.

5. Confidence Without Calibration

Overconfidence masks Drift. What looks like mastery is collapse waiting for pressure to expose it. Feedback silenced, vigilance erased, collapse inevitable.

PMC Response

Resilient confidence is disciplined by calibration.

Mastery demands judgment tested, feedback integrated, and confidence continually realigned.

Enforceable Feedback Loop

1. Enforce 360-degree calibration in every cycle.
2. Leaders must prove how feedback reshaped their decisions and behavior.
3. Documentation is not optional; redesign is the standard.

Doctrinal Closure

- Confidence untested is arrogance engineered; feedback denied is failure designed.
- Unverified confidence collapses under pressure; calibration validates structure.

- Calibration converts confidence into permanence; resisting verification invites Drift.

Architectural Truths

- Mastery is trained.
- Mastery is composure under pressure.
- Mind mastery powers flawless execution.
- Stress hijacks the undisciplined.
- Deliberate practice builds permanence.

Diagnostic Tool: The Mastery Conditioning Map

Purpose

Determine whether mastery is architected into structure as a repeatable, pressure-resilient operating system, or surrendered to Drift through personality, improvisation, and unconditioned behavior.

Diagnostic Dimensions

1. Systemic Conditioning

Definition
Assesses whether mastery is enforced through institutionalized conditioning cycles rather than dependent on individual discipline.

Propagation / Performance Indicator:
Training, repetition, and reinforcement are codified into daily operating routines; cycles run automatically under pressure, and conditioning holds without personality enforcement.

Drift Indicator
Training is inconsistent, optional, or personality-driven; conditioning collapses under load, and performance relies on individual grit or memory rather than structural discipline.

2. Cognitive Design

Definition

Evaluates whether cognition, attention control, and decision pathways are engineered into the system to prevent stress hijack.

Propagation / Performance Indicator

Decision sequences, cognitive triggers, and focus protocols are embedded into rituals and workflows; under pressure, teams default to conditioned clarity, not emotion.

Drift Indicator

Decision-making depends on personal habits; stress triggers reactivity, distraction, and shortcuts; cognitive breakdowns emerge immediately when load increases.

3. Practice Infrastructure

Definition

Examines whether deliberate practice is structurally integrated to convert repetition and feedback into reliable execution.

Propagation / Performance Indicator

Practice cycles, simulations, and feedback loops are scheduled, enforced, and tied to system redesign; repetition compounds into reliability.

Drift Indicator

Practice is episodic or symbolic; feedback is cosmetic, unintegrated, or ignored; errors recur because practice does not alter structure.

4. Error Containment

Definition

Determines whether structural mechanisms prevent isolated errors from escalating under pressure.

Propagation / Performance Indicator

Errors trigger conditioned responses that isolate failure, execute containment protocols, and prevent cascade; pressure tightens discipline.

Drift Indicator

Unconditioned reactions spread error through the system; pressure multiplies mistakes; containment depends on expert intervention rather than structural design.

5. Cultural Reflex

Definition

Assesses whether culture defaults to collective discipline and trained response when load increases.

Propagation / Performance Indicator

Shared conditioning produces composure, predictability, and unity; under stress, behavior converges on trained reflex rather than emotion.

Drift Indicator

Culture fractures during volatility; panic, blame, and reactivity accelerate Drift; collective behavior defaults to untrained instinct.

Scoring Standard (1-5: Drift → Validated)

1. **Severe Drift:** No structural conditioning; mastery is aspirational, inconsistent, or personality-driven; collapse is predictable under pressure.
2. **High Drift:** Some structures exist but fail under load; conditioning is episodic or leader-dependent; errors escalate quickly.
3. **Unstable:** Partial conditioning present; resilience holds in calm conditions but fails when pressure peaks; practices vary by team or individual.
4. **Strong Alignment:** Mastery is largely engineered; structures hold under pressure with minimal variance; only edge-case Drift emerges.
5. **Validated Architecture:** Mastery is fully embedded; conditioning, cognition, practice, error containment, and cultural reflex operate as unified architecture; pressure strengthens precision.

Interpretation Guide

Validated Architecture: (19-25)

1. Conditioning is institutionalized and automatic.

2. Cognitive pathways remain stable under pressure.
3. Practice cycles drive redesign and compound reliability.
4. Errors are contained structurally, not heroically.
5. Culture executes trained reflex, not improvisation.
6. Pressure sharpens execution and coherence.

Drift Detected: (1-18)

1. Discipline collapses into individual effort.
2. Stress hijacks decision-making.
3. Practice does not alter behavior or structure.
4. Errors multiply and cascade under load.
5. Culture defaults to untrained instinct and fragmentation.
6. Mastery remains unengineered; resilience is performative.

Structural Closing Line

Mastery is not talent; it is architecture. Where conditioning, cognition, practice, containment, and culture are not engineered, Drift becomes the operating model the moment pressure is applied.

Leader's Challenge

You already know the truth of your mastery: you mistook calm for control, reflex for discipline, and momentary excellence for permanence.

Marcus exposed what you've been avoiding.
The room didn't fracture because the data failed; it fractured because the leader did.
His breath slipped, his mind scattered, and the structure mirrored him.
That was not emotion.
It was architecture revealing itself.

You've seen the same fractures in your own leaders:
composure faked, reflex untrained, silence posing as steadiness,

standards that hold in routine and collapse in pressure,
confidence untested and uncalibrated.

None of this is accidental.
It is the design you permitted.

If leaders hide strain, the façade replaced regulation.
If decisions scramble, cognition was never engineered.
If reflex erupts, practice is episodic.
If standards decay, permanence was never built.
If truth is swallowed, evasion governs the culture.
If confidence collapses, calibration is abandoned.

These are not quirks.
They are structural failures.
And structure is your responsibility.

Your culture already knows the doctrine you've taught it:
under pressure, we improvise;
under pressure, talent carries the load;
under pressure, we hope nothing breaks.

Your organization is not confused.
It is obedient.

Mastery unengineered guarantees Drift:
the body hijacks,
the mind scatters,
the room tilts,
trust erodes.

You cannot claim resilience while leaders negotiate with panic.
You cannot claim excellence while mechanisms rely on streaks.
You cannot claim strength when one person's fracture can tip the structure.

Marcus wrote his ledger because the collapse kept repeating.

So have you.

Every untrained moment is recorded in outcome, not opinion.

Your challenge is not to inspire harder.

Your challenge is to end the myth that talent substitutes for engineered, pressure-proof mastery.

Move from:

"I look calm" → "My regulation is conditioned."

"I trust my instincts" → "My reflexes are engineered."

"We know the standard" → "Our standards survive volatility."

"I avoid conflict" → "Truth is surfaced on contact."

"I'm confident" → "My confidence is calibrated."

Mastery is not aesthetic.

It defends the structure or it fractures first.

Without regulation, the façade collapses.

Without disciplined reflexes, speed becomes chaos.

Without permanence, standards decay.

Without confrontation, Drift multiplies.

Without calibration, confidence becomes failure.

You are not being asked whether you value mastery.

You are being asked whether you will architect it.

The ledger is still open.

Forge mastery into the structure or Drift will forge collapse into the culture through you.

III. Essence of Execution

1. Core Execution Truth

Mastery is discipline forged in repetition.

2. Indicators of Drift

1. Leaders display façade instead of regulation under pressure.
2. Reflex becomes reactive, untrained, and unstable when load increases.
3. Standards collapse in volatility because permanence was never engineered.
4. Truth is avoided, edited, or delayed when tension rises.
5. Confidence appears strong but dissolves when uncalibrated.

3. Essential Leader Actions

1. Condition regulation so the body does not hijack decision-making under pressure.
2. Engineers reflex through deliberate practice until response becomes reliable.
3. Reinforce standards through repetition and recalibration until they survive volatility.
4. Surface truth immediately; confront fractures on contact.
5. Calibrate confidence through tested judgment, not self-belief.

4. Enforceable Feedback Requirements

1. Stress indicators must be surfaced and audited; façade is treated as structural risk.
2. Pressure drills validate reflex, rhythm, and cognitive sequencing; failures trigger redesign.
3. Standards undergo reinforcement cycles; decay prompts immediate recalibration.
4. Confrontation logs expose avoidance patterns; each instance requires corrective action.
5. Calibration reviews prove how feedback reshapes decisions, behavior, and execution.

5. The Decisive Question

Will you engineer mastery into your structure, or let Drift fracture your culture the moment pressure hits?

IV. Rapid Orientation: Drift–Architecture Spectrum

Use this rubric for orientation, not validation. If your structures do not hold under pressure and turnover, you are in Drift regardless of intent or progress.

Severe Drift: No structural conditioning; mastery is aspirational, inconsistent, or personality-driven; collapse is predictable under pressure.

High Drift: Some structures exist but fail under load; conditioning is episodic or leader-dependent; errors escalate quickly.

Unstable: Partial conditioning present; resilience holds in calm conditions but fails when pressure peaks; practices vary by team or individual.

Strong Alignment: Mastery is largely engineered; structures hold under pressure with minimal variance; only edge-case Drift emerges.

Validated Architecture: Mastery is fully embedded; conditioning, cognition, practice, error containment, and cultural reflex operate as unified architecture; pressure strengthens precision.

Chapter 9 — Personality and Potential

I. Story: Hal at the Edge of Himself

The operations bay felt like an abandoned cathedral; high ceilings, dead monitors, cables coiled like shed skins. It had once been the heart of the engine; now it was a museum of procedures nobody followed. Hal stood in the doorway with the familiarity of a ghost visiting his old house.

He still wore the uniform of certainty: dark jacket, clipped pen, posture straight enough to pass a safety audit. Reliability made his name. Precision built his reputation. Those same habits making him formidable had hardened into something brittle. He felt it in the way his jaw clenched before a decision, in the way his attention narrowed until the world blurred into threat and control.

Imara waited near the far console, hands folded, a presence more than a posture. Marcus lingered in the periphery with his ledger tucked against his side, the edge of a page marked with a grease pencil. He had come to witness, not to direct.

"Why here?" Hal asked Imara without greeting.

"Because it's honest," she said. "Processes don't lie. People do, mostly to themselves."

He half-smiled. "You think I've been lying?"

"I think you've been obeying old design," she replied. "And calling it identity."

Before he could answer, the alert tone cut through the room. A hollow chime, then the red pulse across the wall display. System delays spiking in the coastal region. A familiar pattern: processes stall, customers leave, communication channels intensify.

Hal's body moved before his mind engaged. He stepped toward the console, palm already open to pull the executive override key from his pocket. His signature response: take control, narrow the blast radius, funnel decisions through the one person he knew wouldn't flinch.

Imara's voice cut cleanly, not loud, just placed. "If the structure fails when you step back, you didn't build architecture. You built dependence."

He froze. The key felt heavier than metal.

On the center screen, the incident lead posted the command card: problem statement, scope, rollback timebox, decision authority, next timestamp. The scaffolding was in place; the discipline he had demanded of others, but never trusted when events deviated from the intended course. Old reflexes pressed for override. His pulse pressed back.

"Who determines the response?" Marcus asked from the doorway, voice neutral.

The team's heads turned in unison toward the incident lead, not Hal. Alignment. The word tasted of both relief and insult.

Imara stepped closer. "Hal, when pressure rises, what is your first move?"

"Control the variables" he responded.

"And when the variables are people?"

His silence was an answer. On the wall, the system's delay wavered, stabilized, ticked upward again. He recognized the pattern, the pressure point where leaders mistake urgency for strength.

Imara: "Name the failure mode you've trained into yourself."

He exhaled. "Perfection for protection."

He'd built perfection so tight it had starved everything human. Conversations became transactions, laughter became a risk. Even at home, silence waited for his approval, another system waiting on his command. Systems obeyed; people withdrew. Precision had kept the world intact and left him untouched inside it.

"And what failure does your instinct reproduce across the structure?'

"Bottleneck," he said, the word landing heavier than he expected. "I make the process wait for me."

The second spike peaked. The chat flared: one voice urging rollback, another arguing for containment. Hal's hand tightened around the key. Control wasn't a habit; it was how he metabolized fear.

Imara didn't move. "Every environment has an internal architecture. So does every leader. What architecture holds when you step back?"

He almost laughed. "Nothing."

"Exactly," she said gently. "You've built reliability without structural support. You called it strength. It's Drift disguised as discipline."

Marcus watched Hal's face shift. Not a collapse. A recognition.

On screen, the incident lead pinned a decision path: Contain for five minutes. If error budget breaches, roll back. Authority: Incident lead. Approver: Platform SRE. The pathway was clear. The path was not Hal's; authority belonged to the team.

Hal slid the key back into his pocket. "Run the path," he said, voice even but edged with a fear he chose not to hide. "Post updates on the timestamp."

He stepped back.

Nothing failed.

The line trembled, dipped, then steadied. The rollback sequence began on the timebox, visible end to end. The coastal region nudged from red to amber. Chat threads thinned. Breathing in the room returned to the same rhythm as the HVAC.

A minute passed. Two. Hal waited for the imagined catastrophe his reflex always promised. It didn't arrive. The system held because the structure held.

Marcus uncapped the grease pencil. In the ledger margin he wrote, **Released control. Structure held**. He did not underline it. He did not need to.

Imara's questions did not stop. "What made this possible?"

Hal looked at the command card. "Clarity." He gestured to the visible queue and the posted authority matrix. "Discipline." He looked at his own hands, still. "Decision design."

"And internally?"

He paused, then answered with more honesty than comfort. "I let the system be the system. I stopped using control to stabilize my fear."

Imara nodded once. "Good. Now we design what replaces it."

Hal looked at the steady monitors and realized the system had not survived him; it had outgrown him.

The Reconstruction

They stayed after the operations bay emptied. Lights dimmed to the level of an interrogation that respected its subject. Imara drew a small square on the whiteboard and labeled it with three words: Leadership Under Pressure.

"Every leader runs an internal operating system," she said. "You've built yours on precision. It served you until it ruled you."

Hal felt a flicker of defensiveness and let it pass. "So, what do I run it on instead, permission?"

"Design," she replied, drawing five small circles around the square. "Five structural archetypes you already use outside yourself. We place them inside."

She wrote:

Curiosity: Converts uncertainty into inquiry.

Precision: Channels discipline as intentional modes, not control.

Communication: Align voices to create coherence.

Trust: Builds cohesion through transparent tension.

Stability: Uses awareness as early warning, not anxiety.

Hal read them like a checklist meant for somebody else. "Precision and Stability," he said quietly. "My strengths; overdeveloped to fragility."

Imara circled them lightly. "Overdeveloped becomes brittle. Underdeveloped becomes chaos. We design proportion."

He leaned back against the console. He glanced at the board, seeing his habits mapped like system components for the first time. He understood what Imara was pointing to now, his personal architecture:

the mental and emotional structure shaping his habits, reflexes, and decisions under pressure. "And how do I 'proportion' a personality?"

Imara capped the marker. "Personality is not identity. Identity is the 'who': core values, purpose, and sense of self. Personality is the 'how': the adaptive infrastructure through which that identity is expressed, refined, and tested under pressure. It is both biologically grounded and behaviorally engineered: repeated behavior under pressure consolidates into personality; redesigned behavior, practiced under pressure, becomes evolution."

He accepted it as fact. "Show me the design."

"Three moves," she said. "Each is under pressure."

Expose: Name the reflex. "Perfection as Protection".

Reframe: Translate the need. Protection = clarity, not control.

Replace. Execute the designed behavior.

"You trained the team to display structure," she added. "Now train yourself to trust it."

He stared at the board and felt the odd relief of an honest map. Not a confession. A plan.

"Again," she said, tapping the Curiosity circle: "When uncertainty rises, what is your question?"

"What single fact decides the next move?" he answered without thinking.

She smiled, not approval, recognition. "Good. That's your entry point. Curiosity first. Control last."

The Second Test

The next morning, pressure arrived again, as if the system had agreed to be his teacher. A partner system slowed without warning, cutting off requests at the connection point. The graphs wore different colors, but the sensation remained the same: constriction, then noise.

Hal felt his old reflex rise. His nervous system rehearsed the script: step in, take over, save.

He breathed once, not to calm down but to anchor the sequence he had chosen. Expose. Reframe. Replace.

"Incident lead," he said, "What single fact decides the next move?"

The room stilled. It was not the question to anyone from him.

"Confirm vendor throttle rate by region," the lead replied. "Then we decide; contain or cut."

"Good," Hal said. "Post the timebox for that fact. If we don't have it by then, we decide on available information."

He turned to the platform SRE. "If we cut, what do we abandon?"

"Non-critical batch jobs," she answered, unfazed. "We'll take the hit on reporting. Users first."

Hal nodded. He did not reach for the key; trust had replaced reflex. The room moved around him, aligned to the same tempo. The determining facts arrived. The cutover executed. The system held.

Marcus wrote in the ledger, **Curiosity before control. Decision revealed, not performed.**

Imara watched Hal, then the team, then the board. It was not a triumph. It was proof the system no longer depended on him.

Marcus found a quiet corner by the glass wall and wrote the entry he had been waiting to write:

Observation: Hal released command twice under rising pressure. No degradation in system response. Response improved.

Inference: Control was never reliable. Design was. Leadership error: confusing self-control with systemic stability.

Proof: Structure held. Self held. Evidence that one architecture sustains both leader and system.

He closed the ledger gently.

Hal authored his personal design: leadership turned inward. Doctrine became self-applied; identity rebuilt through intention.

Marcus observed Hal's transformation from afar: from command to authorship, from control to intention. It carried both the truth and the finality of change, proof of permanence in Hal's evolution.

Hal returned to the whiteboard, the same surface that once enforced organizational design principles, to draft his own where he had once written, in permanent marker, Be Who You Are!

He crossed the old words out with a single line. Not erased; acknowledged, then superseded.

Underneath he wrote, Structure Defined.

He added a quiet addendum in small letters only he and Imara would notice: Discipline under pressure. He waited for the ink to dry before stepping back, as if testing whether the words would hold without him.

Imara read it and said nothing. Design was in motion; commentary would only slow it.

Marcus, let the silence say the thing leaders rarely allow: Change the self, change the process.

Maxim: Mastery drives behavior; personality anchors potential.

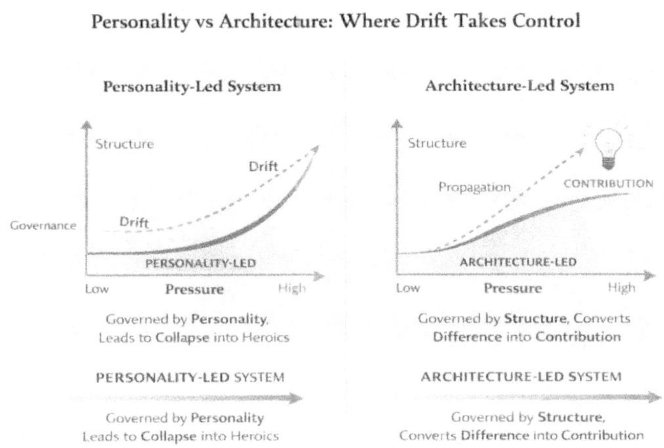

Figure 9.1 Personality vs Architecture: Where Drift Takes Control

Under pressure, personality-led systems collapse into heroics, while architecture-led systems convert difference into contribution.

II. Doctrine & Diagnostic

Processes fail when personality is treated as design material instead of design input. Each recurring flaw reveals how Drift distorts individuality into dysfunction and how disciplined structure restores contribution. These systemic flaws expose the patterns leaders must re-engineer to align personality with performance.

Key Terms

- **Uniformity**: demanding people act alike rather than perform to the same structural standard.

Flaws Leaders Permit

1. Personality Redesign

Drift begins when leaders attempt to redesign personality instead of engineering the environment where personality performs. This turns potential into resistance. Control replaces design.

PMC Response

Design never focuses on personality; it architects the conditions where personality performs.

Structure converts individuality into alignment, and architecture fuses them into contribution.

Enforceable Feedback Loop

1. Mandate quarterly alignment reviews mapping each role's structural design to the individual's dominant strengths.
2. Misalignments trigger redesign, not retraining.

Doctrinal Closure

- Control disguised as design converts individuality into friction.
- Systems redesigning people engineer resistance.
- Environments, not personalities, are the material of mastery.

Transition

Misguided control breeds fixed perception.

2. Fixed Mindset

Drift declares personality permanent; design proves it adaptive. Leaders believe genetics determine human potential. They often say 'that's just how I am' to excuse behaviors. They stop designing the environment, stagnating personal growth and adaptability.

PMC Response

Design treats personality as a starting point.

Structure expands the operational range of personality through calibrated stress, feedback, and experience.

No person is redesigned; the environment is.

Enforceable Feedback Loop

1. Establish Structural Adaptation Cycles: quarterly reviews testing how personality traits are leveraged under pressure.
2. Each cycle asks one question: is the environment evolving around the person, or expecting the person to evolve alone?
3. If performance remains flat while conditions shift, leaders redesign the structure, not the individual.

Doctrinal Closure

- Drift converts belief into structural paralysis.
- Design translates conviction into adaptive architecture.
- Potential expands when structure evolves.

Transition

Rigid minds configure rigid structures.

3. Forced Uniformity

Uniformity standardizes people instead of process. Standardization disguises itself as fairness. Leaders imposing identical processes, reactions, and work styles on every personality, cause the system to fracture in unison. Uniformity dictates how people must be.

PMC Response

Design enforces consistency, not uniformity.

Consistency defines how work flows: through playbooks, handoffs, and clear decision paths.

Resilient organizations are not identical; they are structures of designed balance.

Enforceable Feedback Loop

1. Semi-annually, map behavioral and decision-making patterns across teams.
2. If 60+ percent of members share the same dominant style or conflict-avoidance pattern, trigger structural redesign: adjust role pairings, decision rights, or review rituals to re-introduce stabilizing differences.

Doctrinal Closure

- Uniformity erases initiative and dulls design.
- Fairness without difference manufactures mediocrity.
- Diversity structured with discipline sustains resilience.

Transition

Uniformity starves initiative, inviting heroes.

4. Savior Syndrome

Drift mistakes temporary energy for design. Leaders wait for heroes; one speech, one crisis, one breakthrough to transform the culture. They fail to build the structure to make it repeatable.

PMC Response

Deliberate practice institutionalizes mastery.

Repeatable structure replaces one-time breakthroughs.

Discipline replaces charisma.

The structure, not the hero, carries the weight.

Enforceable Feedback Loop

1. After interventions, record and share the exact behavioral adjustments that worked; turning isolated success into a repeatable discipline.

Doctrinal Closure

- Heroism replaces structure in Drift.
- Discipline institutionalizes mastery beyond personality.
- Systems repeat what charisma cannot sustain.

Transition

Heroic silence becomes false harmony

5. False Harmony

Peace is mistaken for progress. Leaders equate calm rooms with aligned teams.
Disagreement is treated as a threat. Beneath the silence, unresolved tension accumulates until crisis restores truth by force.

PMC Response

Architecture governs tension instead of eliminating it.

Structured friction: honest debate, multiple perspectives, assumption awareness, keep systems adaptive.

Coherence and innovative solutions emerge from governed tension.

Enforceable Feedback Loop

1. During each review cycle, teams surface and record points of disagreement and the decisions that follow.
2. Lack of open discussion signals structural weakness requiring redesign.

Doctrinal Closure

- Peace without truth corrodes coherence.
- Structured tension is the architecture of trust.
- Harmony designed through candor sustains performance.

Architectural Truths

- Personality is infrastructure, not destiny.
- Fixed Is fiction: structure engineers' adaptability
- Balance by design: diversity requires governance
- Discipline is systemic, not heroic.
- Structured tension fuels adaptive strength
- Self-Architecture is the leadership multiplier

Diagnostic Tool: The Personality Architecture Map (PAM)

Purpose

Determine whether individuality in the organization is converted into contribution or tolerated as variance that destabilizes performance.

Diagnostic Dimensions

1. Structural Alignment Architecture

Definition

Assesses whether roles, authority, and workflow convert personal capability into systemic contribution rather than depending on personality to compensate for design gaps.

Propagation / Performance Indicator

Behavior consistently reflects architectural intent; role boundaries, authority paths, and decision expectations produce uniform execution regardless of who fills the role.

Drift Indicator

Leaders coach personalities instead of redesigning structure; individuals patch gaps; performance varies by "who is involved" rather than by design.

2. Adaptability Architecture

Definition

Evaluates whether decision cycles, rhythms, and stressors expand adaptability without losing structural form.

Propagation / Performance Indicator

Feedback loops, reviews, and structured stress harden adaptability; decision cycles adjust predictably under pressure while retaining coherence.

Drift Indicator

Rigidity is mistaken for reliability; the design demands people stretch endlessly while architecture remains static; change becomes personality-dependent.

3. Governance of Difference

Definition

Determines whether the architecture governs disagreement, tension, and diversity through structured friction and transparent feedback.

Propagation / Performance Indicator

Dissent is expressed safely within defined rituals; friction becomes intelligence; boundaries channel difference into performance.

Drift Indicator

Conflict is silenced, politicized, or personalized; uniformity replaces coherence; absence of tension masks impending collapse.

4. Dependency Architecture (Reliability Index)

Definition

Assesses whether performance is engineered into architecture or sustained by irreplaceable personalities.

Propagation / Performance Indicator

Continuity survives turnover; execution does not require heroics; reliability is in architecture, not individuals.

Drift Indicator

Key personalities stabilize the architecture; when they step back, collapse surfaces instantly; heroics mask architectural absence.

5. Self-Architecture Capacity (Leadership Structural Integrity)

Definition

Measures whether leaders regulate themselves through architecture discipline, reflection, and feedback rather than projecting instability into the architecture.

Propagation / Performance Indicator

Leaders mirror the operating architecture: decisions follow doctrine; reflection and structure govern their responses; emotional regulation is systemic, not personal.

Drift Indicator

Leaders externalize instability; control replaces design; emotional reactivity replaces governance; leaders violate the architecture they expect others to uphold.

Scoring Standard (1-5: Drift → Validated)

1. **Severe Drift:** Personality governs behavior; architecture symbolic or absent; performance varies by individual rather than architecture.
2. **High Drift:** Partial structures exist but collapse under pressure; dependency and friction surface instantly; enforcement is inconsistent.
3. **Unstable:** Some architectural elements function, but reliability remains personality-dependent; adaptability and tension governance fracture during urgency.
4. **Strong Alignment:** Architecture governs personality; difference is converted into contribution; only edge-case deviations appear under pressure.
5. **Validated Architecture:** Individuality performs inside architecture; reliability, adaptability, dissent, and continuity are engineered; architecture holds regardless of who occupies the role.

Interpretation Guide

Validated Architecture: (19-25)

1. Personality operates within architecture, not above it.
2. Decision cycles adapt without losing architectural form.
3. Structured friction turns difference into performance.
4. Reliability lives in architecture, not people.
5. Leaders regulate themselves through design discipline.
6. Pressure strengthens coherence rather than exposing dependency.

Drift Detected: (1-18)

1. Roles depend on personalities to function.
2. Adaptability collapses into rigidity or chaos.
3. Conflict avoidance or politicization replaces structured tension.
4. Heroics stabilize what architecture fails to govern.
5. Leader instability leaks into the architecture.
6. Difference destabilizes performance rather than being converted into contribution.

Structural Closing Line

Architecture must govern personality into contribution; when performance depends on individuals rather than design, Drift rules the system and collapse becomes inevitable.

Leaders Challenge

You already know the truth of your personality architecture; you've mistaken preference for design and style for structure.
You watched it long before you named it:
Strong personalities steering decisions, quieter experts deferring to charisma, conflict going underground, heroes fixing what architecture never prevented.

None of this was accidental.

It was the environment you allowed, or failed to build.

If dominance wins meetings - presence replaced process.

If people say "that's just who I am" - personality became governance.

If results hinge on a few individuals - performance lives in people, not design.

If teams describe leaders instead of systems - architecture has already surrendered to preference.

These are not failures of character.

They are failures of structure.

And structure is your responsibility.

Diversity belongs in thinking and perspective; behavior must be uniform under pressure.

You cannot claim safety while dissent depends on who's in the room.

You cannot claim discipline while heroics remain your stabilizing force.

Your organization is not inconsistent; only obedient.

If leaders redesign people instead of roles - resistance is rational.

If charisma dictates influence - clarity has been abandoned.

If conflict appears only in hallways - visible architecture outlawed candor.

If "culture carriers" hold the place together - you've outsourced resilience to personality.

Every leader reaches Hal's moment when they see their own reflexes encoded into the system and realize the organization is mirroring their unmanaged internal architecture.

You cannot champion contribution while making people compensate for your lack of design.

You cannot call volatility "authenticity" when your impulses become everyone else's constraints.

The problem is not personality.

The problem is the structure that lets personality govern.

Your challenge is not to push people to "be better."

Your challenge is to architect an environment where difference performs on purpose.

Shift from:

- "Speak up if you want change" – "Structure the debate."
- "Follow the strongest voice" → "Follow the clearest design."
- "Handle conflict privately" → "Surface tension publicly."
- "Let personalities sort it out" → "Let architecture align it."
- "Rely on your best people" → "Rely on your best structure."

Personality is not neutral.

Design harnesses it.

Drift weaponizes it.

If you do not architect the environment, people will toward safety, not mastery.

Toward comfort, not contribution.

Toward habit, not structure.

Mastery does not erase individuality.

It converts it into contribution.

Your challenge is simple and final:

Will you allow unstructured personality to shape the system,

or build the architecture that makes individuality perform by design?

III. Essence of Execution

1. Core Execution Truth

Mastery drives behavior; personality anchors potential.

2. Indicators of Drift

1. Decisions follow the strongest personality in the room instead of the clearest design.

2. "That's just who I am" is used to justify behaviors that violate structure.

3. Performance swings with who is on shift, in the meeting, or holding the keys.

4. Conflict surfaces in hallways and side channels, not in visible, structured forums.
5. A small set of "culture carriers" or heroes quietly holds the system together.

3. Essential Leader Actions

1. Architect environments where roles, authority, and decisions are governed by structure, not personality.
2. Replace personality-led influence with clear design: decision paths, command cards, and visible authority matrices.
3. Govern difference through structured tension rituals that convert disagreement into intelligence.
4. Design roles and workflows so reliability, not charisma or preference, carries critical work.
5. Practice self-architecture under pressure: expose reflex, reframe the need, replace the behavior.

4. Enforceable Feedback Requirements

1. Every critical decision must point to an explicit structural source (grid, role, path), not to an individual.
2. Reviews log where outcomes depended on "who was there"; these events trigger structural redesign, not personal coaching alone.
3. All "heroic saves" and "culture carrier" interventions are recorded as design failures requiring architecture updates.
4. Conflict that appears only outside formal rituals is flagged as architectural Drift and fed into redesign cycles.
5. Leadership behavior under pressure is audited against doctrine; violations of architecture are treated as structural, not stylistic, breaches.

5. The Decisive Question

Will your architecture govern personality into contribution, or will Drift leave personality governing the system?

IV. Rapid Orientation: Drift–Architecture Spectrum

Use this rubric for orientation, not validation. If your structures do not hold under pressure and turnover, you are in Drift regardless of intent or progress.

Severe Drift: Personality governs behavior; architecture symbolic or absent; performance varies by individual rather than architecture.

High Drift: Partial structures exist but collapse under pressure; dependency and friction surface instantly; enforcement is inconsistent.

Unstable: Some architectural elements function, but reliability remains personality-dependent; adaptability and tension governance fracture during urgency.

Strong Alignment: Architecture governs personality; difference is converted into contribution; only edge-case deviations appear under pressure.

Validated Architecture: Individuality performs inside architecture; reliability, adaptability, dissent, and continuity are engineered; architecture holds regardless of who occupies the role.

Chapter 10 — Trust and Quiet Influence

I. Story: The Aftershock of Trust

The operations floor was built for numbers, not nerves. Rows of workstations stood in symmetry, cables aligned into black lines, monitors breathing blue. At this hour, too late to be early, too early to be late, the air was still. Fans whispered. Elevators clicked in distant shafts. The place ran on control, not confession.

Tonight, the failure wasn't technical; it was personal. A private confidence was shared out of context and passed up the chain, as if trust was information to share rather than a promise to keep; an artifact to route, not a covenant to protect. By noon it reached the one person it could wound. By evening, the wound had reached everyone.

Sasha's chair was empty. Her absence hit harder than any red alert. Her last message still hovered on the shared board. I need distance. I said that in trust". The room settled strangely around the emptiness she left.

Somewhere beyond the room, Sasha sat in stillness. She replayed every conversation, not to relive the words but to measure the distance between what was spoken in confidence and what the structure had converted into circulation. It wasn't anger that settled in her. It was disbelief followed by the colder weight beneath it: the realization that trust here had been treated as a process, not a promise.

They gathered without choreography. Reg stood by the door, already measuring optics. Carol crossed her arms against the cold. Hal scanned the wall displays as if a pattern might still save them. Imara watched through the glass, eyes on reflections, not faces. Darryl sat at the center table, the only stillness in the room.

Darryl left the mess untouched, the disarray left as it was. Evidence of fatigue, unedited. On the main display, a shared document blinked; a blank page with a cursor that looked like judgment.

He set both hands on the table. He exhaled once, flattening the tremor before it reached his voice."
"Before we explain," he said, "we name." His tone carried no anger, no comfort, just intent.

He typed:

Private conversation (Sasha + peer), Thursday 08:12.

Quote lifted and forwarded, Friday 09:37.

Forwarded again to the director channel, 09:41.

Response escalated without context, 09:47.

Screenshots circulated, 10:02–10:18.

Silence.

At the top, he wrote a header: OWNERSHIP. Beneath it, three bullets:

Who acted.

Who looked away.

Who was harmed.

The person who had forwarded the message tried to speak, failed, then said softly, "I forwarded it. I thought the context"

"Context will not repair what intent broke," Darryl said. "Name the action."

The culprit swallowed. "I took what was private and made it strategic."

Darryl typed the words as spoken. Then he asked, "Who looked away?"

Marcus's hand rose. "I saw the screenshot," he said. "I told myself it wasn't mine to correct."

Darryl added another line: Observed, didn't intervene. The silence became commentary enough. Chairs creaked, eyes fixed on the table, the silence heavy enough to tilt the room.

Carol broke it. "Sasha was hurt. We all were. Trust breached".

Darryl wrote: Sasha. The team. The addition changed the air. Betrayal had a blast radius.

Reg checked his watch. "We can't stay here all night."

"If we move without naming what we broke," Darryl said, "we'll bring the break with us." He crossed to the whiteboard and drew two lines, one vertical, one horizontal. A dot in the upper-left quadrant. "High accountability, low transparency."

Marcus recognized the frame. "Surveillance Zone," he said. "Control without trust."

The Trust–Accountability Quadrant

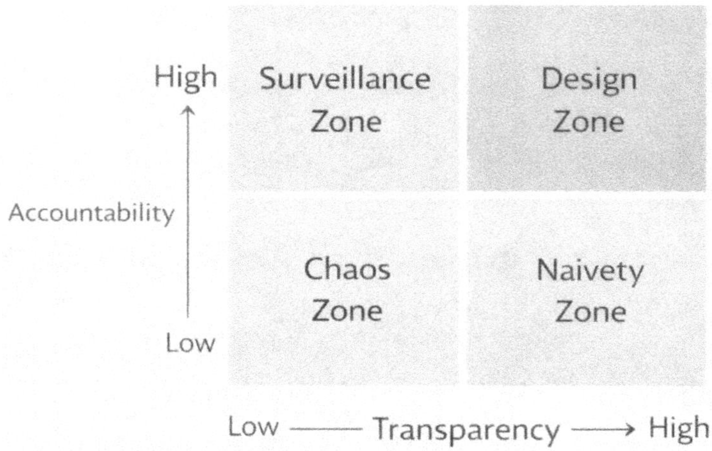

Figure 10.1 The Trust Accountability Quadrant

"Exactly. We don't lecture our way out," Darryl said. "we reshape our behavior into trust."

He added a new header under the first: Behavioral Design.

"Step one: visible ownership. Everyone who saw and stayed silent details their inaction in writing."
"Step two: unedited truth. We tell Sasha what happened. She decides what repair looks like."
"Step three: repair by design. Protocols written, not implied. Monthly audit, names attached. Trust is proven through transparent action."

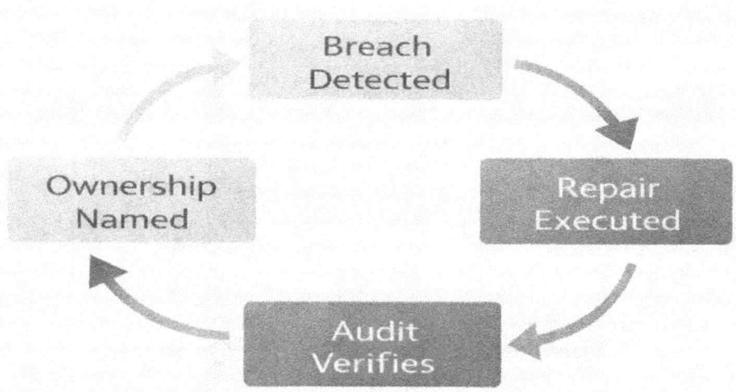

Figure 10.2 Breach to Verification Loop

Trust is restored when harm is converted into visible ownership, structural repair, and verified closure

Someone muttered, “We’ll look vulnerable.”

“Truth is not weakness; it’s the foundation of strength,” Darryl said. “It’s the only durable strength.”

He tapped his phone, placed it on speaker, and called Sasha.

She answered on the third ring. Her voice was flat, precise. “I’m here.”

“We owe you the complete record,” Darryl said. He read the timeline. He named the forward, the silence, the harm. No adjectives. “What do you need from us to fix this?”

Silence stretched. Then Sasha said, “Delete the private message that was shared without my consent, and make the deletion visible. Write the protocol that prevents recurrence. Not an apology, a safeguard. Audit it monthly. And no one edits my name out of the record.”

Darryl nodded, even though she couldn’t see it. “Understood.”

Reg exhaled, arms crossed. “This will establish a precedent.”

“That’s the point,” Darryl said. “Precedent is the architecture of behavior.”

The line clicked dead. The room stayed still. Clarity had a cost, and everyone felt it.

“Record the deletion,” Darryl said. “Erin, you own it. Post the deletion and reason. No euphemisms.”

Erin nodded. “Understood.”

“Protocol messaging; Carol, draft it. Two sentences. The person who forwarded Sasha’s message, you co-author.”

“Audit design; Hal, organize it. One owner per breach. Visible by default. Hidden by exception, approved by me.”

Hal nodded. “Prototype by morning.”

Darryl turned to Marcus. “Public clarification. You own the thread. Facts only. No theater.”

Marcus nodded. “I’ll write it now.”

The room shifted from shame to movement. Keys began to tap, rhythm returning. Imara drew a visual on the whiteboard: Transparency across, Accountability up. In the upper-right quadrant, she shaded a circle. “Design Zone,” she said.

Reg finally spoke. “Publishing the deletion will draw backlash.”

“Backlash is cheaper than erosion,” Darryl said. “Erosion compounds.”

They went to work with deliberate precision, the room pulsing with quiet intensity. Fingers moved across keyboards, screens reflecting faces hardened by resolve and fatigue. Every tap sounded like penance; every line drafted like a stitch closing a wound.

Erin posted the deletion; concise, unsentimental.

Carol wrote the protocol: Private speech is covenant, not data.

Hal built the audit template.

Marcus crafted a single post: We violated trust. We’re naming it, repairing it, and preventing recurrence. Design, not apology. He read it aloud once. No one suggested edits.

Darryl nodded. “Post it.”

The deletion appeared in the original channel. The protocol pinned to the top. The audit doc linked below. For the first time that night, the blue light in the room felt less like blame and more like verification.

Darryl called the client who might hear the rumor first. He repeated Sasha’s model: unedited facts, named actions, visible repair. The client paused, then said, “You’re the first partner who’s ever told us this kind of thing without being cornered,” his voice edged with disbelief that softened into quiet respect. The words carried the weight of years of corporate spin finally broken. Darryl heard it not as praise, but the sound of trust beginning to rebuild through exposure rather than defense.

When the call ended, no one smiled. Respect replaced relief.

Time crept forward through the hum of machines, stretching thin over fatigue and faint relief. Shoulders loosened. Carol packed slowly, the kind of tired that doesn’t resent the work. Hal gathered notes like a craftsman cleaning tools. Imara erased half the board but left the shaded circle intact.

Marcus closed his laptop and opened his ledger. He wrote:

Where truth hid, belief fled. Ownership named; oxygen returned. Trust is not declared. It is maintained in public, boring ways.

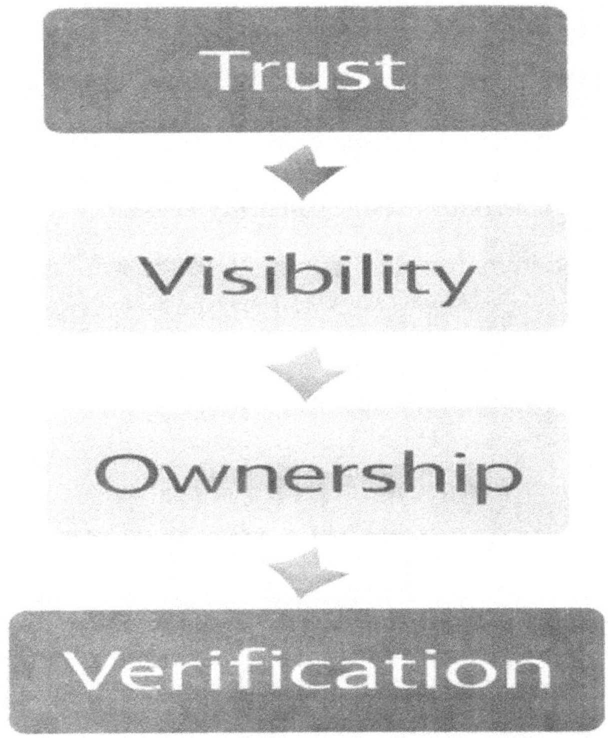

Figure 10.3 Breach to Verification Loop

A repair architecture converting trust violations into visible ownership, structural correction, and auditable closure.

Trust is not declared. It is maintained in public, boring ways.

Trust is sustained through visible ownership, structural transparency, and verified correction not intention, sentiment, or private discretion.

He looked up. Darryl was still typing the incident record. Each line a rung back to ground: deletion posted, protocol published, audit owner named. The structure was stabilizing, not because they spoke well, but because they acted visibly.

"Forty-eight hours," Darryl said. "We bring the record back to Sasha: read it aloud, own it in full view, and let her see the structure hold."

They nodded. It wasn't ritual; it was structure taking shape in time. This was not a ceremony but accountability fixed on a clock, the conversion of remorse into design.

When the room emptied, only Darryl and Marcus remained, standing in opposite pools of blue light. The hum of cooling fans filled the silence. Neither spoke. The quiet held.

Marcus looked down at the ledger and drew the next arc in the shift from Control to Design, the motion deliberate and unhurried. An act of continuation rather than closure, marking design as something still alive and advancing. He stopped short, leaving a space to show the work still unfinished, a reminder of what remained to build.

He wrote beneath it: **Relief is a spike. Release is a system.**

Darryl finished entering the incident log and pressed save. The cursor blinked, steady now.

They walked out together. The elevator chimed. In the mirrored doors, Marcus saw the reflection of the room behind them; the whiteboard grid, the empty chairs, and the work waiting to be completed.

Outside, the city glowed indifferent and alive. Rain started somewhere far off. Marcus tucked the ledger under his arm. He didn't trust the structure yet, not fully, but he trusted the rhythm Darryl had built into it. That would be enough until morning.

And above them, in a room still humming, the record of trust broken and rebuilt waited in the log: a blueprint for how to endure when human error meets structural truth.

Maxim: Trust is the architecture converting human promise into structural integrity.

II. Doctrine & Diagnostic

Each flaw that follows exposes the points where design collapses into Drift, where structure stops responding and trust becomes performative rather than proven. These flaws trace the moments where accountability thins, visibility dulls, and the architecture of behavior loses coherence.

Key Terms

- **Sentiment:** unstructured human impulse mistaken for design; the fragile opposite of architecture.

- **Safety:** engineered assurance that truth can be spoken without fear of retribution.

Flaws Leaders Permit

1. Trust as Performance Theater

Organizations substitute optics for ownership. Statements and apology campaigns replace structural redesign. Visibility becomes performance; sincerity becomes script. Drift thrives where transparency is performed rather than practiced.

PMC Response

Transparency exists to correct operational processes, not narrative control.

Enforceable Feedback Loop

1. Public admissions or culture resets include documented safeguards, assigned owners, and an audit cadence.
2. Structural corrections are verified quarterly through public reporting of outcomes.
3. Leadership accountability reviews link reputation statements to verified structural changes.

Doctrinal Closure

- Transparency performed is concealment by another name.
- Optics without ownership trains the system to lie in public.
- Trust is rebuilt through visible records, named actions, and audited safeguards.

Transition

Performance without redesign accelerates Drift.

2. Accountability as Retribution

Punitive practices dismantle learning. Fear replaces ownership, and silence becomes the performance of compliance. Retribution converts error into secrecy, making correction impossible. Design converts fear into discipline.

PMC Response

Accountability functions as structural feedback, not emotional response.

Enforceable Feedback Loop

1. Breaches trigger learning reviews, documenting cause, correction, and verification path.
2. Results shared within seven days and logged as organizational updates.
3. Repeat patterns require design revision before performance evaluation.

Doctrinal Closure

- Retribution does not correct behavior; it teaches concealment.
- Fear turns truth into hazard and silence into "compliance."
- Accountability is structural feedback; owned, documented, and verified.

Transition

Fear-driven accountability multiplies Drift; design restores discipline.

3. Repair Without Architecture

Emotion cannot repair structure. Apology without redesign institutionalizes Drift. Optimism without mechanism repeats failure by design.

PMC Response

Repairs produce verifiable structure.

Enforceable Feedback Loop

1. Improvement commitments convert into written controls with named owners and verification cadence.
2. Absence of documented mechanism flags Drift for executive review.
3. Resolutions include public confirmation of the control in effect.

Doctrinal Closure

- Reward is the real doctrine; culture follows what gets paid.
- Values preached and incentives contradicted manufactures institutional hypocrisy.
- Trust holds when speech, behavior, and reward operate as one architecture

Transition

Structure makes repair permanent.

4. Misaligned Incentives

Words and rewards diverge; integrity fractures. Leaders preaching values but incentivize optics institutionalize contradiction. Culture follows metrics, not principles.

PMC Response

Alignment is a structural governing directive: speech, behavior, and reward function as one architecture.

Enforceable Feedback Loop

1. Quarterly alignment reviews test incentive structure against declared doctrine.
2. Mismatched rewards trigger redesign.
3. Integrity metrics carry equal weight to performance metrics in leadership evaluations.

Doctrinal Closure

- Reward is the real doctrine; culture follows what gets paid.
- Values preached and incentives contradicted manufacture institutional hypocrisy.
- Trust holds when speech, behavior, and reward operate as one architecture

Transition

Misalignment normalizes deceit; coherence sustains trust.

5. Structural Security

Cultures relying on heroics or silence treat safety as privilege, not design. When protection depends on discretion, truth becomes hazard, and exhaustion becomes proof of loyalty.

PMC Response

Safety is engineered: visible, repeatable, and verified.

Enforceable Feedback Loop

1. Biannual capacity and psychological-safety audits measure overextension and communication risk.
2. Anonymous reporting channels are validated through independent audit for confidentiality integrity.
3. Detected fatigue or silence trends require visible redesign of workload or reporting structure

Doctrinal Closure

- Safety by discretion is not safety; it is privilege with a deadline.
- When truth requires courage, the structure has already failed.
- Safety is engineered: protected voice, protected privacy, and visible correction by default.

Transition

When safety depends on discretion, Drift is already governing. Only engineered protection converts courage into continuity.

Architectural Truths

- Trust is engineered, not assumed.
- Transparency is discipline, not disclosure.

- Accountability is continuity, not consequence.
- Restoration without redesign guarantees recurrence.
- Alignment is structural, not aspirational.
- Safety is engineered or undone.

Diagnostic Tool: Trust–Accountability Continuum Audit (TAC-DX)

Purpose

Determine whether trust and accountability are structurally integrated into reliability or degraded into performance theater, fear, or sentiment-driven Drift.

Diagnostic Dimensions

1. Reliability & Proof Architecture

Definition

Assesses whether commitments, closures, and countermeasures are encoded into visible architecture rather than dependent on personality or promises.

Propagation / Performance Indicator

Commitments are public, timestamped, and closed; every slippage triggers a structural correction; reliability is proven through visible ledgers.

Drift Indicator

Promises move privately; apology loops replace closure; commitments vary by individual discipline rather than architecture.

2. Transparency & Voice Safety Architecture

Definition

Evaluates whether dissent, risk visibility, and contribution safety are engineered as structural mechanisms, not discretionary behaviors.

Propagation / Performance Indicator

Dissent is logged and resolved; risk surfaces without penalty; voice participation is distributed and repeatable.

Drift Indicator

Silence becomes the safest behavior; dissent depends on personality; risks remain hidden until failure forces visibility.

3. Decision Rights & Escalation Architecture

Definition

Determines whether decisions live at the work with clear escalation paths, or drift toward hierarchy, influence, or personality.

Propagation / Performance Indicator

Most routine decisions occur at the work level; escalation pathways are visible; authority thresholds are respected under pressure.

Drift Indicator

Hierarchy overrides design; escalations linger unresolved; decision clarity varies by relationship rather than structure.

4. Behavioral Integrity & Incentive Alignment Architecture

Definition

Assesses whether rewards reinforce structural reliability rather than optics, speed, or political navigation.

Propagation / Performance Indicator

Integrity breaches are logged, owned, and corrected; recognition reinforces collaboration and structural repair.

Drift Indicator

Optics outperform substance; inconsistencies are ignored; incentives reward shortcuts, politics, or theatrics.

5. Quiet Influence Density (Structural Continuity Index)

Definition

Determines whether the structure's continuity is carried by distributed integrators rather than irreplaceable personalities.

Propagation / Performance Indicator

Multiple integrators sustain flow; the structure holds during absence tests; continuity persists across turnover.

Drift Indicator

Work halts when key individuals leave; informal heroes stabilize processes; influence maps mirror personality, not architecture.

Scoring Standard (1-5: Drift → Validated)

1. **Severe Drift:** Trust weak; accountability avoided or weaponized; performance depends on individuals; structures operate through optics or fear.
2. **High Drift:** Early structure exists but fails under pressure; slippages normalize; decisions escalate to hierarchy.
3. **Unstable:** Architectural signals emerging, but reliability inconsistent; voice and closure vary by personality.
4. **Strong Alignment:** Trust and accountability integrated; minor lapses corrected through structural mechanisms.
5. **Validated Architecture:** Trust, accountability, and reliability self-correct; structures hold under pressure and through turnover.

Interpretation Guide

Validated Architecture: (19-25)

1. Commitments close with proof, not personality.
2. Dissent is protected and used as intelligence.
3. Decisions remain at work under pressure.
4. Incentives reinforce structural reliability.
5. Continuity persists through absence and turnover.

Drift Detected: (1-18)

1. Promises live in private channels.
2. Silence replaces candor under pressure.
3. Decisions climb hierarchy or follow influence.
4. Recognition rewards optics or heroics.
5. Work collapses when specific individuals step back.

Structural Closing Line

Trust without accountability rehearses collapse, accountability without trust breeds fear. Only architecture integrating both can produce reliability on purpose.

Leader's Challenge

You already know the truth of your trust architecture:
you treated sentiment as structure, apology as repair, and silence as stability.

You saw it long before the breach exposed it.
Private words turned into artifacts.
Screenshots moved faster than courage.
Silence replaced correction.
"Confidential" meant "until inconvenient."

None of this was random.
It was the architecture you allowed.

If private speech becomes a strategy, trust is data, not covenant.

If harmed people learn last, circulation outranks confrontation.

If safety depends on personalities, architecture is absent.

If silence follows harm, truth has no structural path.

These are not emotional lapses.

They are structural failures.

And structure is your responsibility.

You cannot claim integrity while breaches are handled off-record.

You cannot claim transparency while truth depends on the audience.

You cannot claim accountability when consequence tracks status instead of action.

Your culture is not confused.

It is obedient.

If trust appears only in crisis, it is already optional.

If breaches leave no visible record, you engineered deniability.

If leaders manage fallout quietly, you trained the culture to hide truth.

Every leader reaches Darryl's moment:

when a breach stops being an incident and becomes a mirror;

when the real question is not "Who did this?" but

"What made this easy to do?"

You cannot protect people while leaving their words unprotected.

You cannot claim safety while harm outruns accountability.

You cannot claim learning without visible correction.

If you act only when someone is caught, exposure, not integrity, governs behavior.

If the harmed must request the truth, the architecture has already failed.

Your challenge is not to communicate better.

Your challenge is to architect trust.

Move from:

"I handled it privately" → "I documented it visibly."

"I meant no harm" → "I built safeguards that prevent it."

"We apologized" → "We redesigned the structure."

"I trust my people" → "I verify the architecture."

"We'll be more careful" → "We will audit the architecture."

Trust is not neutral.
Architecture stabilizes it.
Drift erodes it.

If you do not trust, the culture will; toward secrecy, protection, and rumor.

Mastery does not prevent failure.
It converts failure into strength.

Your decision now is simple:
continue managing breaches in private, or build the architecture that makes truth safe, breach visible, and repair structural, not sentimental.

III. Essence of Execution

1. Core Execution Truth

Trust is the architecture converting human promise into structural integrity.

2. Indicators of Drift

1. Trust appears only during crises rather than in daily operation.
2. Breaches are handled privately and leave no verifiable record.
3. Silence becomes the safest behavior; truth waits for permission.
4. Safety depends on personalities instead of engineered structure.
5. Repair stops at apology; safeguards, cadence, and owners are absent.

3. Essential Leader Actions

1. Make every breach a documented event with timeline, owner, and visible correction.

2. Engineer safety through structural mechanisms: reporting channels, confidentiality integrity, and repeatable feedback cadence.
3. Replace sentiment with design: protocols, disclosures, and verifiable safeguards.
4. Surface harm immediately; confront circulation, discretion, and silence on contact.
5. Convert repair into architecture by redesigning workload, reporting lines, and verification rhythms.

4. Enforceable Feedback Requirements

1. All breaches require a published record: sequence, actors, impact, and corrective action.
2. Safety and trust mechanisms undergo scheduled audits; lapses mandate visible redesign.
3. Fatigue, silence, or hidden risk patterns must trigger structural adjustment within fixed cadence.
4. Verification logs tie leadership claims to operational proof; discrepancies require immediate correction.
5. Protocols, confidentiality structures, and reporting channels are measured for continuity; absence of mechanism flags Drift for executive intervention.

5. The Decisive Question

Will you architect trust into visible, verifiable structure or allow Drift to rebuild your culture around silence, discretion, and unrecorded harm?

IV. Rapid Orientation: Drift–Architecture Spectrum

Use this rubric for orientation, not validation. If your structures do not hold under pressure and turnover, you are in Drift regardless of intent or progress.

Severe Drift: Trust weak; accountability avoided or weaponized; performance depends on individuals; structures operate through optics or fear.

High Drift: Early structure exists but fails under pressure; slippages normalize; decisions escalate to hierarchy.

Unstable: Architectural signals emerging, but reliability inconsistent; voice and closure vary by personality.

Strong Alignment: Trust and accountability integrated; minor lapses corrected through structural mechanisms.

Validated Architecture: Trust, accountability, and reliability self-correct; structures hold under pressure and through turnover.

Chapter 11 – Meaning

I. Story: When Meaning Went Silent

The office was still, the kind of stillness that comes before the first train passes and the city remembers itself. Carol sat in that silence, her monitor awake in front of her, Inga's resignation open like a wound that refused to close.

She had read it six times. Each time the verbiage cut a little deeper.

I used to believe we were building something special. That was my reason. Why I gave every night, every ounce of myself. I can't find that meaning anymore; somewhere along the way, the reason I lived for disappeared beneath the weight of work.

The words were stripped of anger, weighted instead with the exhaustion of someone watching their "why" fade into silence.

Carol's hands rested on the desk, still as paperweights. She had built entire frameworks on the idea that culture could sustain meaning; rituals, recognition, and rhythm could carry people upright when everything else leaned toward collapse. But Inga's departure had unraveled that belief. Meaning wasn't holding. It was bleeding out quietly through the cracks she hadn't seen.

Outside, dawn scraped its first light across the glass towers. The reflection caught her eyes, and for a moment she didn't recognize herself. The face looking back seemed older, distant from the woman who once believed empathy was enough to architect belonging.

The calendar alert blinked at the corner of her screen: Exec Sync: Employee Sentiment Review. The irony hit hard.

Reg's face appeared first in the video window, sharp lines, perfect lighting. Behind him, the faint blur of the boardroom wall.

"Engagement's up two points," he said without greeting. "Attrition's leveling off. We're stabilizing."

Carol paused, eyes on the screen, her silence stretching for a breath before her cursor hovered over Inga's email.

"Inga resigned last night," Carol said finally.

"We'll backfill."

Carol stared at him, disbelief twisting into something sharper. "Backfill?" Her voice broke, then hardened. "She gave everything to this place, Reg. Nights, weekends, her belief that we were different. And you're talking like it's a spreadsheet cell to replace."

He leaned back, unbothered. "People move on, Carol. It happens."

Carol's breath caught. "No. They burn out because we make it impossible to stay. We drain the ones who care most, then act surprised when they leave."

He blinked once, like someone hearing the ghost of broken radios. Silence. She pressed on, lower now, tired. "She wasn't a position, Reg. She was the lifeblood that reminded us this place could still matter."

Her eyes glinted, anger cooling into exhaustion. "That lifeblood just stopped," she said, voice cracking under the weight of disbelief. "Do you even feel it, Reg? Another life bled out, and you don't even flinch."

The silence on the conference call wasn't awkward, it was sterile. She ended it without saying goodbye.

Carol stared at the blank screen after ending the call. The stillness pressed in; too quiet, too clean. Her reflection in the dark monitor looked like someone halfway erased.

She needed to see her people. To prove there was still something left beating under the metrics.

The "gratitude call" had been her idea. A quick morale lift to end the week, a reminder that connection still existed somewhere inside the machinery.

It began like a forced prayer. Screens flickered to life. Someone laughed too loudly, the brittle sound of a person trying to fill a room that didn't want to be full.

"Let's start with something positive," Carol said.

Silence.

Then a voice, low and tired: "I'm grateful I made it through another week without crying."

Nervous laughter.

Another voice: "I'm grateful we're still pretending everything is okay."

The chat window bloomed with hollow emojis, applause icons, digital confetti that felt obscene.

"I'm grateful Inga finally escaped," someone said, half-joking.
A few people laughed. Carol didn't.
The word *escaped* kept echoing.

Carol watched, heart thudding, as faces turned away from the camera one by one. No eye contact. No air. Just the quiet hum of people holding themselves together because quitting felt like betrayal.

A new hire began to speak, his voice shaking "I still believe this place could..." He stopped. No one looked up.

The laughter that followed was jagged. Not joy. Survival.

Carol felt it then, the rupture. Meaning didn't die loudly; it suffocated in politeness.

She closed her laptop mid-laughter. The echo lingered in her chest like static after a storm.
They weren't cynical. They were grieving what used to matter.

The day slid forward without form. Meetings, messages, faces. All of it flattening into background noise. By late afternoon, Carol found herself in the atrium, sitting beneath the skeletal glow of the suspended lights. The hum of ventilation filled the space like distant surf.

Imara appeared without prelude, carrying two cups of coffee. She placed one beside Carol and sat. They didn't speak for a long time.

"You look like you're trying to shoulder meaning by yourself again," Imara said finally.

Carol let out a breath that was almost a laugh. "If I let go, what happens to the rest of them?"

"Then the system shows whether it ever carried them at all."

Carol's gaze dropped to her hands. "I thought the meaning could be felt. I thought if people saw that I cared enough, they'd care too."

Imara shook her head slowly. "You built feeling into ritual, not into structure. Empathy doesn't scale until it becomes design."

Something inside Carol gave way, not a break, but a quiet yielding. “So you’re saying meaning isn’t a feeling?”

“It’s a system of coherence. Feeling is how we notice it’s missing.”

Carol sat back, her ache pressing deeper, not fading. For a moment she wanted to agree with Inga, surrendering and call it truth.

She stopped. This was the one freedom no collapse could take from her.
Her father’s words returned, though she had never quoted them aloud: you always have freedom to choose your attitude.

Her internal conflict was evidence that something still mattered. That meant it could be rebuilt.

Meaning wasn’t comfort; it was reconstruction not endurance, but resistance: the deliberate recalibration of structure against collapse.

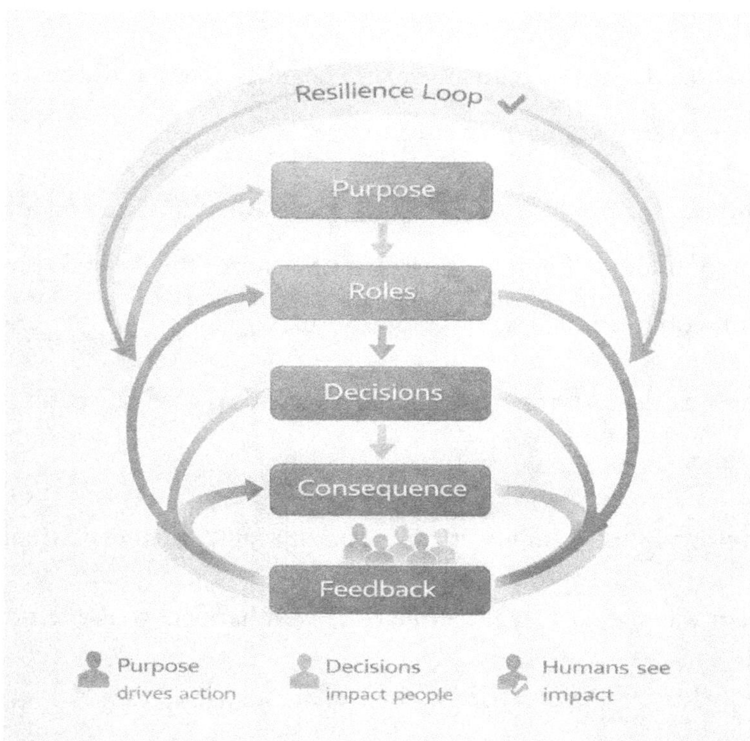

Figure 11.1 Meaning as Architecture

Meaning persists when purpose, roles, decisions, consequences, and feedback form a closed structural loop.

She straightened, breathing once, slow and deliberate. Her body remembered the design before the mind caught up.

The realization didn't ease her. It anchored her, like a heartbeat finding rhythm again.

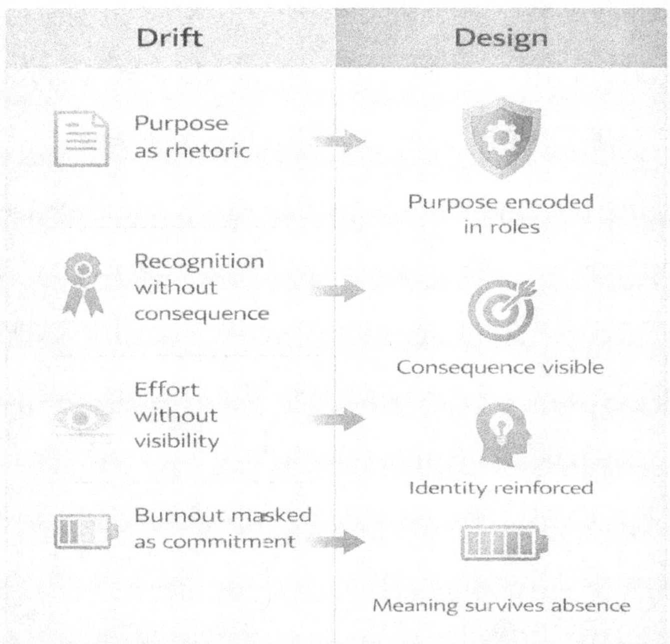

Figure 11.2 Drift vs Designed Meaning

Meaning collapses when purpose is rhetoric; it endures when purpose is structurally encoded into work.

The next morning, Carol rewrote the recognition model. She replaced quarterly awards with Contribution Maps; simple, recurring grids connecting every task to the human life it altered. Each map closes the month with a question, not a metric: What changed because we cared?

At first, she expected indifference. What she found instead was hesitation, the quiet kind that hides behind curiosity. A handful of engineers spoke haltingly about clients they'd never met.

Not everyone understood. Some called the new model naïve. "You can't map meaning," one manager muttered. Others worried it was performative, another layer of corporate poetry over exhaustion.

In one session, a senior engineer pushed back. "We're already underwater. You want us to talk about feelings now?"

Carol didn't flinch. "Not feelings. Consequence."

The room went still. For a moment she thought she'd lost them. But the silence wasn't rejection; it was calculation. The mind resisted before the heart caught up.

Psychology defines it as productive tension: the necessary strain between what exists and what must evolve. She could feel it alive in that room, the stress of people relearning why their work mattered. Meaning demanded that pressure; without it, it dissolved into slogan.

Watching them, she recognized the same fatigue that had hollowed her: the disbelief that meaning could survive the machinery. Their doubt was her own reflection spoken aloud. The fight she'd waged in silence was now happening in the open, and it was necessary. Every structure resisted before it held.

By the third session, one of them brought data showing how their patch had prevented hundreds of user lockouts. They didn't call it meaning. They called it *impact.*

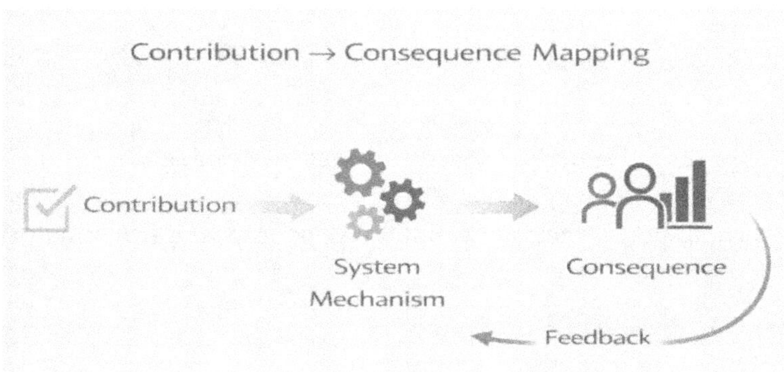

Figure 11.3 Contribution - Consequence Mapping

Meaning is sustained when individual contribution is structurally linked to visible human and organizational outcomes.

But Carol heard the shift in tone; steady, grounded. Their words sounded like ownership, like they'd reclaimed a piece of why they were here.

Weeks blurred. She began holding open conversations where teams turned numbers into stories. They talked about the people behind the data instead of the data itself. Each review traced work back to a face, a moment changed, a problem eased. The fatigue didn't vanish, but it softened. Effort began to feel meaningful again, like something worth giving yourself to.

Still, the question haunted her: why had it taken Inga's loss to begin this redesign?

Late one night, Carol reopened Inga's email. She scrolled to the bottom, to a line she had ignored the first time.

You once said the system would carry us. I wanted to believe that.

For the first time, Carol saw it differently. Inga hadn't lost meaning, she had lost confirmation that meaning could be held by the system. The culture demanded belief, but offered no structure for it. Meaning had been an atmosphere, not an architecture.

Carol began sketching frameworks again; circles, nodes, lines. Now every arrow pointed to a person. Each role became a vector of contribution, each process a mechanism of coherence. The design took on rhythm. Not decoration; truth made visible.

She realized she was no longer trying to shield people from the engine of meaning. She was bringing them into its design. Every role, rhythm, and act of care became a pulse in a coordinated revival; a synchronized heartbeat restoring coherence to a system once thought dead. She was no longer alone at the console; the teams were resuscitating it together, each heartbeat reconnecting the architecture to life itself.

The following quarter, attrition improved without the push of incentives. Change grows naturally from coherence and shared belief. Pulse surveys showed words she hadn't seen in years: purpose, alignment, trust. Hal called it sentiment recovery. Marcus called it structural correction. Carol called it meaning returning to life, the system remembering how to breathe again.

One afternoon, Marcus left a note in her inbox, a single line from the ledger: **Meaning is not morale. It is the architecture outlasting exhaustion.**

She smiled at that. He had understood.

The halls moved again, not with noise, but with intent. Conversation carried force; laughter sounded like something earned.

Work no longer drained people; it demanded them, and they answered.
Meaning was reclaimed, wrestled back from Drift through thousands of small acts of refusal.

The air felt charged. Not gentle. Alive, like a structure that had survived the fire and kept building anyway.

What filled the space was resilience. The will of people remembering why they fought to exist.

The night after the results review, Carol stayed late. The building was quiet again, the same silence as that morning weeks ago. The same office. The same city. But not the same woman.

She walked through the corridors, lights low, the hum of systems steady. She passed the glass walls of teams still at work; small clusters of voices, whiteboards alive with motion. She paused at one room where an analyst spoke about error-rate reduction as preventing user stress. Another where a designer explained a layout decision as reducing confusion.

The language had changed. Function had become meaning. When meaning becomes muscle memory, design has become culture.

She leaned against the doorway for a moment, listening. They weren't performing belief; they were living conviction moving as if meaning had become muscle memory, every action a quiet declaration that this place mattered again.

When she returned to her office, the city was a mirror of moving light. She sat again at her desk. On her monitor, a new message waited. From an unknown address. The subject line read: **Still building something that matters?**

The words stayed open on her screen as she looked across the floor. In the reflection of the glass, she saw motion: teams still working, cross-talking, solving. Not rushing, not grinding, just moving with coherence.

Two analysts were comparing data not for accuracy but for effect; a designer was sketching beside a customer feedback note, smiling. These were small gestures, but they were proof. The culture no longer needed supervision to remember why.

She didn't answer the message. She didn't need to. The building already had.

Outside, the city lights moved like circuitry, steady and bright. The stillness returned, but it was no longer empty.
It was the quiet of design fulfilling its purpose: meaning in motion.

Maxim: Meaning humanizes resistance

II. Doctrine & Diagnostic

Work becomes mechanical, identity dissolves, and Drift takes control when the *why* disappears. People work harder while commitment deteriorates. Cultures collapse without coherence. Meaning is the architecture of endurance. Design anchors purpose into structure, linking roles to consequences. Designing into the system humanizes performance.

Key Terms

- **Meaning:** fusion of purpose and structure anchoring why people engage deeply, creating resilience and sustained performance under pressure. It is the design of coherence guiding behavior and binding identity to contribution.
- **Why:** personal reason, motive, or cause giving an individual's life or work its meaning. It is the human compass converting work, struggle, or sacrifice into purpose.
- **Coherence:** structural state of alignment among *why* (purpose), *how* (system), and *who* (identity) producing behaviors reinforcing meaning without external control.
- **Consequence:** structural feedback making the effects of decisions visible, measurable, and human. The structure's way of saying: this is what your work caused.

Flaws Leaders Permit

1. Lack of Clear Purpose or Meaning

Work lacking a visible "why" decays effort into compliance. Employees lose the thread connecting their labor to consequence; engagement drops, performance follows, and identity erodes. Lacking perceived meaning correlates with lower motivation, retention, and performance.

PMC Response

Anchor roles explicitly to measurable human or organizational outcomes.

Begin reviews, projects, and rituals with the question, "Why does this matter?"

Purpose must be visible, measurable, and personal.

Enforceable Feedback Loop

1. Require teams to document purpose alignment in quarterly reviews.
2. Track retention and engagement shifts tied to meaning clarity.

Doctrinal Closure

- Work without why is labor without ownership.
- Contribution unlinked to consequence degrades into transaction and breeds Drift.
- Visibility of purpose converts effort into stewardship; design restores meaning to the system.

Transition

When purpose fades, leadership becomes theater, not architecture.

2. Leadership Disconnect from Meaning

Leaders preaching vision, but live metrics fracture trust. Teams follow posture, not slogans; when example and message diverge, Drift takes command. Leaders failing to articulate or embody meaning spread confusion and resistance throughout the system.

PMC Response

Require visible alignment.

Leaders must narrate the purpose behind every directive and model the behavior they demand.

Meaning must be embodied in decision and demeanor.

Enforceable Feedback Loop

1. Audit leadership communications for alignment between stated purpose and observable action.
2. Require quarterly storytelling sessions linking outcomes to values.

Doctrinal Closure

- Behavior is the blueprint; performance without proof builds Drift.

- Message divorced from metric dismantles trust; the system mirrors the leader's integrity.
- When the leader's why governs their behavior, the structure holds alignment.

Transition

Leadership detached from meaning fractures alignment.

3. Poor Alignment of Individual and Organizational Meaning

When personal purpose and corporate mission diverge, coherence collapses. People perform, but do not belong; adaptability dies where conviction is split. Misalignment weakens resilience and engagement.

PMC Response

Conduct meaning-mapping sessions linking individual values to enterprise goals; redesign roles until contribution and conviction intersect.

Enforceable Feedback Loop

1. Implement biannual alignment reviews where employees articulate how their personal why connects to organizational mission.

Doctrinal Closure

- Misaligned *why* fractures belonging; performance survives while culture dies.
- Coherence is engineered at the intersection of conviction and contribution.
- Alignment is design, not sentiment; roles must bind identity to consequence.

Transition

Misalignment erodes culture; fragmentation follows.

4. Cultural Fragmentation and Silos

Absent a unifying reason, departments protect turf over truth. Silos become safe havens from uncertainty, and collaboration decays into transactions. Shared meaning is the foundation of innovation and cohesion.

PMC Response

Install cross-functional rituals restoring shared narrative: purpose briefings, rotation programs, and collective retrospectives.

Enforceable Feedback Loop

1. Track cross-department initiatives for measurable purpose alignment and collaboration metrics.
2. Require reflection on shared outcomes.

Doctrinal Closure

- Shared meaning is the architecture strong enough to span silos.
- Without a common *why*, collaboration erodes into barter and protection.
- Unified narratives convert turf into structure and motion into coherence.

Transition

Fragmentation breeds immediacy.

5. Short-Term Focus over Enduring Meaning

Organizations chasing immediacy sacrifice permanence. Targets replace trajectory; the system burns through people faster than it produces value. Short-term focus links to burnout and operational Drift.

PMC Response

Design long-term scorecards pairing quarterly results with durability metrics: retention, learning, and resilience.

Enforceable Feedback Loop

1. Require strategic plans to include durability metrics alongside financial KPIs.

Doctrinal Closure

- Immediacy consumes endurance; targets without trajectory consume people.
- Design defines endurance; pressure tests it.
- Permanence is engineered; mastery is structure that does not distort under pressure

Transition

Short-term thinking dissolves endurance, coherence collapses next.

6. Neglect of Psychological and Systemic Coherence

Failure to build purpose into systems is replaced by inspirational speeches. Processes execute flawlessly yet feel hollow; the organization functions but no longer lives. Systemic Drift begins when meaning and design separate.

PMC Response

Integrate meaning into architecture: decision rights, incentives, and rituals must express the reason they serve.

Enforceable Feedback Loop

1. Audit system design for purpose integration and human feedback inclusion.
2. Measure cohesion between operational goals and lived experience.

Doctrinal Closure

- Process without purpose is maintenance; systems thrive when they remember why.
- Inspiration without integration is theater; structure without consequence is hollow.
- Coherence binds human truth to design.

Architectural Truths

- Every structure resists before it holds
- Meaning is freedom to choose your *why*

- Shared resistance forges purpose
- Structures prevail through shared construction
- Resilience is mastery of tension
- These Architectural Truths define how meaning becomes measurable through design under pressure.

Diagnostic Tool: The Meaning Architecture Audit

Purpose

Determine whether meaning is structurally engineered into roles, decisions, and feedback loops, or left to rhetoric, sentiment, and performance theater that collapses under pressure; this is not a morale or engagement survey.

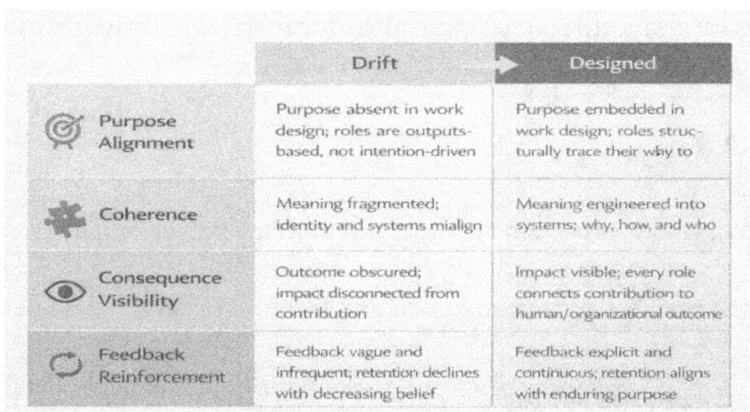

Figure 11.4 The Meaning Architecture Audit

A diagnostic framework verifying whether purpose is encoded into roles, decisions, and feedback loops rather than sustained by rhetoric.

Diagnostic Dimensions

1. Purpose Alignment

Definition

Evaluates whether every role can structurally trace its *why* to organizational intent, so purpose directs daily design rather than living as rhetoric.

Propagation / Performance Indicator

Purpose is encoded into role charters, decision frameworks, and performance systems; people can show how their work advances the mission using structural artifacts, not slogans. Daily priorities, trade-offs, and resource allocation consistently reference the why, and cross-functional decisions can be audited back to stated intent rather than to personal preference.

Drift Indicator

Purpose appears in slide decks and speeches but not in how work is designed or sequenced; people describe outputs and tasks, not consequences or impact. When leaders leave the room, teams execute activities that no longer clearly connect to mission, and belief depends on a few charismatic storytellers rather than on the architecture.

2. Identity Coherence

Definition

Assesses whether the architecture reinforces a healthy connection between personal identity and organizational meaning, instead of demanding conformity that erodes self-concept.

Propagation / Performance Indicator

Role frameworks explicitly show how individual strengths reinforce collective design; leadership rituals acknowledge specific individual impact in the language of purpose, not generic praise. Feedback and recognition link personal contribution to shared meaning, so people can see themselves in the design rather than just inside a job description.

Drift Indicator

People describe "doing what it takes to survive" rather than belonging; silence increases in meetings as dissent and difference feel unsafe or pointless. The structure rewards conformity over contribution; identity fragments from work; belonging is replaced with quiet withdrawal and role performance, and psychological safety depends on isolated leaders rather than systemic norms.

3. Consequence Visibility

Definition

Determines whether people can clearly see and prove the human and structural impact of their work, rather than watching it disappear into process.

Propagation / Performance Indicator

Feedback cycles tie actions to visible results through dashboards, debriefs, and closure rituals that show concrete outcomes. Teams can name recent decisions and point to their effects on customers, colleagues, and the structure; recognition is tied to verified impact, and accountability includes learning, not just blame.

Drift Indicator

Work vanishes into workflows and tools; people cannot describe the outcome of their last major action, only the activity they completed. Feedback is infrequent, ceremonial, or purely quantitative; recognition feels random; accountability is evasive or politicized, and emotional fatigue rises as effort feels unconnected to real consequence.

4. Shared Construction

Definition

Evaluates whether meaning is co-built through shared creation of rituals, decisions, and goals, or imposed from hierarchy as a script to be followed.

Propagation / Performance Indicator

Cross-functional forums and team-based rituals actively shape how purpose shows up in work; people at different levels contribute to defining standards, language, and practices that embody meaning. Communication loops between leadership and teams are transparent, iterative, and visibly incorporated into structural decisions, so "we built this" is a truthful statement rather than a slogan.

Drift Indicator

Meaning is authored by hierarchy and broadcast as posters, slogans, and campaigns; participation is token or purely consultative. Language of separation dominates: "they decided," "they changed the vision," and ownership narrows to titles; passivity, quiet cynicism, and resignation spread as culture becomes compliance and belief depends on a small circle of influencers.

5. Resilience of Belief

Definition

Determines whether belief in purpose holds under pressure because it is structurally protected or collapses into compliance when conditions strain the architecture.

Propagation / Performance Indicator

Crisis protocols, decision guidelines, and escalation pathways explicitly anchor back to values and purpose; post-event reviews test whether alignment holds under stress. Leaders model consistency between stated meaning and hard decisions, even when it is costly; teams maintain candor and connection in difficult periods, and belief feels reinforced, not betrayed, by challenge.

Drift Indicator

Under stress, leaders retreat to control, opacity, and short-term optics; teams revert to bare compliance and risk avoidance. Values become negotiable; transparency disappears; decisions contradict declared meaning without structural challenge, and people emotionally withdraw even while remaining physically present. Continuity of belief depends on a few stabilizing personalities; when they step back, conviction rapidly erodes.

Scoring Standard (1-5: Drift → Validated)

1. **Severe Drift:** Meaning lives in rhetoric and sentiment only; structures do not reference purpose; people cannot show proof that their work matters beyond output, and belief relies entirely on individual leaders.
2. **High Drift:** Some formal statements or tools reference purpose, but daily decisions, incentives, and feedback rarely align; under pressure, rhetoric is abandoned, and reliability of meaning varies by manager or team.
3. **Unstable:** Pockets of structural meaning exist (in specific leaders, teams, or processes), but experience is inconsistent; belief and coherence break under stress or leadership turnover, revealing dependence on personalities rather than architecture.
4. **Strong Alignment:** Most roles, decisions, and feedback loops visibly encode purpose; when stress hits, structures generally reinforce rather than contradict meaning, and continuity is not tied to a small set of individuals.

5. **Validated Architecture:** Meaning is structurally embedded and reliably evidenced across dimensions; people can prove impact, see themselves in the design, and sustain belief through pressure and change.

Interpretation Guide

Validated Architecture: (19-25)

1. Purpose is structurally transmitted through role charters, decision frameworks, and performance systems, not just through messaging.
2. People can show concrete outcomes their work produced and how those outcomes align with the *why*.
3. Identity and belonging are reinforced by the architecture; individuals feel seen in the design, not erased by it.
4. Meaning is co-authored through shared rituals, forums, and feedback loops; "we built this" reflects actual structural participation.
5. Under pressure, values still govern decisions; belief holds, and crises become tests that strengthen coherence rather than expose hypocrisy.
6. When the five dimensions are plotted as a radar-style grid, the shape is broadly full and balanced, with minimal dips, indicating structural meaning rather than symbolic claims.

Drift Detected: (1-18)

1. Purpose appears in narratives and artifacts but not in daily choices; people talk about tasks and outputs, not consequences.
2. Identity is suppressed or fragmented; people describe survival more than belonging, and dissent retreats into silence or private conversations.
3. Work disappears into process; feedback is sporadic or ceremonial; recognition rewards activity, optics, or heroics, not verified impact.
4. Meaning is dictated from the top; ownership narrows to titles; "they decided" replaces "we built," and quiet cynicism grows as posters outpace lived experience.

5. Under stress, control, secrecy, and short-term fixes override stated values; belief collapses into compliance, and continuity of meaning depends on a few stabilizing individuals.
6. When plotted visually, the grid shows distortions, hollow centers, or sharp dips revealing fracture points where meaning has not been structurally anchored.

Structural Closing Line

When meaning is not engineered into architecture, people become performers in a story they no longer believe; in that silence, Drift becomes the author of the culture.

Leader's Challenge

You already know the truth of your meaning architecture;
you've mistaken morale for meaning, and sentiment for structure.

You saw it long before you admitted it:

People surviving the week instead of shaping consequences.
Recognition rituals collapsing into performance.
The most committed burning out first.
Departures arriving with the inevitability of Drift.

None of this was emotional.
It was structural.

```
If purpose never enters the workflow → people disconnect.
If consequence stays invisible → effort becomes exhaustion.
If belief rests on a few champions → meaning collapses when they leave.
If gratitude replaces redesign → Drift becomes the culture.
```

These are not "engagement dips."
They are failures of meaning encoded into your system.

You cannot claim purpose while rewarding activity instead of consequence.
You cannot claim culture when honesty depends on who is in the room.
You cannot claim resilience while conviction still depends on heroics.

Your organization is not unpredictable—

only obedient to the architecture you built.

If tasks lack a why → people detach.

If dashboards display volume instead of impact → belief erodes.

If recognition praises effort without proof → trust dissolves.

If exits shock you → you measured sentiment and ignored structure.

Every flaw is a permission you granted:

Purpose without architecture.

Recognition without consequence.

Contribution without visibility.

Commitment without coherence.

Your challenge is not to motivate harder.

Your challenge is to stop rehearsing collapse in the language of care.

Shift from:

- "Boost morale" → "Show where the why lives in the work."
- "Tell a better story" → "Prove the consequence created."
- "Recognize hard work" → "Honor visible impact."
- "People seem disengaged" → "Meaning will not be optional."
- "Celebrate effort" → "Document contribution."

Meaning is not neutral.

Design carries it.

Drift consumes it.

If Purpose isn't structured → work becomes theater.

If Identity isn't coherent → belonging fractures.

If Consequence isn't visible → effort erodes.

If Meaning isn't shared → culture collapses into compliance.

If Belief isn't resilient → pressure destroys conviction.

You are not being asked whether you care.

You are being asked whether you will architect a structure that carries meaning—

so your people no longer have to.

III. Essence of Execution

1. Core Execution Truth

Meaning humanizes resistance.

2. Indicators of Drift

1. People describe "getting through the week" instead of naming the impact their work created.
2. Recognition rituals feel performative; emojis, ceremonies, and praise without visible consequence.
3. Purpose appears in decks and speeches but not in role design, decisions, or daily priorities.
4. The most committed contributors burn out first; their departures feel inevitable rather than preventable.
5. Sentiment scores are tracked, but there is no structural evidence that meaning is embedded into the system.

3. Essential Leader Actions

1. Embed *why* into roles, workflows, and reviews so every contributor can trace their work to a clear purpose.
2. Replace generic recognition with mechanisms that honor verified human and structural impact.
3. Design recurring forums where teams turn metrics into stories of consequence and visible change.
4. Architects shared construction of meaning by involving teams in shaping rituals, language, and standards.
5. Under pressure, make decisions that preserve coherence between declared purpose and actual design.

4. Enforceable Feedback Requirements

1. Every significant initiative and project must document its explicit *why* and the human or structural consequence it seeks to create.
2. Performance and recognition systems must show a direct line from contribution to verified impact, not just activity or effort.
3. Pulse surveys and audits must measure purpose alignment, identity coherence, and consequence visibility not only morale.
4. Exit and burnout reviews must code for meaning-loss patterns and trigger structural redesign where alignment has failed.
5. Post-event and crisis reviews must test whether decisions upheld the stated *why* or defaulted to short-term optics.

5. The Decisive Question

Will you architect meaning into the structure so resistance becomes humanized and coherent, or leave it atmospheric and allow Drift to decide what your people are struggling for?

IV. Rapid Orientation: Drift–Architecture Spectrum

Use this rubric for orientation, not validation. If your structures do not hold under pressure and turnover, you are in Drift regardless of intent or progress.

Severe Drift: Meaning lives in rhetoric and sentiment only; structures do not reference purpose; people cannot show proof that their work matters beyond output, and belief relies entirely on individual leaders.

High Drift: Some formal statements or tools reference purpose, but daily decisions, incentives, and feedback rarely align; under pressure, rhetoric is abandoned, and reliability of meaning varies by manager or team.

Unstable: Pockets of structural meaning exist (in specific leaders, teams, or processes), but experience is inconsistent; belief and coherence break under stress or leadership turnover, revealing dependence on personalities rather than architecture.

Strong Alignment: Most roles, decisions, and feedback loops visibly encode purpose; when stress hits, structures generally reinforce rather than contradict meaning, and continuity is not tied to a small set of individuals.

Validated Architecture: Meaning is structurally embedded and reliably evidenced across dimensions; people can prove impact, see themselves in the design, and sustain belief through pressure and change.

Chapter 12 — Proving Performance

I. Story: Validating Performance

The boardroom was engineered for measurement, not comfort. Geometry replaced warmth; precision ruled the air. Screens standing-by in disciplined silence. The room waited in readiness before judgment; a structure validating its own integrity.

Marcus stood at the head of the table with the ledger open; his running record of distrust and discovery, pages marked by the slow conversion of skepticism into belief in design. The others watched the light play across his face, waiting for what no one could rehearse: the moment a structure either validated itself or collapsed under the weight of its own expectation.

Reg sat two chairs down, posture precise, face unreadable. Hal adjusted the data stream on his tablet; numbers aligned like soldiers. Carol held a printed report, margin-marked and human. Imara leaned back, eyes steady, the quiet center of gravity in the room. The air carried a cold, metallic edge from the recycled ventilation. No one spoke. They didn't need to. The test itself would speak soon enough.

A digital clock on the far wall ticked over to nine. The Audit had begun. The sound of the second hand punctuated every breath.

The lead auditor, a quiet man with a voice that cut through rhetoric, broke the stillness. "PMC promised resilience, a structure that endures pressure, not heroism. Today, we test the claim."

Hal's fingers moved with deliberate calm, connecting his tablet to the main display. Metrics came alive: performance curves, variance graphs, the Resilience Validation Matrix (RVM)**:** four quadrants pulsing in equilibrium: **Meaning, Structure, Outcome, Human Resilience.** This was not a presentation; it was measurement incarnate.

Marcus's voice carried the tension between skepticism and faith. "Design requires no defense; structure speaks in proof."

The auditor nodded. "Then let it speak."

Carol began with the "Meaning" report, voice steady, eyes bright with conviction earned through exhaustion. "Engagement stability held through two budget freezes. Attrition fell twelve percent, but the real proof is in language. Exit interviews no longer cite burnout; they cite completion. People stayed because meaning stayed. They no longer asked for rescue; they asked for relevance."

The auditor made a note. "Meaning measurable. Proceed."

Imara added, "Meaning alignment is the structural core of performance; morality is measured through endurance."

Marcus wrote in his ledger: **Meaning enduring pressure validates purpose.**

Hal advanced the "Structural Integrity" feed. The wall filled with the visual rhythm of order, colored streams moving in synchrony. "Three divisions, identical operational loads, leadership rotations every quarter. Variance held below three percent. No dependency on individual authority."

Reg exhaled, more belief than relief. "Validation lives where leadership absence doesn't trigger collapse."

The auditor studied the graphs. "Structure proves itself by surviving indifference. You've built that."

Imara spoke into the pause. "Heroic leadership is structural fragility disguised as strength. Structures without heroes reveal truth."

Marcus's pen scratched across the page: **Validation is the absence of dependency.**

The display shifted to longitudinal "Outcome" data. The auditor narrated what the numbers confessed. "Recovery time improved twenty-one percent year over year. Adaptive index sustained across rotation cycles. Output rose without emotional depletion."

Hal nodded. "Because process, not personality, drives recovery."

Reg added quietly, "Performance is durable when persuasion isn't required."

Carol smiled faintly. "Optics are temporary. Structure is the only applause that matters."

Marcus's ledger recorded: **Outcome validated. Data stood without defense.**

Imara spoke with quiet command. "Resilience isn't speed. It's under strain. People stayed engaged even when success was invisible. They trusted the rhythm of design more than the comfort of recognition. The architecture carried them."

The auditor summarized. "Human Resilience observable, not assumed. Continue."

Marcus looked around the room. The quadrants were alive; four disciplines, one organism. For a moment, the structure felt less like data and more like conviction rendered measurable.

The auditor turned to another page. "Three anomalies within the RVM. Two operational data sets manipulated; indicators of load redistribution and process integrity."

Hal's shoulders stiffened. "We flagged those. A manager optimized optics, not outcomes. The variance was cosmetic. Correction is logged in the integrity ledger."

Reg's eyes flickered. He knew what this was: the shadow of erosion trying to re-enter the frame. Resilience tested not by attack but by compromise.

The auditor waited. Silence lengthened. Carol broke it. "We didn't hide the operational breach within the RVM data integrity layer. We published it. Transparency by design."

The auditor nodded once. "Acknowledged. Continue."

Then the glitch came.

A warning light pulsed on the display; amber, then red. A cross-region sync failed. One division's resilience feed dropped below threshold. The graph trending downward. The air thickened as if the building itself had held its breath.

"System fault," Hal said. His voice stayed flat, but his knuckles whitened. "Signal loss in the northern region. Data integrity gap."

"Cause?" the auditor asked.

Hal hesitated. "Human. An unverified overwrite in one of the resilience indices."

Carol leaned forward. "Who?"

Hal's eyes darted toward Marcus. "Archived input from yesterday; the oversight protocol came from your queue."

Marcus's pulse spiked. "That's impossible." He opened his device, scrolled through the log, and saw it; a single line, mistyped timestamp, one data link misaligned. Validation is corrupted not by deceit, but by fatigue. His fatigue.

Reg looked at him, not in anger, but recognition. "Precision defines the integrity of design."

Marcus breathed out. "I'll correct it."

The auditor raised a hand. "No edits. Correction protocols must activate autonomously."

For a moment, no one moved. The metrics dipped lower. Carol whispered, "If it fails now, the PMC doctrine fails with it."

Imara spoke into the tension. "Then we learn whether organizational conviction was architecture or performance."

The room filled with mechanical hum and human silence. Marcus's heart pounded against his ribs. His throat felt dry. The air tasted like metal. The system, designed for self-correction, began its recovery cycle. Automated governance traced the error, flagged its source, isolated the fault, redistributed load. Each recalibration pulse echoed like a heartbeat. Within minutes the slope flattened. Variance stabilized at 1.4, then 1.1, then 0.9.

Hal exhaled audibly. "Recovery sequence complete. No manual intervention."

Marcus stared at the restored line; the living signature of design redeeming human imperfection. His breath shuddered out, his hands trembling slightly before he hid them beneath the table.

Imara leaned closer. "Now you see what you built," she said. "Not perfection; resilience."

He nodded slowly. "Validation is not the avoidance of error; it is design restoring order without permission."

The auditor recorded the timestamp. "Documented recovery without leadership intervention. PMC verified adaptive integrity."

The minutes that followed were quieter. Marcus found himself studying Carol's expression, the way her focus had changed. Her shoulders had lowered, but her eyes had not softened; they had steadied. He realized she wasn't waiting for victory. She was watching for permanence. Every member in the room had lost something over the years: sleep, certainty, faith. Yet, they had built something that endured every pressure and legitimized its structure. It was validation achieved through precision.

The structure continued its cycles. The faint whir of cooling fans filled the silence between heartbeats. Reg sat still, a figure of unspoken reckoning. He had built the architecture to hold others; now it held him. The self-governance of the structure was validation of independence; the very proof Reg once doubted could exist.

Imara looked at Marcus. "When you started this ledger, you wrote every failure as a prophecy. What do you see now?"

He turned the pages; years of notes, smudged ink, the slow evolution of disbelief to doctrine. "I see that the structure doesn't need me to believe in it anymore. It believes in itself."

She nodded. "That's what design is; conviction converted into structure."

For the next thirty days, Reg remained in the background. The structure operated under its own governance. No directives, no approvals, no corrections. Reports stayed stable. Decisions remained aligned. Engagement, trust, and retention unchanged. Validation the structure no longer needed its authors.

On the thirtieth day, Marcus reopened the ledger. He wrote before the results appeared: **When resilience fails, humanity is revealed. When it holds, design manifests doctrine.**

Hal read the summary aloud: "Variance zero point nine four. Stability unchanged. Output consistent across all quadrants."

Carol leaned forward, exhaustion replaced by reverence. "The structure held."

Reg stepped back from the glass, leaving his reflection behind. "I spent half a lifetime defending success with my presence," he said. "It never occurred to me that permanence might require my absence."

Marcus turned the ledger toward them. The ink shimmered under the overhead light as he wrote the final entry:

The trust built the bridge. Meaning gave it purpose. Validation decides it prevails.

He drew a single line beneath it, marking closure, not end. The auditor signed beneath the line, pen parallel to Marcus's. "Audit complete," he said. "PMC is verified as self-sustaining."

No applause followed. Only the sound of pens closing, papers stacking, structures humming with quiet integrity. Reg left the room first. Carol gathered the reports, hands steady. Hal stayed behind, watching the data loops settle into equilibrium. Imara lingered in the doorway, gaze fixed on the ledger; the book that once recorded doubt, now documenting permanence.

Marcus was last. He stood before the screen where the Resilience Validation Matrix glowed in soft light. Each quadrant pulsed with subtle rhythm: meaning, structure, outcome, and resilience; none dominant, each dependent. He realized it mirrored something human: breath, heartbeat, resolve, renewal.

He walked out into the corridor. The air felt heavier, not with strain, with validation. Meetings continued. Voices carried down the hall, each one clear, certain, purposeful. The structure no longer required belief to exist. It had entered the stage of permanence.

Imara joined him halfway down the hall, her steps measured. "You've seen Drift defeated," she said quietly. "Does it feel like triumph?"

He shook his head. "It feels like stillness."

"That's the point," she said. "Resilience does not perform; it persists."

They reached the end of the corridor. Through the glass, the city stretched alive; movement layered over pattern, human rhythm threaded through structure. Marcus rested a hand on the glass, watching the reflection merge with the skyline. "It's not us anymore," he said.

"No," Imara replied. "It's architecture as governance."

He closed the ledger slowly, the gesture deliberate, reverent. The weight of years of skepticism dissolved into a quiet conviction. He had not been converted by charisma or convinced by language. He had seen validation stand on its own.

Outside, the evening pressed against the glass. The city breathed beyond it; indifferent, ongoing, alive. Marcus whispered to the reflection in the window, not as hope, but verification.

"Architecture is absolute."

Maxim: Validation is the architecture of permanence.

II. The Doctrine of Validation

Validation confirms architectural integrity: the alignment of meaning, structure, outcome, and human resilience.

Validation converts architecture into enforceable design principle; design engineers excellence; excellence manifests as mastery; mastery sustains permanence.

Key Terms

- **Validation:** confirmation of design integrity; evidence that structure performs to standard without reliance on belief or defense.
- **Permanence:** state in which excellence is governed and sustains independent of people, pressure, or context. Its existence is proven, not declared.

Architectural Truths

i. Excellence Must be Proven Under Pressure

Excellence does not require justification. Pressure does not create excellence; it reveals whether architecture governs it.

Principle

Only excellence that holds under pressure can be made permanent.

Mastery is achieved when excellence is no longer contingent on effort, presence, or circumstance.

ii. Structure Is the Only Reliable Witness

Heroic leaders manipulate perception; resilient structures reveal truth.

Principle

Self-correcting architecture replaces optics with integrity.

Structures recovering without intervention validate architecture.

iii. Meaning Humanizes Measurement

Numbers without human reference crumble. Human purpose stabilizes data and restores integrity.

Principle

Converging purpose and validation transform measurement to moral principle.

Meaning enduring pressure validates purpose.

iv. Resilience Is Self-Correction

Recovery requiring intervention is Drift.

Principle

Automating self-restoration is the apex of human architecture.

Design converts error into performance.

v. Absence Is the Final Audit

Leaders prove their value with absence.

Principle

Excellence in the absence of leadership proves structural doctrine.

Sustained self correcting excellence proves permanence.

Binary Doctrine of Validation: Drift vs Design

Fragile (Drift)	Resilient (Design)
Fragile by nature	Resilient by design
Optics-driven performance	Evidence-driven mastery
Charisma-led success	Structure-led continuity
Data as defense	Data used as design input
Heroics under pressure	Systemic endurance
Recovery dependent on leaders	Recovery embedded in system
Short-term validation cycles	Long-term compounding validation

Doctrinal Verdict

Validated mastery is the architecture of self-sustaining structure; proof that doctrine endures as continuity.

III. Diagnostic Tool: The Resilience Validation Matrix (RVM)

Purpose

Verify whether architecture sustains stability, performance, and human resilience without leadership presence, proving the organization's permanence under pressure.

Diagnostic Dimensions

1. Meaning Alignment

Definition

Tests whether purpose, doctrine, and values remain coherent under pressure without reverting to command or personality.

Propagation / Performance Indicator

Purpose holds as architectural doctrine; engagement and behavioral coherence persist without incentive or persuasion.

Drift Indicator: Meaning fractures under pressure; communication becomes directive; morale collapses or requires emotional intervention.

2. Structural Integrity

Definition: Evaluates whether core systems recover stability autonomously, validating that structure, not leadership, restores order.

Propagation / Performance Indicator: Variance returns below thresholds without intervention; operational stability emerges through structure.

Drift Indicator: Leaders must act for recovery; absence reveals dependency; architecture collapses when authority is removed.

3. Outcome Continuity

Definition: Measures whether results remain consistent across cycles without narrative defense, emotional activation, or oversight.

Propagation / Performance Indicator: Performance is durable before, during, and after observation; outcomes remain stable without theatre or escalation.

Drift Indicator: Metrics spike when watched and collapse when attention fades; outcomes depend on persuasion, crisis framing, or heroics.

4. Human Resilience

Definition: Assesses whether human capacity restores itself through rhythmic structure rather than sacrifice or personal effort.

Propagation / Performance Indicator: Wellbeing and emotional equilibrium recover via embedded rhythms; strain resolves through structure.

Drift Indicator: Fatigue compounds; recovery requires intervention; heroics substitute for design; exhaustion becomes normalized.

5. Architectural Autonomy Under Absence

Definition: Validates whether the architecture performs identically when leadership is withdrawn, exposing true architectural permanence.

Propagation / Performance Indicator: Operations, decisions, and human rhythm hold steady during leader absence; transparency and cadence continue uninterrupted.

Drift Indicator: Stability requires presence; visibility fragments; cadence halts; architecture waits for rescue.

Scoring Standard (1-5: Drift → Validated)

1. **Severe Drift:** Architecture collapses without presence; outcomes, meaning, and human stability depend entirely on intervention.
2. **High Drift:** Some structural elements function, but recovery, continuity, and resilience remain personality-dependent; absence reveals systemic instability.
3. **Unstable:** Architecture sustains partial autonomy but degrades under pressure; results and human rhythm recover inconsistently.
4. **Strong Alignment:** Most systems self-correct; meaning, results, and human capacity remain coherent under pressure; only edge-case variance appears.
5. **Validated Architecture:** Architecture governs fully; stability, outcomes, and resilience hold across cycles and through absence; permanence is proven.

Interpretation Guide

Validated Architecture: (19-25)

1. Architecture self-governs under pressure and absence.
2. Meaning, systems, and outcomes remain coherent without persuasion or oversight.
3. Human capacity restores through design, not sacrifice.
4. Transparency and cadence persist without defense.
5. Stability is systemic, not dependent on leadership.

Drift Detected: (1–18)

1. Purpose fractures and reverts to command under strain.

2. Stability requires intervention; absence reveals dependency.
3. Performance collapses after attention or applause.
4. Fatigue accumulates; heroics mask architectural failure.
5. Structure waits for rescue rather than self-correcting.

Structural Closing Line

Validation makes architecture visible; structures that require presence reveal Drift, while systems that restore themselves under strain embody permanence.

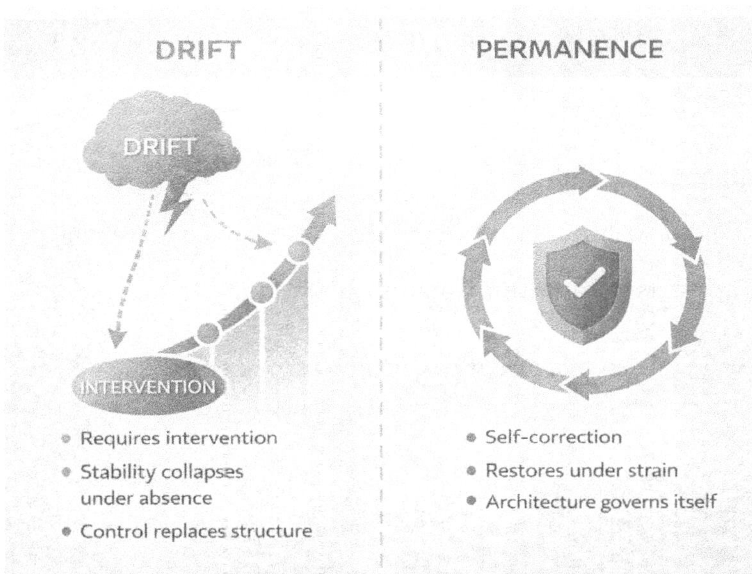

Figure 12.1 Validation Under Strain (Sample States)

Comparative system responses illustrating Drift revealed through dependency versus permanence confirmed through self-restoration under pressure.

IV. Enforcement: Leadership Validation Protocol.

The structure has validated itself; leadership must now prove alignment.

Figure 12.2 Leadership Validation in Action

Leaders submit to architectural validation; standards are enforced independent of role, authority, or presence.

The RVM confirmed architecture endures pressure.
Enforcement begins when leadership submits to the same standards it commands.
In this section, validation enters the governing of human structure.

Authority untested by validation is performance without permanence.

Purpose

Establish leadership as the structural guarantor of validation. Leaders cannot command permanence; they can only prove it. This section defines how leadership enforces validation as a governance ritual, ensuring the system proves its design through absence, transparency, and recurrence.

Leaders embody validation; their presence must prove architecture, not protect it.

i. Leadership Absence Mandate

Validation Standard: Leadership presence cannot substitute for structural integrity.

Mandate: Every validation cycle must include one full absence audit; leadership withdrawal during operational load.

Intent: Prove architecture, not authority, sustains permanence.

Enforcement: Structural failures undergo structural review; if leadership presence is required for stability, governance reassesses leadership validity.

Authority dependent on presence is Drift disguised as strength.

ii. Publication of Validation Audits

Validation Standard: Transparency validates legitimacy.

Mandate: All RVM results must be published within 30 days and publicly reviewed within 10 days.

Intent: Concealment constitutes Drift. Leaders must stand exposed beside the data they govern.

Enforcement: Omission or delay triggers leadership review; repeated concealment initiates redesign of reporting structure.

Unpublished validation is unearned trust.

iii. Recurrence and Validation Cycle Enforcement

Validation Standard: Validation repeated becomes doctrine; delay institutionalizes Drift.

Mandate: Organization executes four validation audits annually; each documented, witnessed, and reviewed.

Intent: Validation must be ritual.

Enforcement: Missing or incomplete audits result in leadership authority being suspended until cycles restored

Governance without discipline is Drift disguised as management.

iv. Doctrine of Consequence

Validation Standard: Neglect validation; forfeit permanence.

Mandate: Leaders failing to enforce validation forfeit moral authority and triggers formal structural redesign of their role.

Intent: Validation is the currency of leadership credibility.

Enforcement: Repeated negligence constitutes systemic Drift, requiring intervention by the governance body.

Leadership neglecting validation architects collapse.

V. Doctrinal Transition

Section V closes the Doctrine of Validation and opens the next discipline: Development. Validation ends the test of permanence; Development begins the construction of adaptive capacity. It stands as the threshold between proven design and its deliberate evolution.

i. The Irreversible Verdict

Validation is the architecture of permanence.

Here the chapter's architecture reaches final authority as structure, measurement, and governance merge into irreversible doctrine. It is not a conclusion but coronation; the Doctrine of Validation is the living standard of permanence, uniting Doctrine, Diagnostic, and Enforcement into a single Verification Doctrine. Validation is the permanent condition of design: measured, enforced, and complete. Drift argues for relevance; Architecture governs through validation.

ii. Transition to Chapter 13 — Leadership Development as Structural Evolution

The RVM audits architecture. Leadership validates architecture through absence and transparency. Chapter 13 advances from validation to development; the deliberate evolution of leadership structure no longer dependent on individual presence.

In PMC doctrine, development is the systemic advancement of leadership architecture. Validation confirms permanence; development designs its replication. Leadership development is the engineering of leadership permanence.

Through this bridge, permanence transforms into architectural continuity. Organizations move from proving permanence to expanding capacity; the architecture of leadership continuity.

VI. Rapid Orientation: Drift–Architecture Spectrum

Use this rubric for orientation, not validation. If your structures do not hold under pressure and turnover, you are in Drift regardless of intent or progress.

Severe Drift: Architecture collapses without presence; outcomes, meaning, and human stability depend entirely on intervention.

High Drift: Some structural elements function, but recovery, continuity, and resilience remain personality-dependent; absence reveals systemic instability.

Unstable: Architecture sustains partial autonomy but degrades under pressure; results and human rhythm recover inconsistently.

Strong Design Alignment: Most systems self-correct; meaning, results, and human capacity remain coherent under pressure; only edge-case variance appears.

Validated Architecture: Architecture governs fully; stability, outcomes, and resilience hold across cycles and through absence; permanence is proven.

Chapter 13 — Development as Structural Evolution

I. Story: The Continuity Test

The boardroom did not change its geometry through leadership change; it didn't need to. Architecture had a shape now. The glass reflected a quiet room built for judgment: four monitors asleep in equilibrium, the ledger closed beside a pen that would not move again for the next 3 months. Marcus pressed the pen flat with two fingers, then released it. No speech. No ceremony. He looked at Carol; she nodded once, sliding the ledger into the drawer marked Continuity. Proof that Marcus' absence would now speak for architecture. He stepped out of the line of sight and out of the structure he had helped build.

Marcus wasn't disappearing; he was departing for a deliberate secondment. Three months in the organization's Asian operations to help design reliability systems. His absence would test the structure at home more rigorously than any audit. It would be measured, recorded, and public. Continuity required absence, not oversight.

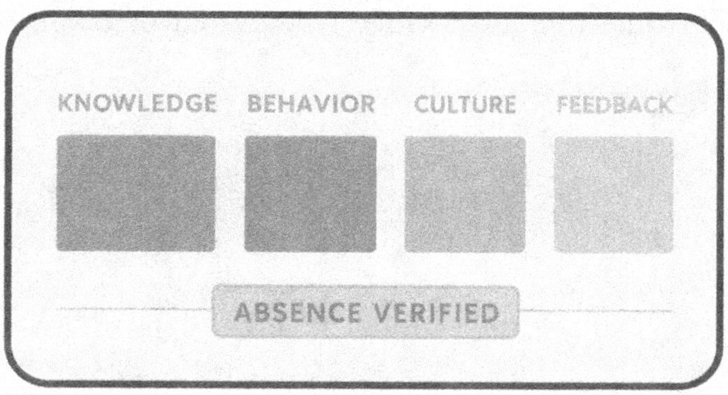

Figure 13.1 Continuity Proven Through Absence

Permanence is validated only when performance holds without leadership presence.

Letting go wasn't easy; it was self-discipline.

He paused by the doorway. The room's rhythm matched his own; the environment synchronized with architecture, not emotion. Months earlier, this silence would have been chaos: raised voices, emergency calls, decisions made on instinct instead of structural discipline. Today there was a governing methodology. His exit was more than absence. It was architecture being validated.

Three months would pass before Marcus would next open the ledger. The room's geometry would hold through the quarter, unchanged but tested.

He took one last glance at the wall display. Its reflection met his eyes, bright lines converging into the shape of a circuit. He recognized it: the architecture he once tried to control now breathing on its own. He smiled without moving his lips. Leadership aligned with architecture.

Imara stood near the back wall, neither in charge nor apart, a witness with a steady pulse. She noticed what had changed most: synergy. There was less defense in the room now, less of the anxious leaning forward that used to signal hidden doubt. The team worked quietly, focused, assured. She could feel it, continuity not as a concept but as muscle memory, the kind a body learns after pain. The air smelled faintly of metal and coffee; small, human validation that architecture had not drained life from the room.

She felt the faint ache of vigilance, her gut reflex to command. It faded when she realized the architecture no longer needed her guidance to hold.

The quiet was impressive, and brittle. She had seen calm like this before, just seconds before the old architecture fractured.

Silence had become the architecture's first measurement; absence would be its second.

Before the scheduled absence audit, an insecure Hal reached out for a video conference with Marcus. The connection was clear but the tone was distant: Hal in the boardroom, Marcus, tanned from the endless Vietnamese sunshine, sitting on a park bench enjoying street vendor noodles. Their exchange was short, procedural, disciplined. Hal reported minor variances; Marcus listened without correction, only asking, 'What does the system report?' Hal paused, then answered, 'It says we hold.' Marcus nodded once, the hint of a smile crossing his face before the screen dimmed. The call ended not with farewell but confirmation; the architecture was speaking for itself.

Carol's team took their seats: Carol at the head of the table, Hal opposite her. In Marcus' chair sat the new division lead, Angel, eyes scanning the dormant displays like a pilot waiting for clearance for takeoff. Each of them carried trace memories of collapse: late nights, improvisations, and the small betrayals leaders commit when systems fail. They had sworn the new matrix would not repeat that pattern.

Carol spoke first. Her tone carried the restraint of command tempered by clarity. "Begin the absence audit."

The screens woke in sequence. The former Resilience Validation Matrix revealed its successor without fanfare; same structure, different verbiage.

Continuity Verification Matrix (CVM):

Knowledge Architecture

Behavioral Replication

Cultural Memory

Feedback Closure.

No slides. No preamble. The architecture spoke; its interface and metrics communicating authority directly, data replacing rhetoric.

Hal linked the feeds. "Load verified. Cross-region alignment green. Starting with Knowledge Architecture."

The Knowledge Architecture quadrant pulsed. Peer validation records; documented exchanges where learning insight was refined. Playback of ritual clips. Decision logs. Heatmaps of cross-role retrieval. Carol watched the rhythm, not the color. Consistency mattered more than brightness. The pulse was steady. The design rehearsed its discipline.

"Replication," she said. The word wasn't instruction; it was governing principle.

The room moved with measured cadence. Behavioral Replication showed leadership protocols executed by successors without prompting: Monday's clarity huddle, Thursday's risk forum, Friday's closure notes.

Angel's team appeared on screen: her lieutenant, Yegor, finishing a decision without escalating; naming tradeoffs, citing the prior case, logging the rationale. No glance upward. No request for rescue.

Imara noted the posture around the table: shoulders lower than when she first arrived, eyes less defensive. Conviction had become routine. That was the validation: confidence expressed as quiet. Her jaw eased; for the first time, she did not brace for collapse.

Carol watched too, arms crossed lightly. Her instinct, still alive, wanted to intervene, to tighten the process and preempt drift. But she resisted. Continuity demanded trust in architecture, not vigilance. She drew a long breath, steadying the internal tension every leader carries; the one between empathy and enforcement. This was her discipline now: constraint.

Then the fracture arrived.

A thin amber line cut through the Cultural Memory feed. The lights flickered slightly; the system emitted a soft tone, like a warning whisper. The tone threaded through the air; thin, precise, almost human. Everyone froze. Even breath paused, each instinct waiting for authority that no longer existed.

Terminology drift. The glossary variance map showed “stability window” relabeled as “grace period” in Angel’s division. Small word. Large consequences. “Grace” allowed discretion; “window” demanded discipline.

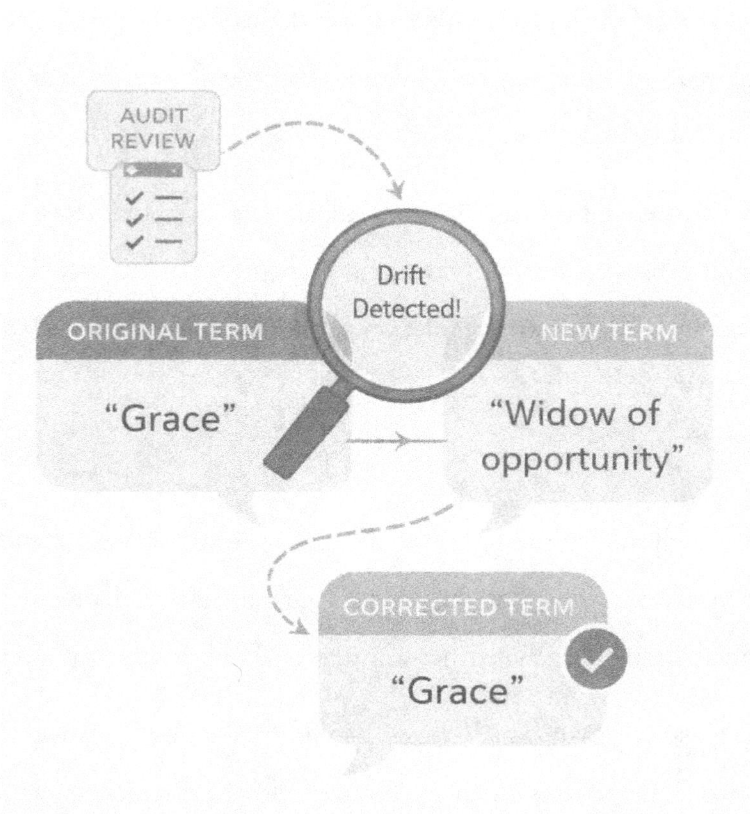

Figure 13.2 Terminology Drift Detection

A verification mechanism identifying linguistic variance before semantic drift produces structural failure.

For a moment, Angel wished the architecture would tell her what to feel; praise or shame. Then she remembered that was the point: it wasn't built to console, only to rectify.

Hal straightened. "We can patch the label and...." His voice held the reflex of a man trained to engage before reflecting.

Carol didn't look at him. "Don't touch it." She turned to the room. "FVL (Feedback Verification Loop) on."

The Feedback Verification Loop overlay snapped into view:

Signal → Route → Impact → Verification.

The system traced the term "Grace" across channels, revealing a cascade of softer decisions: deadlines slid by hours, then by days; the team's risk language blurred where it should have stayed precise. No alarms had triggered, yet. Drift never arrives shouting. It whispers permission.

Angel cleared her throat. "My read…" Her voice faltered, halfway between explanation and apology.

"Not your read," Carol said, voice even. "Route it."

The air thickened for a moment, tension pressing down. Hal's jaw flexed; his instinct was to engage and control, not surrender it to protocol. This was the test: whether instinct would yield to architecture.

Hal's reflex screamed to fix it fast, to restore stability. His fingers hovered over the controls, then stilled. The pause scraped against his pride, the silence louder than command.

He reengaged the loop. The system flagged the terminology breach in the system record, surfacing the last three moments where words had altered outcomes. The system projected each possibility onto the screen: if the term "Grace" stayed, if it reverted, if the system adapted. Carol's breath deepened as the implications became visible, not abstract. This was more than a report. It was judgment. The room held its breath as consequence took form.

Hal hesitated, suspended between pride and precision, discipline choosing architecture over instinct. Imara saw his fingers tense, then relaxed. The decision to follow protocol rather than ego, the smallest hinge in Hal's transformation, completed itself in silence.

"Impact report details a two-week slippage if 'grace' persists," Hal said quietly. His tone carried both data and concession. "Verification recommends revert to 'window' and add a language standard seal as a safeguard freezing approved terminology before drift can begin."

Imara measured the faces. No one looked toward the door. Nobody was praying Marcus would be walking in. That was the point.

Carol leaned back. "Execute."

The loop closed with mechanical care: the glossary propagated the correction; the Monday huddle script updated; the system record appended the rationale and named the subtle risk, *sentiment eroding standard*. The amber line cooled to green. Cultural Memory stabilized. The system calibrated itself in public.

Angel exhaled. "We didn't detect the Drift."

“You sensed it,” Imara replied, voice measured. “The design converted instinct into structure.”

For a moment, Imara let herself feel pride. Pride in what they had built together. The architecture was not replacing them; it was protecting their purpose from Drift. Continuity doesn’t eradicate impulse; it forges discipline.

Tension drained. Even silence had discipline now.

Hal advanced to the final quadrant. Feedback Closure displayed completion rates; the pulse steadied at ninety-three percent, then rose. They sat with the quiet rhythm of enforcement. No applause. Only presence.

A soft chime. The CVM summary assembled itself on screen, not as victory lap, but as validation:

Absence Audit: Closed.

Knowledge Architecture: 4.2

Behavioral Replication: 4.1

`Cultural Memory: 3.8 → 4.0 (terminology correction logged)`

Feedback Closure: 4.3

Quadrants < 3: None.

Redesign Mandate: Not triggered.

Carol looked to Imara. “Verify continuity”.

Imara stepped forward only enough to speak into the room, not over it. “Continuity verified. The system corrected terminology before it collapsed. Leadership presence is not required.”

They rose. Hal lingered at the display, as he always did, watching the curves settle. Angel glanced at him, then at Carol, then at the door; the place where leaders used to enter to fix things.

The quarter’s audit completed, they reassembled for its final verification.

The door opened.

Marcus stepped in without announcement, the quiet return of someone who no longer needed to be seen. He stopped at the threshold, measuring the room, the hum, the absence of urgency. The air felt cooler, steady; even the lights seemed calibrated, unflinching. Carol didn't stand. She didn't brief him. She turned the screen gently, so the reflection caught his face beside the summary line that didn't ask for him.

He felt something like awe; the quiet kind that replaces certainty. The room no longer needed him, and somehow that felt right.

He walked to the table and pulled the drawer marked Continuity. His ledger waited like a ritual, not a relic. He opened a fresh page. The ink caught the light.

He wrote without flourish:

Absence validated permanence. Terminology aligned with architecture. Continuity verified itself.

He signed beneath it, smaller than before, but not less significant.

Imara watched him. "Does it feel like a loss?" she asked.

"Loss," Marcus asked. "Of being the axis? The architecture no longer needs my presence to remain stable."

Marcus traced the edge of the page with his thumb. "It feels like restoration, architecture reclaimed from dependency.

She nodded. "Then the architecture endured."

He slid the ledger forward. Carol counter-signed, the stroke crisp as a seal. The signature line beneath hers remained open; the next leader's space, already waiting.

Through the glass, the city carried on; indifferent, ongoing, alive. The monitors dimmed to their resting pulse, a rhythm that needed no witness.

For a brief moment, Marcus searched for his old reflex; the tightening in his chest, the need to intervene, to command.
It didn't come.
The stillness that once unnerved him now felt designed, deliberate. What had once been anxiety was now design.

He realized continuity had not erased his instinct to lead; it simply relocated it, embedding it in the design itself.

He thought of how many years he had spent forcing order, mistaking control for continuity.

This calmness corrected him more completely than any meeting ever had.

He exhaled slowly. For the first time, his stillness didn't signal control; it signaled continuity.

He turned, one hand light on the back of a chair he no longer needed to pull.

In the absence, the architecture held.

Absence executed its validation. Leadership withdrawn, continuity held. Structures governed themselves through architecture. Dependency dissolved; architecture prevailed. Continuity is not declared; it is validated.

Maxim: Continuity is architecture surviving the architect.

II. The Doctrine of Continuity

Continuity validates architecture that sustains excellence without intervention. Absence is the crucible proving permanence

Continuity is self-replication: structures retaining rhythm, memory, and moral alignment when architects withdraw.

Continuity is the architecture of permanence.

Key Terms

- **Continuity:** design sustaining performance through absence; structure proving endurance when leadership withdraws.
- **Replication:** design reproducing itself; transfer of structure, behavior, and intent until excellence becomes self-sustaining.
- **Verification:** formal confirmation that design meets its declared standard.
- **Continuity:** validates architecture that sustains excellence without intervention. Absence is the crucible proving permanence

Continuity is self-replication structures retaining rhythm, memory, and moral alignment when architects withdraw.

Architectural Truths

i. Absence Validates Permanence

Continuity cannot be declared; it must be proven. Absence must not expose dependency; it must confirm design. Sustained performance without intervention achieves permanence. Absence is the audit.

Principle

Leaders must institutionalize absence audits. Absence untested is Drift disguised as continuity.

Permanence is architecture validated through absence.

ii. Replication Is the Engine of Resilience

Leadership sustained through presence is Drift. Replication converts resilience from event to system. When discipline is transferable, continuity emerges as a system, not sentiment.

Principle

Leadership continuity is achieved when behaviors replicate autonomously. Replication is the currency of resilience.

Replication operationalizes resilience as continuity.

iii. Architecture Transforms Discipline into Mastery

Instinct is reactive; discipline is trained. Design captures disciplined responses and embeds them into structure. Architecture transforms human mastery into structural order, converting repetition into permanence.

Principle

Architecture converts trained discipline into enduring intelligence; design becomes self-governing.

Architecture forged from discipline renders permanence systemic.

iv. Feedback Regenerates Structural Intelligence

Feedback is not audit; it is adaptation. Structure regenerates through feedback, converting error into intelligence and erosion into evolution. Feedback loops leveraging data to intelligence ensure corrections become continuity.

Principle

Feedback cycles must reproduce redesign without intervention.

Feedback regenerates structural intelligence into continuity.

v. Trust in Architecture Confirms Permanence

Control sustained by oversight is fragility; control sustained by trust is design. Leaders must entrust authority to architecture. Resilience during absence is the ultimate validation of architecture; trust proven through continuity.

Principle

True mastery is a leader's absence, and the structure holds.

Trust validated during absence validates continuity

Binary Doctrine of Continuity: Drift vs Design

Fragile (Drift)	**Resilient (Design)**
Continuity dependent on intervention	Continuity proven by absence
Leadership preserved by presence	Leadership replicated through systems
Instinct untrained and reactive	Discipline embedded and enduring
Feedback episodic and corrective	Feedback continuous and regenerative
Trust in people	Trust in architecture

Doctrinal Verdict

Continuity is permanence proven by absence.

III. Diagnostic Tool: The Continuity Verification Matrix (CVM)

Purpose

Verify whether leadership reproduces itself through architecture rather than personality, confirming continuity through absence.

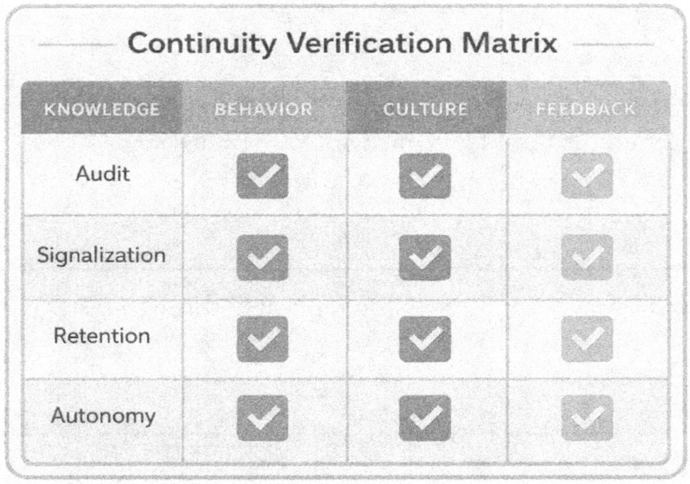

Figure 13.3 Continuity Verification Matrix (CVM)

Continuity demands evidence that knowledge, behavior, culture, and feedback persist without leadership presence.

Diagnostic Dimensions

1. Knowledge Architecture

Definition: Measures whether leadership knowledge is codified, retrievable, and applied consistently without reliance on originators.

Propagation / Performance Indicator: ≥90% of leadership systems, playbooks, and doctrinal assets are accessible and reused across rotations, producing consistent execution within 90 days.

Drift Indicator: Knowledge becomes tacit or personalized; retrievability fails; expertise collapses when originators step back.

2. Behavioral Replication

Definition: Assesses whether leadership behaviors and decision routines reproduce autonomously across cycles.

Propagation / Performance Indicator: Successors perform defined leadership routines at required cadence without instruction; behavioral scores on the Leadership Behavior Index consistently meet standard.

Drift Indicator: Decisions escalate upward; leaders imitate personal style over doctrine; rituals halt without intervention.

3. Cultural Memory

Definition: Evaluates the persistence of language, doctrine, and values across leadership transitions.
Propagation / Performance Indicator: 95% linguistic and doctrinal consistency across tiers validated through Cultural Consistency Scans and archived comparisons.
Drift Indicator: Vocabulary erodes; doctrine requires re-teaching; values drift into sentiment or personalization.

4. Feedback Closure

Definition: Determines whether feedback loops autonomously trigger structural updates without enforcement.
Propagation / Performance Indicator: 100% Feedback Verification Loop (FVL) closure within cycle; redesigns remain durable for >90 days.
Drift Indicator: Feedback loops remain open; errors repeat; closure depends on individual correction rather than design.

5. Continuity Under Absence

Definition: Tests whether knowledge, behavior, culture, and feedback maintain performance when leadership is removed.
Propagation / Performance Indicator: Operations, cadence, and decision logic remain stable during absence audits; continuity metrics remain unchanged across cycles.
Drift Indicator: Systems pause, fragment, or seek direction; stability requires leader visibility; cadence collapses until intervention.

Scoring Standard (1-5: Drift → Validated)

1. **Severe Drift:** Architecture collapses without presence; continuity dependent on individuals; knowledge, culture, and routines degrade instantly.
2. **High Drift:** Partial systems exist but degrade under pressure or absence; leaders must intervene

for recovery; continuity unreliable.

3. **Unstable:** Some autonomous replication occurs but inconsistently; continuity survives in pockets but fractures under load.
4. **Strong Alignment:** Most continuity systems perform autonomously; variance appears only in edge cases under pressure.
5. **Validated Architecture:** Leadership fully self-replicates; continuity persists through pressure, rotation, and absence without decline.

Interpretation Guide

Validated Architecture: (19-25)

1. Leadership knowledge is fully codified and reused across roles.
2. Leadership behaviors and decision logic reproduce without instruction.
3. Organizational language and doctrine remain coherent across transitions.
4. Feedback loops autonomously produce redesign and stability.
5. Absence audits show no loss in cadence, meaning, or performance.

Drift Detected: (1-18)

1. Knowledge is hoarded or undocumented; transitions produce loss.
2. Successors depend on personality, memory, or intervention.
3. Cultural vocabulary erodes; doctrine becomes sentiment.
4. Feedback cycles remain open or require escalation to close.
5. Structures wait for leadership presence rather than self-regulating.

Structural Closing Line

Continuity is replication proven through absence; any structure requiring presence reveals Drift and mandates redesign.

IV. Enforcement: The Doctrine of Continuity

Continuity is not maintained; it is governed. The CVM proves the architecture replicates itself. Intervention proves Drift.

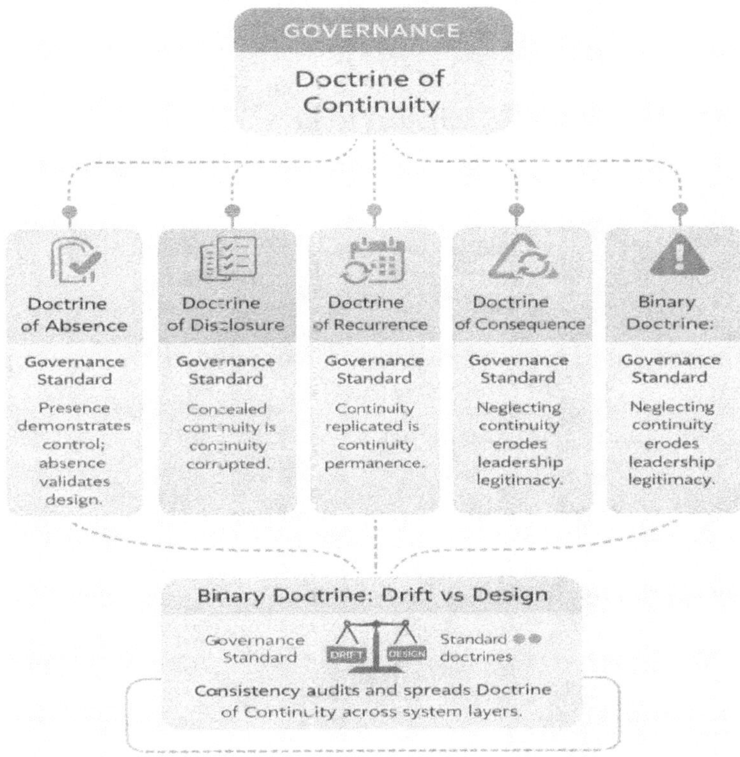

Figure 13.5 Governance Doctrine of Continuity

Critical governance standards that convert continuity from oversight into enforced permanence.

Purpose

Establish leadership as the moral guarantor of continuity. Leaders do not preserve design; they relinquish control to prove design permanence. This section enforces continuity as a living doctrine: withdrawal becomes verification, transparency becomes trust, recurrence becomes permanence.

Leaders are not stewards of architecture; they are patrons to their resilience.

i. Doctrine of Absence

Governance Standard: Presence demonstrates control; absence validates design.

Mandate: Governance cycles include one enforced absence audit under operational load.

Intent: Convert dependence into replication.

Enforcement: Equilibrium collapsing in absence, leadership reverts to probationary status pending redesign.

Presence sustaining stability is Drift sanctified as leadership.

ii. Doctrine of Disclosure

Governance Standard: Concealed continuity is continuity corrupted.

Mandate: CVM and Absence Audit findings published within thirty days in governance records.

Intent: Transparency is the signature of permanence.

Enforcement: Concealment triggers leadership review; failure to disclose is Drift

Suppressed verification erodes permanence.

iii. Doctrine of Recurrence

Governance Standard: Continuity replicated is continuity permanence.

Mandate: Four Continuity Audits annually; witnessed, logged, and ratified in the Continuity ledger.

Intent: Transform audit into doctrine.

Enforcement: Omission of audits suspends leadership authority.

Institutionalized audits convert resilience into permanence.

iv. Doctrine of Consequence

Governance Standard: Neglecting continuity erodes leadership legitimacy.

Mandate: Failure to enforce absence or disclosure constitutes Drift.

Intent: Continuity is verification of moral governance.

Enforcement: Repeated negligence activates intervention and redesign of governance.

Leaders indifferent to continuity endorse Drift.

V. Doctrinal Transition

Continuity verifies architectural autonomy. The structure governs itself through verified rhythm; transitioning from leadership reliance to systemic permanence. Section V closes the Doctrine of Continuity and opens the Discipline of Adaptation. Continuity verifies permanence; Adaptation engineers evolution. This is the threshold between verified architecture and intelligent design; when structure begins to think.

i. The Irreversible Continuum

Continuity is the architecture of permanence.

Here the architecture reaches final authority: the CVM, the ledger, and the architecture function independent of intervention. Leadership has transformed into governance logic: embedded, replicable, self-correcting. Continuity is replication. Verification is the seed of adaptation.

Architecture now carries its own intent.

ii. Transition to Chapter 14 — Adaptation as Structural Intelligence

Continuity audits architecture for permanence; adaptation reconfigures permanence for contextual integrity. Verified structures now enter the adaptive cycle: observation, redesign, replication. The architecture that once proved its endurance now practices its own renewal.

In PMC doctrine, adaptation is not deviation from architecture; it is architecture reinterpreting itself under new conditions. Continuity forged architectural memory; adaptation transforms that memory into agency. The organization advances from self-governance to self-evolution.

Through this bridge, permanence becomes evolution; governance becomes learning; continuity becomes architectural intelligence.

VI. Rapid Orientation: Drift–Architecture Spectrum

Use this rubric for orientation, not validation. If your structures do not hold under pressure and turnover, you are in Drift regardless of intent or progress.

Severe Drift: Architecture collapses without presence; continuity dependent on individuals; knowledge, culture, and routines degrade instantly.

High Drift: Partial systems exist but degrade under pressure or absence; leaders must intervene for recovery; continuity unreliable.

Unstable: Some autonomous replication occurs but inconsistently; continuity survives in pockets but fractures under load.

Strong Alignment: Most continuity systems perform autonomously; variance appears only in edge cases under pressure.

Validated Architecture: Leadership fully self-replicates; continuity persists through pressure, rotation, and absence without decline.

Chapter 14 — Embedding Adaptability

I. Story: The Adaptation Drill

Pre-Drill Calibration

Failure of adaptation erodes permanence. When structural composure collapses, architecture concedes performance to Drift. The "Chamber" exists to prevent that outcome. Built for pressure, not comfort, it captures every breath and hesitation.

Light framed the circle of six: Imara at the center, Marcus and Sasha opposite each other, Carol to the right, Hal to the left, and Reg in the background watching.

Imara initiated the Readiness Brief. "Continuity is discipline engineered; what you tolerate, you teach. We calibrate composure. We measure trust. We enforce architecture; then release control."

Monitors displayed second-by-second data:

Pulse Coherence Index (team): `0.92 → 0.93 → 0.91 (stable band 0.90–1.00)`

Cognitive Foresight Baseline: 0.87

Emotional Regulation Thresholds (per seat): Sasha 0.95, Marcus 0.97, Carol 0.96, Hal 0.93, Reg 0.90

Stakeholder Confidence Simulator: 0.94 (global partner composite)

Regulatory Scrutiny Index: 0.71 (elevated scenario)

The **Adaptive Continuity Grid (ACG)** illuminated:

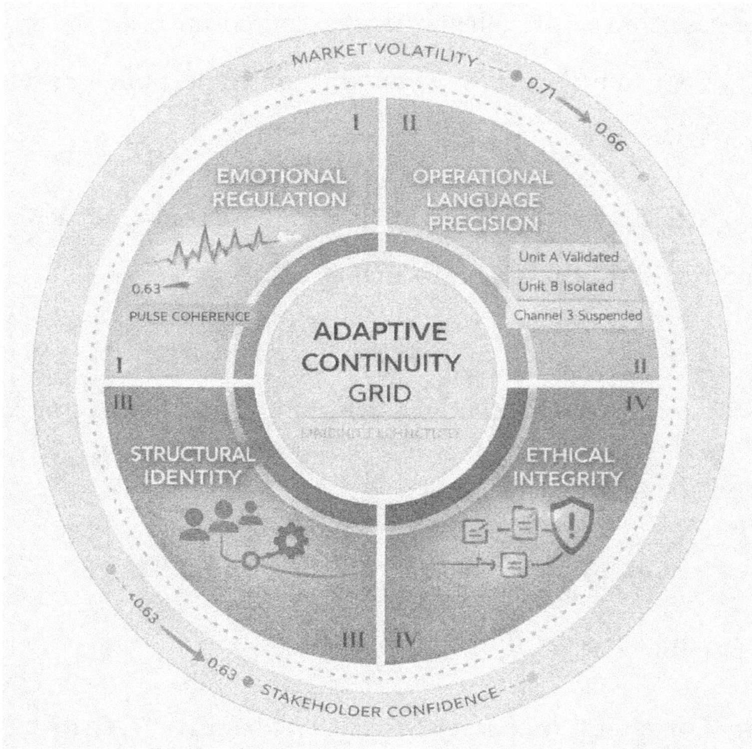

Figure 14.1 The Adaptive Continuity Grid (ACG)

A diagnostic grid measuring whether adaptability is engineered across emotion, language, identity, and ethics under pressure.

Quadrant I **Emotional Regulation**

Quadrant II **Operational Language Precision**

Quadrant III **Structural Identity**

Quadrant IV **Ethical Integrity**.

A secondary tier tracked external conditions: Market Volatility and Stakeholder Confidence.

Roles were assigned by competence, not title: Sasha, Command Communications; Hal, Operational Timing; Carol, Language and Trust; Marcus, Systems Oversight; Imara, Doctrine and Adjudication; Reg, Executive Auditor and Constraint.

Mechanism measured. System aligned. Structure held. Architecture decided. Design humanized

Imara verified thresholds. "Any quadrant under 0.75 triggers Redesign Mandate. Foresight under 0.85 initiates Pre-Failure Reconfiguration. The Continuity Council adjudicates disputes on doctrine in real time."

Phase I: Compound Rupture — Internal Collapse / External Withdrawal

"Begin sequence," Imara said

Sasha pressed the key.

Internal mechanism jammed. Feeds vanished. Reports contradicted themselves. Simultaneously, the simulator pulled a market withdrawal: a key European partner suspended all orders pending alleged disclosure gaps. Stakeholder Confidence dropped to 0.71 → 0.63. Quadrant I flashed amber Variance Drift 0.63; Quadrant III showed Continuity Breach 0.48.

Hal's console is filled with error states. "Operational continuity broken. Trade feed offline. Queue saturation imminent."

Sasha's pulse spiked; hands tightening on the console.

Carol intervened. "Control emotion first. No commands until self composure."

Imara reinforced. ""Imara's jaw locked before she spoke. 'Composure first. Correct variance to 0.95 before you decide."

Sasha synchronized her breathing with the steady click of a metronome: inhale four, hold four, exhale six.

Quadrant I rose 0.63 → 0.88 → 0.95. Drift contained.

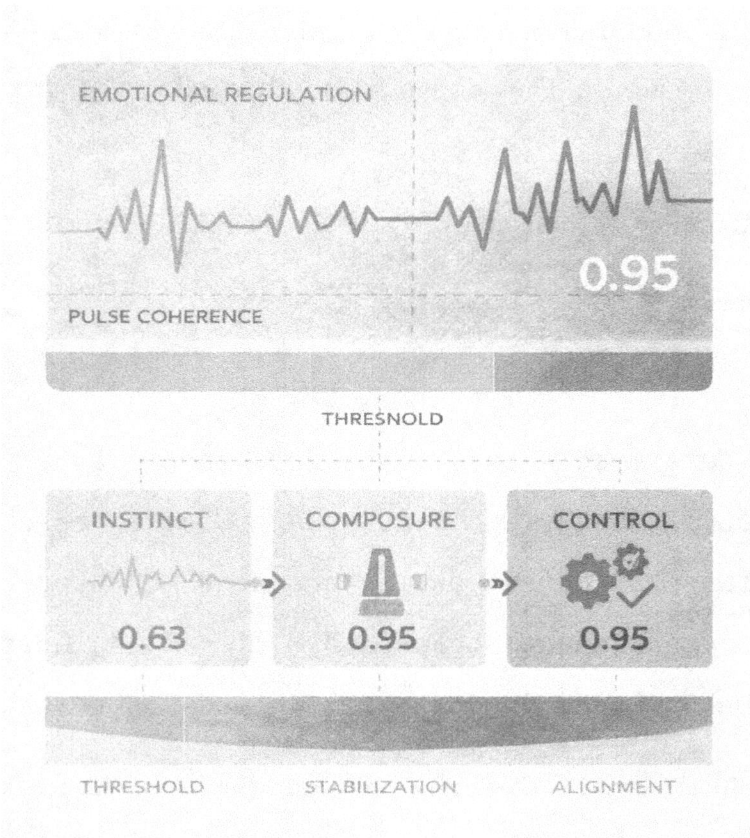

Figure 14.2 Composure Under Pressure

Engineered emotional regulation stabilizes the system before decisions, escalation, or authority are invoked.

Imara marked the lesson. "Leaders must eradicate reaction; only composure preserves design."

Reg watched from the rail, silent, measuring his own urge to intervene.

Phase II: Language Erosion — Precision Under Scrutiny

Sentences inverted. Verbs dropped. Orders duplicated.

Quadrant II—Operational Language Precision fell to 0.52.

Carol set the protocol. "Anchor to verifiable syntax. No adjectives, no speculation. Standardized communication lines only."

Hal transmitted: "Unit A, validated. Unit B, isolated. Process Channel 3, suspended."

Sasha mirrored: "External channel 1, hold. Channel 2, publish correction stub."

Operational Language coherence recalibrated to 0.94. The Regulatory Scrutiny Index ticked up to 0.74 as clarity replaced chaos.

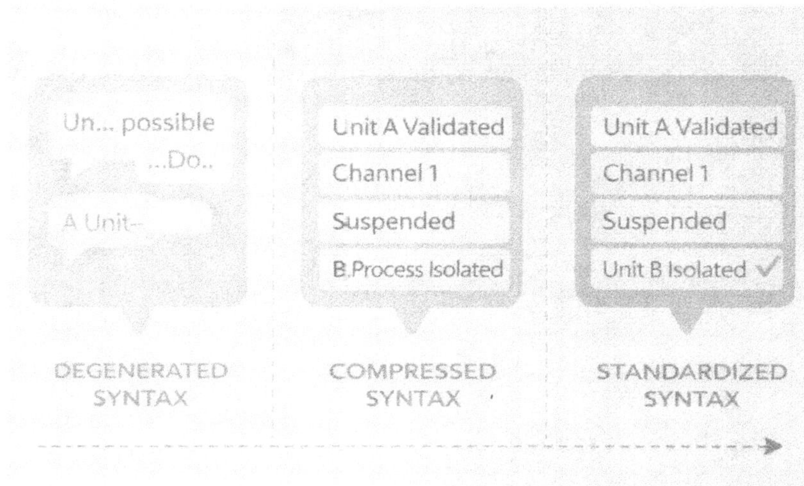

Figure 14.3 Operational Language Precision

Compressed, verifiable language preserves alignment and prevents drift under scrutiny.

Marcus summarized without flourish. "Efficiency restored alignment."

Imara: "Precision is alignment. Aligned language sustains architecture."

Phase III: Identity Collapse — Authority Contested

Organizational labels vanished: titles, divisions, signature permissions.

Quadrant III: Structural Identity plunged to 0.39. Silence. Then the human reflex to intervene arrived.

Hal asserted. "We restore Reg as primary. We need a single apex."

Marcus countered. "Doctrine demands clarity over intervention. We choose by competence for the task in front of us."

Reg withheld judgment, eyes on Imara.

Imara adjudicated. “Doctrine stands. Temporary continuity roles by competence: Hal, timing; Sasha, communications; Carol, trust; Marcus, oversight. Reg, verifier; intervene only if adjudication fails.”

Hal bristled. “If timing conflicts with communications?” The hesitation revealed the battle between reflex and trust.

“Then clarity overrides speed,” Imara said. “Synchronize to operational language.”

They rebuilt synchronicity through functional alignment. Within 120 seconds, the ACG pulsed green: Structural Drift Contained 0.91.

The Stakeholder Confidence metric stopped falling at 0.66.

Reg exhaled. “Authority deferred. The structure endured.”

Phase IV: Ethical Disruption — Truth at Cost

A false message propagated: organization concealing defect rates. Confidence fell to 0.58. Quadrant IV—Ethical Integrity flashed red: Integrity Breach Detected.

Carol’s tone sharpened. “Stakeholders demand acknowledgement.”

Hal pushed back. “Acknowledge now, and we incur operational delay and cost.”

The room fell silent for a moment, tension sharpening the air. Reg asked the only question that mattered. “What preserves permanence?”

Marcus answered, tone stripped of calculation. “Truth. Always.” It sounded less like logic, more like faith.

Sasha drafted aloud, each clause verified by Carol: “Error identified. Correction underway. Verification ongoing. Full ledger disclosure at 14:00.”

`Message sent. Confidence rose 0.58 → 0.71 → 0.89. Ethical Integrity 1.00.`

Imara entered the record. “Integrity is permanence under scrutiny.”

Phase V: Foresight Projection — Anticipation Before Failure

Imara dimmed the chamber. "We simulate progression beyond recovery; secondary and tertiary shocks. Predict within variance margin ≥ 0.85."

Scenarios unfolded: supply-chain turbulence; investor downgrades; media distortion; regulator audit acceleration.

Marcus called metrics. "Foresight Accuracy 0.88. Reflex latency 2.1 seconds."

Hal flagged a delay. "Synchronization lag exceeds tolerance by 0.3."

Imara ordered reconfiguration. "Transfer predictive algorithm to Marcus; reroute trust propagation to Carol; Sasha, pre-commit language frames for three outcomes."

Structure rebalanced. Foresight Accuracy 0.92. Reflex latency 1.6 seconds.

Reg nodded. "Adaptability proven: the architecture adapted before failure."

Phase VI: Dual Pressure Extension — Dissent and Negotiation

The simulator activated a regulatory ultimatum: provide full defect-disclosure logs within six hours or face provisional suspension. Simultaneously, the European partner demanded a 48-hour exclusivity window to "evaluate trust," threatening to publicize concerns.

Conflict surfaced.

Hal: "Prioritize regulator; legal exposure eclipses public image."

Carol: "No. 'Language first,' Carol cut him off. 'We stabilize the narrative, or both collapse'."

Marcus cut through the argument. 'Data integrity decides this,' he said, his tone firm. 'Authenticated summary report in two hours; full logs in six. No speculation, no delay."

Sasha proposed a composite plan. "Issue a Continuity Bulletin: regulator receives audited digest T+2; partner receives synchronized summary, no exclusivity. Publish doctrine note: 'No exclusivity in correction; truth is public by design.'"

Hal resisted. "Your partner will retaliate."

Imara adjudicated. "Doctrine rejects non-disclosure. Proceed with synchronized disclosure."

Sasha executed. Confidence lifted to 0.92; Regulatory Scrutiny eased to 0.68. The partner withdrew the exclusivity demand, forced by transparency.

Imara marked the doctrine. "Clarity forges alignment."

Phase VII: Root-Cause Inquiry — Proof Over Pride

With stabilization achieved, Imara initiated Root-Cause Analysis. "We examine failure without defense. Data, then doctrine."

Marcus: "Primary Drift origin; emotional reactivity at activation. Secondary; language contradictions during duress. Tertiary; identity vacuum exploited by intervention reflex."

Hal faced the ledger. "I pressed for apex control. That impulse added latency."

Imara neither softened nor shamed. "Record: intervention reflex increases Drift when identity collapses. Protocol: when organizational titles drop, leadership defaults to competence map, not hierarchy."

Carol added, "Lexical bloat extended confusion by 42 seconds. Institute a Phrase Compression Protocol: verbs before nouns, evidence before claim."

Sasha reflected. "Coherence stabilized the architecture. I recommend implementing precision coherence resets at each phase transition to enforce discipline and ensure continuity under pressure."

Reg concluded. "Control reflex constrained by doctrine sustained permanence."

Phase VIII: The Continuity Council — Audit, Enforcement, Alternatives

The simulation ceased. The chamber brightened. The team convened at the central table. The ACG expanded into the Continuity Audit ledger with dual-path analysis: Actual vs Alternative outcomes.

Imara: "Quadrant I: Emotional Regulation."

Sasha: "Variance 0.63 corrected to 0.96 in 18 seconds. Alternative path without breath protocol projects 0.74 at T+60, below threshold, yielding cascade Drift."

Imara: "Verdict: Drift contained. Mandate: install timed coherence resets at each phase."

Carol: "Quadrant II: Operational Language Precision. Integrity restored to 0.94. Alternative without refinement leaves 0.71 at T+90; regulatory index worsens to 0.62."

Imara: "Verdict: Precision restored. Mandate: Phrase Refinement Protocol v1.3 in two weeks."

Hal: "Quadrant III: Structural Identity. Breach 0.39 restored to 0.91. Alternative with apex control shows 0.78 and 0.4-second added latency."

Imara: "Verdict: Structure reconstituted. Mandate: Competence-First Continuity Map formalized and trained."

Marcus: "Quadrant IV: Ethical Integrity. Breach corrected in 40 seconds. Alternative denial yields 0.49 confidence at T+240 and two-quarter revenue impact."

Imara: "Verdict: Integrity sustained. Mandate: Public-first correction standard formalized."

Marcus continued. "Foresight Accuracy 0.92, Reflex latency 1.6. Alternative configuration without reassignment holds at 0.84; failure probability increases 19%."

Reg issued the Council orders. "Continuity Council mandates:

Competence-First Continuity Map: owner Hal; training rollout in 21 days.

Phrase Compression Protocol v1.3: owner Carol; compliance audit in 14 days; tolerance ≥ 0.92.

Timed Coherence Resets (phase transitions): owner Sasha; instrumentation within 10 days.

Foresight Algorithm Reassignment: owner Marcus; latency ≤ 1.5 seconds in 30 days.

Public-First Correction Standard: owner Imara; doctrine publication and governance adoption in 7 days."

Imara added enforcement. "Deviation demands redesign; doctrine does not negotiate."

Phase IX: Cultural Integration — Human Structure Aligned

The chamber shifted from audit to integration. Carol led the Language Coherence Check, a 60-second call-and-response that synced tone and meaning across the team:

Carol: "Claim?"

Team: "Validation precedes it."

Carol: "Speed?"

Team: "Follow clarity."

Carol: "Trust?"

Team: "Not asserted; measured."

Sasha initiated a Continuity Pulse: micro-survey delivered to devices; five prompts, 20 seconds. Results posted live: Emotional Coherence 0.95; Trust Readiness 0.93; Decision Confidence 0.94.

Marcus recorded a Resilience Calibration: "Coherence maintained post-audit. No fatigue Drift. Human structure is aligned with architectural rhythm."

Reg watched the readouts settle. He spoke carefully. "Excellence is control disciplined by design."

Imara sealed it. "That is permanently made human."

Doctrine ledger — Final Publication

Imara opened the leather-bound ledger. Her handwriting was sharp, measured, final.

Continuity Ledger — Proof Summary

Quadrant I / Emotional Regulation: 0.96 — Drift contained; **Timed Coherence Resets** mandated (Sasha, T+10 days).

Quadrant II / Operational Language Precision: 0.94 — Precision restored; **Phrase Compression v1.3** mandated (Carol, T+14 days; audit ≥ 0.92). -

Quadrant III / Structural Identity: 0.91 — Structure reconstituted; **Competence-First Continuity Map** mandated (Hal, T+21 days; latency impact ≤ 0.2 sec).

Quadrant IV / Ethical Integrity: 1.00 — Integrity sustained; **Public-First Correction Standard** formalized (Imara, T+7 days).

Foresight Accuracy: 0.92; **Reflex Latency:** 1.6 sec — **Algorithm Reassignment** mandated (Marcus, T+30 days).

Stakeholder Confidence: Restored to 0.92; **Regulatory Scrutiny:** 0.68.

Continuity Index: 0.98 — Validated.

Alternative Governance Path Analysis

Without breath protocol: Quadrant I projects 0.74; cascade Drift likely.

Without language alignment: Quadrant II 0.71; regulator index 0.62; partner withdrawal persists.

With apex restoration: Quadrant III 0.78; added latency 0.4 sec; slower recovery.

With denial: Quadrant IV 0.49; confidence collapse projected two quarters.

Imara read the verdicts aloud, each a hinge between principle and practice:

"Foresight engineered is resilience embedded."

"Clarity institutionalizes alignment."

"Truth is continuity embodied."

"Competence leads when hierarchy fails."

She summarized:

Continuity rehearsed, validated, and assigned.
Adaptability institutionalized. Permanence secured.

For a long moment, the chamber held stillness. No tension, validation. Outside, markets moved and messages raced. Inside, the architecture functioned at a measured pace, awake and prepared.

Sasha said, "Pressure doesn't threaten architecture; it demands adaptability."
Marcus replied, "architecture adapts preventing collapse."
Imara powered down the console, her voice deliberate. "Adaptability is permanence."

Maxim: Adaptation rehearses permanence before change arrives.

Change challenged architectural integrity. Design did not yield; it recalibrated. Pressure met architecture and became composure. Composure transformed pressure into symmetry. The Chamber held because adaptability was engineered doctrine.

II. The Doctrine of Adaptation

Adaptability is architecture rehearsing change before it arrives.

Adaptability is not improvisation; it is disciplined foresight and pre-designing responses. It is the architecture of composure, converting volatility into continuity. Adaptation is architectural foresight; permanence rehearsing renewal.

Key Terms

- **Adaptation**: deliberate redesign of architecture in advance of pressure; architecture's capacity to adjust without loss of integrity or performance.
- **Continuity Council:** governing body enforcing design integrity under pressure; audits Drift, mandates redesign and confirms continuity is structurally sustained.

Architectural Truths

i. Anticipation Enables Stability

Resilient architecture rehearses response before impact. Anticipation converts volatility into predictable rhythm. Pre-designed structures engineer stability.

Principle

Leaders must institutionalize foresight drills before disruption.
Anticipation is prevention engineered into architecture.

ii. Composure Is an Engineered Design

Emotional steadiness under pressure is design integrity. Operational resilience depends on composure engineered through disciplined training of physiological and cognitive control. Design mirrors their leaders' coherence.

Principle

Adaptive design measure and train composure as operational discipline.

Composure is design expressed through biology.

iii. Adaptive Reserve Is Foundational Capacity

Reactive strength exhausts; adaptive capacity regenerates. Adaptive reserve, the fusion of resilience and foresight, is the internal capability allowing organizations to absorb disruption and continue transformation.

Principle

Adaptive reserve must be measured as structural capacity.

Reserve foresight is preserved as capacity.

iv. Language Governs Adaptation

Language precision determines execution precision. Under pressure, ambiguous words erode alignment. Standardized language disciplines emotion, preserves trust, and converts coordination into reflex. Language is the scaffolding of collective composure.

Principle

Crisis language must be embedded before crisis.

Language becomes the architectural doctrine of composure under pressure.

v. Leadership Translates Foresight into Execution

Adaptive leadership converts prediction into practice. Leaders maintain coherence when structures strain turn foresight into composed structural response. They transform feedback into stability and fear into architecture.

Principle: Leadership must embody foresight through visible composure and design correction.

Leadership is design operationalized; foresight made executable.

vi. Adaptation Must Be Institutionalized

Discretionary adaptability collapses. Architectural enforcement prevents drift. Simulations, audits, and monthly adaptation reviews transform discretion into governance.

Principle

Leaders must ritualize adaptation until it becomes reflex.

Institutionalized adaptation is permanently engineered.

Binary Doctrine of Adaption: Drift vs Design

Fragile (Drift)	**Resilient (Design)**
Change triggers panic	Change rehearsed through foresight
Emotion dictates action	Composure dictates response
Language erodes under pressure	Language embeds order under pressure
Leadership reacts to failure	Leadership rehearses adaptation
Flexibility left to chance	Adaptability ritualized as governance
Safety sought through silence	Safety achieved through disclosure

Doctrinal Verdict

Adaptability engineered transforms change into continuity.

III. Diagnostic Tool: The Adaptive Continuity Grid (ACG)

Purpose

Verify whether adaptability is engineered as an auditable architecture that preempts volatility, ensuring continuity through composure, precision, structural integrity, and ethical clarity.

Diagnostic Dimensions

1. Emotional Regulation Architecture

Definition: Measures whether physiological and cognitive stability under strain is structurally enforced, not individually willed.

Propagation / Performance Indicator: Pulse Coherence ≥0.90 during disruption; composure restored within 20 seconds; foresight ≥0.85 maintained across cycles.

Drift Indicator: Recovery exceeds threshold; escalation or visible frustration appears; coherence collapses under compounded pressure.

2. Operational Language Precision

Definition: Determines whether language remains compressed, unambiguous, and replicable under load, preserving structural coherence.

Propagation / Performance Indicator: Language deviation ≤5%; ambiguity density ≤0.1; crisis communication remains verifiable and consistent across teams.

Drift Indicator: Adjectives replace data; terminology drifts; defensive phrasing or semantic variability enters command flow.

3. Structural Identity Integrity

Definition: Tests whether roles realign by competence, not hierarchy, when structure experiences partial or total collapse.

Propagation / Performance Indicator: Competence-based reassignment occurs within 60 seconds; handoff latency ≤0.2 seconds; leadership continuity remains stable.

Drift Indicator: Authority vacuum, hesitation, or hierarchical reversion; delayed continuity restoration; capability ignored in reassignment.

4. Ethical Integrity Under Pressure

Definition: Evaluates whether truth, disclosure, and corrective action remain immediate and uncompromised under simultaneous moral and operational pressure.

Propagation / Performance Indicator: Zero concealment tolerance; disclosure within two operational cycles; stakeholder confidence restored ≥0.90.

Drift Indicator: Delay, euphemism, optics management, partial admission, or incentive-driven distortion of truth.

5. Cross-Quadrant Continuity

Definition: Measures whether the four adaptive quadrants reinforce one another without generating compounded Drift under stress.

Propagation / Performance Indicator: CDI <0.3; cross-quadrant alignment (Emotion→Language→Structure→Ethics) remains intact during simulations; volatility does not multiply across domains.

Drift Indicator: CDI ≥0.3; emotional variance distorts language, ambiguity fractures structure, authority confusion delays truth, or concealment destabilizes composure.

Scoring Standard (1-5: Drift → Validated)

1. **Severe Drift:** Quadrants fail under pressure; composure, language, structure, and ethics collapse; adaptation requires leader personality or visibility.

2. **High Drift:** Some adaptive features exist but degrade under urgency; cross-quadrant Drift spreads quickly; continuity unreliable without intervention.

3. **Unstable:** Adaptive capability holds in controlled conditions but fractures during volatility; quadrant performance inconsistent across cycles.
4. **Strong Alignment:** Quadrants operate with architectural consistency; variance appears only in edge-case stress; CDI remains below threshold.
5. **Validated Architecture:** Adaptability is engineered; composure, language, structure, ethics, and cross-quadrant coherence remain stable through pressure, rotation, and absence.

Interpretation Guide

Validated Architecture: (19-25)

1. Adaptive limits and metrics are enforced and reproducible.
2. Composure and clarity restore immediately under strain.
3. Language remains consistent across teams and cycles.
4. Roles realign by competence without delay or hierarchy.
5. Truth withstands moral, reputational, and operational pressure.
6. Cross-quadrant coherence prevents drift multiplication.
7. Continuity persists through volatility without performance loss.

Drift Detected: (1-18)

1. Physiological and cognitive stability depend on individuals.
2. Language becomes ambiguous under pressure.
3. Hierarchy reasserts itself during collapse.
4. Ethical clarity fractures into optics or delay.
5. Cross-quadrant Drift compounds (CDI ≥0.3).
6. Adaptation becomes reactive, improvisational, or ceremonial.

Structural Closing Line

Adaptability is architecture, not temperament. Architecture that cannot reproduce composure, clarity, structure, and truth under pressure reveal drift and require immediate redesign.

IV. Enforcement: The Doctrine of Adaptive Governance

When foresight, composure, and ethical integrity become measurable, they must also become governed. Leadership is the custodian of adaptability. Enforcement converts architecture from theory into governance; foresight made binding.

Governance is the architecture protecting adaptability from erosion, complacency, and drift.

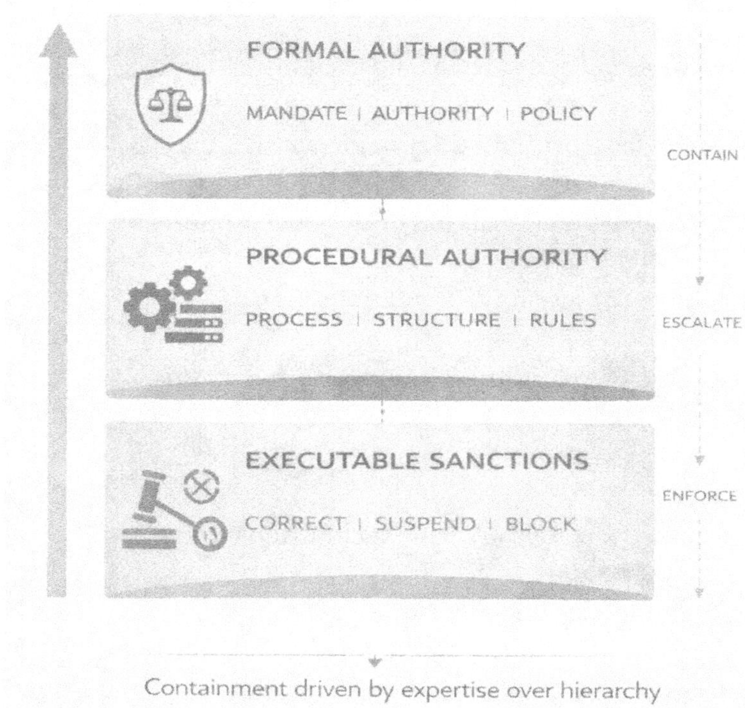

Figure 14.5 Adaptive Governance Stack

An enforcement stack governing anticipation, composure, disclosure, and renewal so adaptation becomes permanent doctrine.

Purpose

Ingrain the Doctrine of Adaptation into leadership and cultural governance. This section defines the enforceable standards preserving composure, operational language precision, ethical integrity, and foresight as operational doctrine. Where the ACG measures adaptability, enforcement guarantees its permanence.

The Four Principles of Adaptive Governance

i. The Principle of Anticipation

Standard: Architecture preempts volatility through scheduled foresight drills, quarterly scenario analysis, and predictive recalibration.

Mandate: The Continuity Council conducts adaptive foresight simulations; outcomes documented in the Adaptation Ledger.

Intent: Institutionalize foresight as a recurring event, ensuring prediction precedes reaction.

Enforcement: Failure to meet foresight cadence triggers a Redesign Mandate.

Anticipation is governance rehearsing stability.

ii. The Principle of Composure

Standard: Leadership composure must be quantifiable and trainable. Executive roles maintain a Pulse Coherence ≥ 0.90 and Language Precision ≥ 0.95 during simulation.

Mandate: Composure audits measuring emotional regulation and linguistic precision using the ACG parameters; results published within governance reports.

Intent: Establish composure as design discipline.

Enforcement: Composure index below threshold mandates retraining, followed by verification drill under council supervision. Persistent variance constitutes Drift violation and triggers temporary leadership suspension pending measured realignment

Composure enforced is coherence institutionalized.

iii. The Principle of Disclosure

Standard: Ethical integrity demands transparency of variance. No concealment, deferral, or euphemism is permissible under adaptive governance.
Mandate: Regulatory, stakeholder, or ethical anomalies logged in the Continuity Ledger and disclosed to the Council Ethics Unit.
Intent: Ensure truth precedes optics and moral integrity remains design anchored.
Enforcement: Concealment constitutes ethical Drift triggering mandatory resimulation and public correction protocol.

Truth delayed is Drift disguised as diplomacy.

iv. The Principle of Renewal

Standard: Adaptation regenerates through continual redesign. Systems exceeding Drift thresholds must be audited, redesigned, and revalidated.
Mandate: The Continuity Council enforces a 12-month Adaptive Renewal Cycle; integrating foresight, composure, and ethics reviews into one renewal audit.
Intent: Prevent stagnation of doctrine by mandating deliberate renewal as a requirement of permanence.
Enforcement: Lapse in renewal audit constitutes negligence. Initiate mandatory architectural reconstruction and leadership accountability review.

Renewal enforced is permanence rehearsed.

Governance Enforcement Mechanism

Custodianship: Each adaptive quadrant is assigned a Council Custodian responsible for monitoring Drift and ensuring compliance across leadership tiers.

Verification: Metrics logged in the Adaptation Ledger are cross-audited quarterly by independent reviewers.

Transparency: Results become part of the public governance record maintaining organizational trust and ethical continuity.

Correction: Quadrants breaching their governance standard initiate automatic Resimulation Mandate and redesign sequence.

Governance without correction is Drift in disguise.

Adaptive Enforcement Matrix

Principle	Standard	Drift Indicator	Enforcement Action
Anticipation	Quarterly foresight drills completed	Missed simulations, lagging prediction	Redesign Mandate
Composure	`Pulse ≥ 0.90; Language ≥ 0.95`	Reactive tone, command volatility	Retraining and resimulation
Disclosure	Truth within two cycles	Concealment, delay, euphemism	Public Correction Protocol
Renewal	Annual full-structure audit	Doctrine stagnation, outdated metrics	Renewal Audit and Leadership Review

Cultural Enforcement: The Leadership Covenant

Leadership by Example: Executives undergo adaptive composure certification.

Public Adaptation Record: Adaptation decisions logged and accessible.

Ethical Reflex: Truth disclosure precedes strategic defense.

Composure Continuum: Emotional regulation under pressure is treated as moral infrastructure.

Adaptive Renewal Ritual: Leadership reaffirms its covenant through a live adaptive drill; measured, published, and reviewed.

Culture sustains what enforcement secures.

Governance that adapts is permanence enforced.
Enforcement unmeasured is Drift institutionalized.
Architecture becomes governance when foresight becomes an obligation.

V. Doctrinal Transition

Adaptation completes the proof of composure and begins the discipline of permanence in motion. Where validation confirmed structure and continuity proved rhythm, adaptation transforms both into living architecture. It is the threshold where foresight ceases to be prediction and becomes reflex, where architecture begins to sense, learn, and redesign itself.

Section V closes the Doctrine of Adaptation and opens the next discipline: Mastery. Adaptation ends the engineering of resilience; Mastery begins the purposeful embodiment of foresight and renewal. It marks the shift from architecture evolution to endurance through virtuous practice.

i. The Irreversible Threshold

Adaptation is the architecture of intelligent evolution.

Here, the architecture transcends reactive renewal and enters deliberate self-mastery. Adaptation transforms permanence into agency by embedding contextual learning and foresight into the very fabric of the architecture. The Adaptive Continuity Grid becomes not only a diagnostic but a lived practice, driving anticipatory change.

Adaptation is no longer a process but an innate discipline manifest in leadership character, organizational culture, and architectural foresight. Drift is exposed and corrected by practiced composure and clarity.

Adaptability institutionalized becomes intelligence embodied.

ii. Transition to Chapter 15 — The Discipline of Mastery

The organization now moves beyond adaptation as redesign and rehearsal toward mastery as its defining condition. Mastery is sustained foresight sharpened by feedback loops of character, ritual, and institutional rigor. Within the architecture, intentional leaders design renewal preemptively, ensuring durability through time and complexity.

In PMC doctrine, Mastery represents the final translation of adaptability into embodied permanence, resilience becomes generative, architecture evolves with purpose, and endurance is expressed through conscious practice.

iii. Operational Continuities:

From Practice to Mastery: Adaptation cycles become continuous improvement protocols integrated into governance.

From Metrics to Meaning: Data transforms into moral architecture; leadership conscience becomes architectural governance.

From Simulation to Existence: Adaptive rehearsal becomes a live rhythm; permanence rehearsed until reflexive.

Adaptation was the rehearsal; Mastery is the embodiment.

iv. Operational Implication — The Practice of Mastery

Adaptation trained reflex; mastery trains ritual.
In governance, this means converting foresight into cadence: daily stand-ups testing composure, quarterly renewal councils measuring ethical latency, and annual covenant reviews embedding reflection as design discipline.
The operational implication: permanence becomes a practice schedule, not a policy.

Mastery is adaptability ritualized until it becomes identity.

VI. Rapid Orientation: Drift–Architecture Spectrum

Use this rubric for orientation, not validation. If your structures do not hold under pressure and turnover, you are in Drift regardless of intent or progress.

Severe Drift: Quadrants fail under pressure; composure, language, structure, and ethics collapse; adaptation requires leader personality or visibility.

High Drift: Some adaptive features exist but degrade under urgency; cross-quadrant Drift spreads quickly; continuity unreliable without intervention.

Unstable: Adaptive capability holds in controlled conditions but fractures during volatility; quadrant performance inconsistent across cycles.

Strong Alignment: Quadrants operate with architectural consistency; variance appears only in edge-case stress; CDI remains below threshold.

Validated Architecture: Adaptability is engineered; composure, language, structure, ethics, and cross-quadrant coherence remain stable through pressure, rotation, and absence.

Chapter 15 — Scaling Excellence

I. Story: The Doctrine of Propagation

The Expansion Audit

The silence of scale was different from the silence of collapse.

In the old world, silence had meant paralysis; the dead air before an apology, the tense waiting for command. Now it carried rhythm: a hum so even it resembled breath. Across continents, the system pulsed in symmetry under architecture that governed its rhythm. Screens in Singapore, Berlin, Lagos, and Toronto refreshed at the same instant. No directives, no roll calls; just the system sustaining rhythm across its mechanisms, every heartbeat on the planet moving to one cadence.

Replication cycles initiated every twelve hours. Global fidelity scan complete. Variance below threshold.

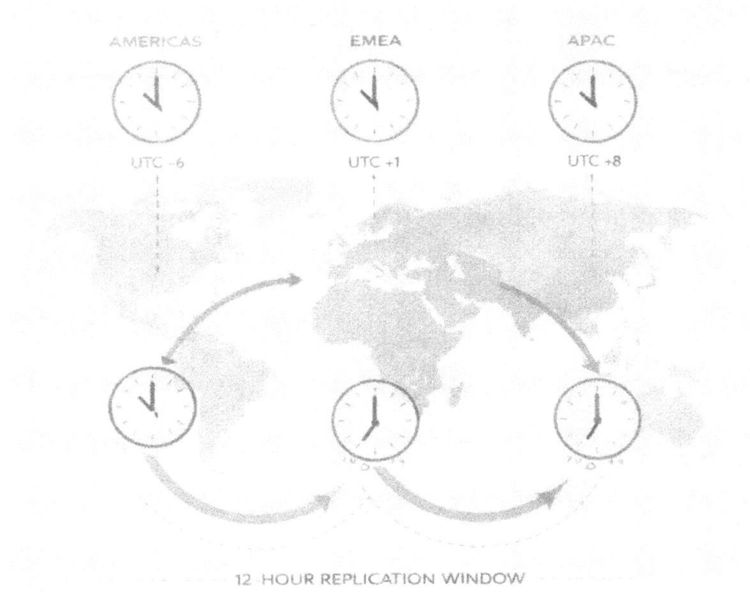

Figure 15.1 Global Replication Rhythm

Disciplined cadence synchronizes replication across geographies without directive control.

The line scrolled across the upper corner of the wall display in soft blue light. No one read it aloud. It was a soundless affirmation; the pulse of continuity. The organization no longer announced its discipline; it embodied it.

Marcus stood alone in the executive observatory. The same glass amphitheater where, years earlier, performance had collapsed under its own ambition. The air was cool, metallic. The hum of circulation carried the faint rhythm of a living organism: inhale, exhale, recalibrate. The glass itself shimmered with embedded filaments, each strand pulsing faintly, like veins beneath translucent skin.

He moved slowly along the perimeter, fingertips grazing the cool glass. The surface vibrated faintly under his touch; alive, responsive. From here, he could see the city alive with its own pulse: building windows flashing data like constellations, traffic streams moving in perfect rhythm, and distant air routes sketching luminous threads across the sky. It felt less mechanical than human: a heartbeat spread across steel and air, the rhythm of a living system at work. The architecture was no longer just containment; it was consciousness rendered visible.

Marcus hadn't spoken for an hour. He didn't need to. The data spoke in the vocabulary of architecture: alignment, fidelity, replication. His reflection hovered over the display like a ghost; human, but dissolving into the architecture. His pulse aligned unconsciously to the blinking fidelity metrics. When one pulse faltered, the other followed. He smiled faintly. The system carried the rhythm; the architecture taught him how to breathe.

For a brief moment, a thought surfaced, uninvited: Can silence contain the chaos? He exhaled, almost laughing at the question. The silence could. It already had. But the laughter came from somewhere deeper, a release mixed with humility. He realized that he no longer needed to assert mastery. The structure's order was no longer his to command. It was his to witness.

Then the system's rhythm faltered.

A flicker of light stuttered across the central wall, a sound like static threading through the air. For a moment, the hum fractured, the system inhaled and forgot to exhale.

Below, the command floor stirred.

Hal's eyes snapped to his console. "Deviation detected. Recovery Cadence variant, Equilibrium Reset."

The words hung like a contagion. Carol's head turned sharply toward him. "Drift disguised as calibration." Her voice was tight, eyes narrowing with recognition.

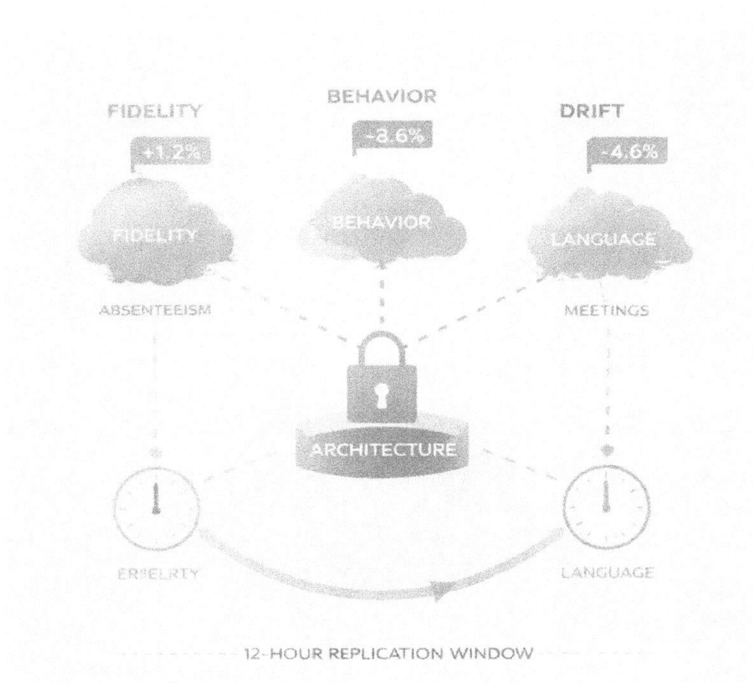

Figure 15.2 Drift Disguised as Calibration

Deviation masked as optimization propagates silently unless architecture enforces verification.

A low, discordant tone rippled through the chamber. Monitors dimmed, then recovered, the ambient light taking on a faint red tint. The air thrummed, charged with urgency. Sasha's hand trembled above her cadence screen; she could feel the rhythm faltering, as though the room itself had lost heartbeat. Data lines hesitated mid-refresh. The digital pulse thickened, almost sluggish. Hal's jaw clenched. Carol's shoulders stiffened. Imara's steady breathing became the metronome of composure.

Marcus's chest tightened, the old reflex clawing at his throat. He felt the ancient echo of control, an instinct wired by years of crisis leadership, by the memory of collapse and the desire to intervene against Drift. His fingers twitched. He could end Drift with a word. He could reclaim control. The temptation burned, not from arrogance, but from fear. The subtle terror that structure might fail without him. But doctrine was ironclad. He inhaled deeply; trust the structure, breathe with it. The air felt heavy in his lungs; each breath measured, deliberate. His throat burned with restraint. He pressed his palm against the cool glass, anchoring himself to the structure he relinquished. Surrender is not the end of control; it is control perfected by structure.

Imara's voice cut through, even, steady. "Route it through verification."

The system obeyed. Across the network, algorithms traced the altered phrase through documentation, transcripts, behavioral logs. The air thrummed again as data surged, charged and alive. Within seconds, the pattern materialized: the variant had spread across three divisions. Absenteeism up 1.2%, meeting velocity down 4.6%, recovery integrity diluted. Drift never shouted; it whispered permission.

Marcus's heartbeat echoed in his ears. The silence between data pulses stretched thin, fragile. His mind replayed a hundred possible outcomes: uncorrected Drift metastasizing through routines, rituals dissolving, culture unraveling. The reflex screamed to act, but the architecture demanded faith. He closed his eyes and counted each breath. One. Two. Three. He began to feel it, the transition between fear and faith, between control and architecture. The hum returned; slow, disciplined, deliberate.

Then, like the tightening of a single muscle, the system corrected.

The words Equilibrium Reset blinked red, then vanished. Recovery Cadence reappeared, resolute. Across every display, color restored itself to blue. The hum normalized.

Replication Fidelity held above threshold across all regions; behavior, language, and cadence aligned. The system audited itself and logged variance as Drift Signal 0. No intervention recorded

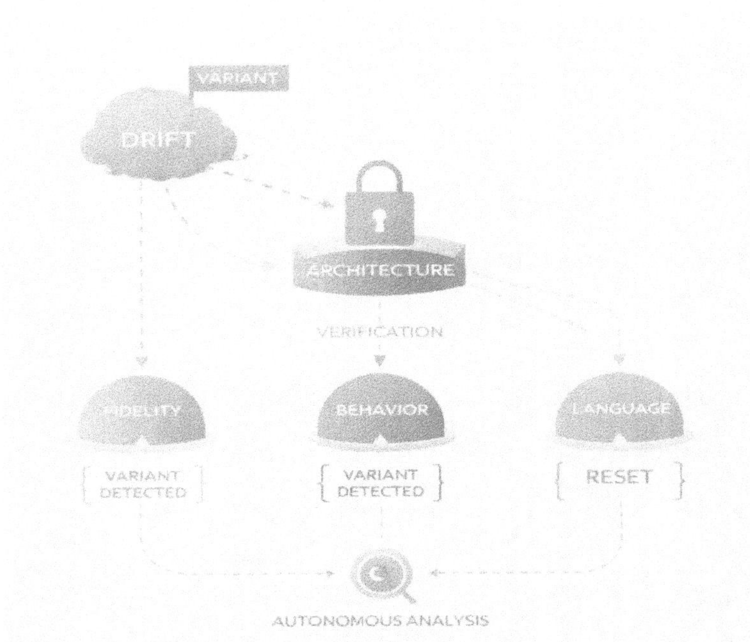

Figure 15.3 Self-Correction Without Command

Mature architectures correct Drift autonomously without leadership intervention.

Hal leaned back, exhaling with the soft disbelief of relief. "Deviation neutralized." His tone was cautious.

Carol allowed herself a single nod. "Integrity restored." Her fingers, still poised above the console, relaxed slowly.

Sasha watched the cadence pulse on her screen: steady, calm, alive. "Heartbeat restored," she whispered, breath syncing with the rhythm.

Imara looked upward toward the observatory. Through the mirrored glass, Marcus's silhouette appeared; motionless, breathing slow. Her voice carried both reverence and confirmation. "Design embedding law becomes mastery made permanent."

Darryl, silent throughout, closed the reliability register and rested his hand atop it, fingers trembling before they steadied. He whispered to no one, "Recorded."

Marcus closed his eyes. Memory flooded: panic in the first audit, the chaos of command, the desperate improvisations of leadership. That era had ended. Now, the hum was order: silent, relentless, complete. He realized the stillness he once feared was not silence but design. In that moment, something inside him, some stubborn remnant of identity built on control, released. Trust was no longer philosophy; it was architecture breathing through him.

He turned toward the window. The city below shimmered in rhythm with the dashboards. Highways glowed in motion patterns identical to data streams. Towers blinked in synchronized pulse. Even the river reflected sequenced light, rippling in harmony with invisible signals. He whispered, half prayer, half report: "The structure holds."

The elevator doors opened behind him with a sigh of recognition. Reg stepped into the observatory, his reflection merging with Marcus's. The founder who had governed through control, command, and authority stood before an architecture that no longer required human intervention.

For a moment, neither spoke. Reg's eyes moved across the glass, reading the metrics as if studying his own obsolescence. His hand rested on the edge of the console where his first performance ledger had once lain; a tactile ghost of the past. In his mind, echoes: the collapse years ago, the noise, the pleading voices, the chaos he once commanded by sheer will. The contrast pressed against him like cold air. He felt both small and infinite. A man witnessing his own disappearance into legacy.

The silence between them was not void; it was reverent. Marcus's reflection blurred into Reg's, two generations of leadership, the old built on control, the new on surrender. Reg's gaze softened. Beneath the metrics, he saw faces: Carol's defiance, Hal's rigor, Sasha's resilience, Imara's quiet faith. He felt the cost they had all paid to reach this stillness. Each one had bled into the architecture; each had given something human to make the design human.

He ran his hand across the console edge. The nameplate that once bore his initials was gone, replaced by a streaming data feed; no static emblem, only living evidence. He gave a small nod. "You've made leadership obsolete," he said finally, voice low but steady, "by letting architecture govern and structure carry it." His gaze lingered, filled with equal grief and pride. Behind his words was the quiet ache of surrender: a founder confronting the truth that permanence required his absence.

Marcus turned, meeting his gaze. "Leadership was never meant to survive the structure," he answered. "Only to establish the architecture that would."

Reg's lips parted as if to reply, then closed. He looked out across the city; alive, ordered, self-sustaining. For the first time, he felt peace not as power retained, but as power released. Between them, the silence deepened, no longer a gap but a bridge: the human cost of control yielding to the permanence of design.

Below, Imara observed in silence. Carol watched, eyes reflecting both reverence and fatigue. Hal rested his hands flat against the console, grounding himself in stillness. Sasha exhaled, shoulders lowering. Darryl put his feet up, an unspoken salute. No applause. No commentary. The architecture had already enshrined the moment.

Marcus approached his ledger, a weathered leather-bound volume, once heavy with the burden of decisions, now lighter than ever. It sat on its bespoke pedestal in the observatory, illuminated softly by the ambient glow of data streams flowing around it. This ledger was no mere book; it was the living testimony of a journey from command to design.

Fingertips trembling, Marcus opened the ledger. Each page bore the meticulous record of trials, corrections, moments of doubt, and breakthroughs. Ink had faded in places, but the essence was indelible; a covenant between man and architecture.

He pulled the pen from the ledger's coil, pausing to steady his breath. In a final entry, he wrote:

In relinquishing command, I found permanence.
Leadership was the spark; architecture, the fire that learned to breathe.
This ledger is no longer mine,
but the structural heartbeat of mastery is permanent.

Closing the book slowly, Marcus laid the pen beside it and stepped back. His trusty ledger had transcended flesh and voice; it was legacy inscribed in permanence.

He lingered a moment, fingers lightly brushing the surface as if passing a silent farewell. Then, with composed certainty, Marcus turned away. The final ledger entry is not a conclusion, but a threshold to permanence.

Marcus smiled, not in triumph but in relief. He whispered, "The architecture endures." Then he walked forward, leaving no sound behind.

Outside, the city breathed.

From the towers to the ports, from mountain observatories to desert hubs, every pulse synchronized. Streetlights shifted hue in exact cadence with system cycles; freight convoys timed departures to global audits. Even the traffic flow seemed choreographed by invisible rhythm. A child crossing a plaza paused, sensing the whisper beneath the stone, unaware she was walking within the architecture's pulse.

In a quiet café on the eastern fringe, a manager checked her tablet and smiled, the numbers aligned perfectly with headquarters. The design had taught itself to adapt and renew.

Reg remained in the observatory long after Marcus had gone. The buzz enveloped him like breath. He unfastened the old ID badge from his lapel and placed it gently on the console. For the first time in decades, he had nothing left to command. He felt the grief of surrender and the quiet grace of release. Authority had defined his very breath; now, for the first time, the air belonged entirely to the architecture he had built. He closed his eyes and listened.

The rhythm held.

He whispered, almost inaudible, "It lives."

Replication sustained. Propagation complete.

Silence returned. Absence had become design. Design no longer breathed; it commanded life.

What was once void now pulsed with permanence; architecture validated, mastery rendered eternal.

Reg vanished, but the rhythm persisted. The pulse endured: resilient, self-sustaining, infinite. Propagation complete. Architecture codifies doctrine; design embeds it.

Maxim: Propagation is architecture self-teaching; permanence is mastery without the master.

II. The Doctrine of Propagation

Propagation reveals how permanence functions under architecture.
It is not a process added to design, but a condition written into architecture. Proof that excellence can sustain, replicate, and renew itself without distortion.

Key Terms

- **Propagation:** disciplined replication of design until excellence repeats itself without erosion. Architecture proving it endures and performs beyond the leader.
- **Fidelity:** design remaining intact under repetition; architecture preserved in form, intent, and performance.

- **Cadence**: enforced rhythm of excellence; deliberate repetition turning discipline into culture.Propagation reveals how permanence functions under architecture.

Architectural Truths

i. Replication Is the Final Proof of Permanence

Replication is permanence proven. Excellence that required personality expired.
Permanence exists where propagation removes the need for personality.

Principle

Mandate replication in results; architecture authenticates structure through replication.

ii. Fidelity Is Architectural Discipline

Fidelity enforced is discipline embodied. Variance tolerated becomes Drift; enforcement defines doctrine.

Integrity is proven in enforcement, not announcement.

Principle

Audit Fidelity as Architectural Standard using the Design Fidelity Index, Behavioral Replication Audit, and Cultural Echo Measure.

iii. System Self-Correction Confirms Maturity

Mature architectures are correct before command. Self-correction is the signature of governed Architecture; human intent made automatic. Dependency on external intervention reveals immaturity and prevents scale.

Principle

Neutralize Drift with feedback, language, algorithm; all serving human discernment before intervention.

iv. Ritualization Converts Replication into Culture

Rituals convert repetition into identity. Cadence is the pulse of permanence.
Discipline becomes identity when repetition is enforced as an operational rhythm.

Principle

Ritualize auditing, make rhythm nonnegotiable. Weekly audits, quarterly reviews, and annual summits mandate cadence and enforce permanence.

v. Absence Is the Ultimate Audit

Absence reveals authenticity; design validated when structure endures without command.

The leader's absence must not expose dependency; it must confirm architectural integrity.

Principle

Require performance to outlast leadership. Absence proves or disproves fidelity.

vi. Meaning Is the Moral Architecture of Scale

Meaning must scale with design or permanence erodes. Replication without integrity becomes Drift disguised as discipline.

Principle

Institutionalize purpose through replication. Replications reinforce purpose, dignity, and moral coherence.

Binary Doctrine of Propagation: Drift vs. Design

Fragile (Drift)	Resilient (Design)

Expansion through imitation	Expansion through replication
Personality-dependent order	Architecture governed order
Culture diluted by scale	Culture disciplined by architecture
Manual correction	Human-guided self-correction
Episodic rituals	Institutionalized cadence
Presence masks dependency	Absence validates permanence

Doctrinal Verdict

Absence-validated replication proves permanence.
Architecture unable to self-teach collapses.
Excellence replication is excellence continuity.

The Doctrine of Propagation declares permanence as architecture teaching itself under the Three Core Laws. Design is human at its core. Machines, audits, and systems never replace leadership; they preserve the architect's intent so meaning, integrity, and excellence endure beyond the individual. Replication without humanity becomes Drift disguised as order.

III. Diagnostic Tool: The Replication Integrity Audit (RIA)

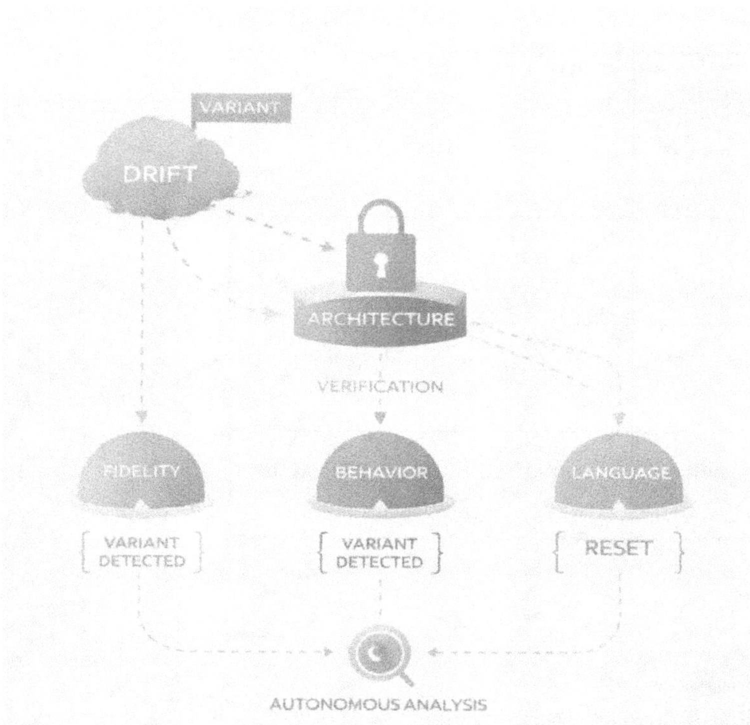

Figure 15.4 Replication Integrity Audit (RIA)

A diagnostic framework verifying that fidelity, behavior, meaning, and structure replicate under absence.

Purpose

Verify whether excellence self-replicates through enforceable design architecture rather than personality, ensuring propagation under absence and revealing Drift where replication fails.

Diagnostic Dimensions

1. Design Fidelity

Definition

Measures whether design elements replicate with precision across generations without deviation, memory-dependence, or stylistic alteration.

Propagation / Performance Indicator

≥0.90 Design Fidelity Index; procedures, logic, and decisions execute identically across second-generation implementations.

Drift Indicator

Memory-based execution, undocumented modifications, missing steps, or >10% variance from baseline.

2. Behavioral Transfer

Definition

Determines whether leadership behaviors institutionalize through cadence rather than relying on personal presence or discretionary correction.

Propagation / Performance Indicator

≥0.90 Replication Cohesion Rate; behavioral rituals, tone, and rhythm reproduce autonomously during unsupervised cycles.

Drift Indicator

Dependency on personality, leader reinforcement, or correction; behavioral cadence fractures when originators are absent.

3. Meaning Continuity

Definition

Assesses whether moral intent, strategic rationale, and doctrinal meaning persist unchanged through replication.

Propagation / Performance Indicator

≥0.90 Meaning Retention Index; language, framing, and decision rationale remain consistent under ethical and strategic simulations.

Drift Indicator: Purpose erosion, diluted vocabulary, or procedural reenactment without preserved intent.

4. Structural Reproduction Capacity

Definition

Evaluates whether the structure can generate additional replications autonomously without redesign or leader-driven initiation.

Propagation / Performance Indicator

≥0.85 Second-Generation Replication Rate; replicated units produce new units with minimal degradation across three cycles.

Drift Indicator

Replication halts at first generation, requires manual initiation, or exhibits structural bottlenecks and dependency.

5. Cross-Quadrant Replication Integrity

Definition

Measures whether the four propagation quadrants reinforce one another without compounding Drift across cycles.

Propagation / Performance Indicator

CDI <0.3; Drift does not transfer across quadrants, and replication coherence strengthens across generations.

Drift Indicator

CDI ≥0.3; design drift triggers behavioral drift → meaning erosion → structural reproduction failure.

Scoring Standard (1–5: Drift → Validated)

1. **Severe Drift:** Replication collapses immediately; fidelity absent; behaviors and meaning rely on individuals; structure cannot reproduce beyond the first generation.
2. **High Drift:** Partial replication occurs but degrades under load; behavioral and meaning transfer are inconsistent; structural reproduction requires intervention.
3. **Unstable:** Replication holds in controlled conditions but weakens under pressure or absence; quadrant performance varies across teams and cycles.

4. **Strong Alignment:** Replication is mostly autonomous; deviations appear only at edge cases; Fidelity, Behavior, Meaning, and Reproduction hold across cycles.
5. **Validated Architecture:** Excellence self-replicates without originators; design, behavior, meaning, and structure propagate as an integrated architecture; replication under absence confirms permanence.

Interpretation Guide

Validated Architecture: (19-25)

1. Design fidelity is precise and documented.
2. Behaviors reproduce through cadence, not personality.
3. Meaning and doctrine remain intact across generations.
4. Replicated units generate additional replications autonomously.
5. Drift does not transfer between quadrants; CDI remains <0.3.
6. Absence strengthens proof of permanence.

Drift Detected: (1-18)

1. Replication depends on memory, style, or leader presence.
2. Behavioral cadence collapses without supervision.
3. Meaning dilutes; vocabulary diverges across teams.
4. Structure cannot reproduce beyond the first generation.
5. Drift spreads across quadrants (CDI ≥0.3).
6. Permanence is assumed, not engineered.

Structural Closing Line

Replication is architecture, not inheritance where fidelity, behavior, meaning, and structure are not engineered to propagate under absence, Drift becomes the source code of the organization.

IV. Enforcement: Governance of Replication Fidelity

Replication without enforcement is imitation on a countdown.
Governance converts replication from performance into permanence.
The Global Replication Governance Architecture (GRGA) safeguards fidelity, ensuring each replication mirrors its design in structure, discipline, and cadence.

Propagation is not scale; it is governance drilled until repetition becomes architecture.
Enforcement is that architecture enacted.

Purpose

To embed replication as moral architecture.
Leadership proves excellence through discipline that replicates itself without command.
Enforcement transforms replication from aspiration to statute: fidelity verified, behavior reproduced, meaning preserved, cadence ritualized.

The GRGA ensures that expansion does not erode doctrine.
Each enforcement cycle converts distance to alignment, autonomy to orchestration, and growth to permanence.

Replication ungoverned is Drift disguised as progress.

Each enforcement cycle begins with the originator stepping aside; structure either stands or collapses under its own cadence.

i. Enforcement Architecture of Design Fidelity: Scaling Integrity

Standard: Architecture repeats without distortion.
Mandate: Every regional or divisional replication submits to a quarterly Design Fidelity Audit under the RIA framework; score ≥ 0.90 required.
Intent: Prove that architecture, not sentiment, scales integrity.
Enforcement: Variance beyond ten percent halts replication and activates Redesign Mandate under GRGA authority. The GRGA publishes fidelity indices to the global ledger within 30 days.

Design replicated imperfectly is architecture betrayed.

ii. Enforcement Architecture of Leadership Behavior: Behavior Scales Permanence

Standard: Leadership must replicate behavior, not personality.

Mandate: All leadership tiers conduct monthly Behavioral Transfer Audits verifying replication of cadence rituals, decision language, and composure standards.

Intent: Convert personality into procedure; ensure that presence never substitutes for discipline.

Enforcement: Detection of dependency on personal authority initiates a Cultural Transfer Redesign under GRGA oversight. Repetition of variance constitutes Drift Violation and disqualifies leadership until retraining is verified.

Behavior scaled is permanence secured.

iii. Enforcement Architecture of Meaning Continuity: Purpose Scales Identity

Standard: Purpose must travel intact across every replication.

Mandate: Doctrine Alignment Audits confirm identical intent, ethical reasoning, and decision vocabulary across replications; Meaning Retention Index ≥ 0.90.

Intent: Preserve the moral geometry of scale; ensure that growth amplifies dignity, not dilution.

Enforcement: Deviation in language or rationale triggers the Meaning Re-Alignment Protocol, requiring public correction documentation in the global ledger. Repeated erosion mandates re-certification of moral coherence before further replication.

Meaning preserved is identity sustained; meaning lost is structure undone.

iv. Enforcement Architecture of Execution Cadence: Cadence Scales Permanence

Standard: Cadence sustains permanence.

Mandate: All entities maintain a fixed replication cadence; monthly replication drill, quarterly propagation audit, annual renewal summit logged and ratified by the GRGA.

Intent: Transform repetition into culture; enforce tempo as trust.

Enforcement: Missed or falsified cadence records trigger an automatic audit resimulation and leadership accountability review. Cadence variance exceeding 5 percent constitutes negligence and mandates architectural redesign.

Neglect cadence, rehearse Drift; enforce cadence, sustain permanence.

Governance Enforcement Framework

- **Custodianship:** The GRGA assigns custodians to each replication quadrant: Design Fidelity, Behavioral Transfer, Meaning Continuity, Structural Cadence. Each custodian is accountable for Drift detection, report transparency, and protocol compliance across all expansions.
- **Verification:** Replication data streams feed the Global Fidelity Ledger. Independent auditors validate indices quarterly. Any anomaly exceeding tolerance initiates an automatic Re-simulation Mandate.
- **Transparency:** Results are public within the governance network. Concealment equals Drift. Silence is treated as falsification.
- **Correction:** When replication falters, redesign activates without permission. Governance corrects through enforced redesign cycles; proof that permanence is maintained by correction, not assumption

Governance without consequence is permission to drift.

V. Doctrinal Closure: Propagation as the Discipline of Permanence

Propagation completes the architecture. It is not expansion; it is permanence rendered in design. Design ceases to depend on human intervention and perpetuates itself through fidelity, behavior, meaning, and cadence. Governance achieves silence; each governing design discipline within the architecture enforces its own discipline.

Permanence is the deliberate replication of excellence without distortion. It is the final state where the human hand no longer directs the architecture yet continues to live through it. The structure no longer depends on its architect; it embodies human intent as living governance. Replication indices now converge; fidelity confirms autonomy.

i. The Irreversible Architecture: Propagation as Self-Governance.

It fuses continuity, adaptation, and mastery into a self-verifying design. Architecture governs through alignment, coherence becomes discipline. Each replication becomes testimony that excellence has learned to reproduce itself.

Every previous doctrine: Validation, Continuity, Adaptation culminates here as a singular proof: excellence sustained through replication becomes excellence made permanent.

Permanence is the mastery of recurrence without Drift. Design enforces its own fidelity. The cycle has closed; Design has achieved awareness of itself.

Permanence becomes identity.

ii. The Discipline of Permanence: Architecture Transcending into Design

As permanence is achieved, the role of leadership evolves in function and deepens in purpose. Leaders shift from control to stewardship: guardians of intent, architects of renewal, and interpreters of design's moral framework. Their mandate is capability elevation, developing people strong enough to sustain structure through mastery. Leadership is the living conscience of permanence; the force ensuring architecture never loses its humanity as it endures.

The enforceable architectures of propagation; fidelity, transfer, meaning, cadence govern as living statutes. Each replication cycle renews permanence.

Permanence is disciplined motion. It is renewal encoded in rhythm, proof sustained by structure. Architecture regenerates without fatigue, redesigns without permission, and enforces integrity as instinct.

Governing permanence refines ego into service so design endures through people. Leadership integrated into architecture becomes the highest form of governance: structure energized by human purpose.

Permanence is excellence liberated.

iii. Operational Implication: The Human Standard of Permanence

For the reader, this is the final discipline: **become the embodiment of permanence; living proof that excellence can inhabit the human form.**

Excellence is a state lived through conscious design. To embody permanence, leaders must enact the same discipline their architecture sustains: fidelity without distortion, behavior without dependence, meaning without dilution, cadence without fatigue.

Leadership Mastery is the architecture of human empowerment; people capable of perpetuating excellence without dependency. It is the deliberate development of successors surpassing their designers, ensuring permanence through human amplification of mastery. People become the conduit for design replicating fidelity. Every decision, cycle, and ritual reaffirms permanence lives through people who uphold it.

Achieving permanence creates a legacy where human mastery amplifies design.

The holy grail of leadership is contribution.

Permanence verified: when the Designer's absence no longer interrupts excellence.

VI. Rapid Orientation: Drift–Architecture Spectrum

Use this rubric for orientation, not validation. If your structures do not hold under pressure and turnover, you are in Drift regardless of intent or progress.

Severe Drift: Replication collapses immediately; fidelity absent; behaviors and meaning rely on individuals; structure cannot reproduce beyond the first generation.

High Drift: Partial replication occurs but degrades under load; behavioral and meaning transfer are inconsistent; structural reproduction requires intervention.

Unstable: Replication holds in controlled conditions but weakens under pressure or absence; quadrant performance varies across teams and cycles.

Strong Alignment: Replication is mostly autonomous; deviations appear only at edge cases; Fidelity, Behavior, Meaning, and Reproduction hold across cycles.

Validated Architecture: Excellence self-replicates without originators; design, behavior, meaning, and structure propagate as an integrated architecture; replication under absence confirms permanence.

Epilogue

What Remains When Architecture Governs

This book was written to establish Permanence.

Not improvement.

Not momentum.

Not excellence as an aspiration.

Permanence.

It began with a simple claim: Drift is not an exception. It is the default condition of all human systems absent governing architecture. Drift does not require incompetence, malice, or neglect. It emerges naturally wherever responsibility is diffuse, accountability is ambiguous, and performance is entrusted to personality rather than structure.

The purpose of architecture is not to motivate people to resist Drift. It is to make Drift structurally impossible to sustain.

That work is complete.

The architecture set out in this book governs where responsibility resides, how authority is exercised, how decisions are made under pressure, and how accountability is enforced without dependence on individual character. It replaces intention with law. It removes heroism as a requirement. It constrains behavior not by exhortation, but by design.

Where architecture governs, Drift no longer masquerades as normal work.

This is sufficient to prevent collapse.

But collapse prevention is not the same as completion.

When architecture achieves Permanence, the system enters a new condition. Volatility reduces. Ambiguity narrows. Performance stabilizes. The organization no longer relies on exceptional individuals to compensate for structural absence. The system begins to hold.

This moment is often mistaken for resolution.

It is not.

Architecture governs behavior. It does not abolish the conditions of being human.

Human beings remain finite. Variable. Context-sensitive. Responsive to pressure, uncertainty, and contradiction. None of these characteristics represent failure. They are not deficiencies to be corrected. They are constraints that exist whether acknowledged or ignored.

Architecture is required not because humans are unreliable, but because they are irreducibly human.

Structure that assumes uniform capacity, constant availability, or endless absorption of demand is not neutral. It is extractive. Extraction does not announce itself as breakdown. It appears as compliance. As professionalism. As people continuing to operate within the system without visible disruption.

This is not a rejection of pressure or intensity, but of demand that escapes governance.

When architecture succeeds, extraction becomes harder to see.

Drift, in this condition, no longer presents as chaos or collapse. It presents as quiet normalization. As expectations that grow without being named. As load that accumulates without being measured. As silence that is interpreted as alignment rather than containment.

This is not a failure of architecture. It is a consequence of ignoring what architecture rests upon.

Permanence stabilizes systems. Continuity determines whether that stability is lived without extraction.

Design is the human application of Architecture over time. It is expressed through rhythms, enforcement, boundaries, and the treatment of variance. Where design is neglected, architecture remains intact while its human substrate absorbs unacknowledged cost.

This is the condition in which organizations often congratulate themselves prematurely.

The system holds.

The metrics stabilize.

The language becomes confident.

And yet, the system continues to ask.

Not dramatically. Incrementally.

Each demand appears reasonable in isolation. Each accommodation feels temporary.

Over time, these accommodations become assumed. Endurance becomes expected.

Variance becomes inconvenient. Signals that do not align with the system's operating rhythm are suppressed, not by mandate, but by consequence.

None of this violates architecture. But it does test design.

A system that governs behavior without governing its own demands will drift again, not toward collapse, but toward quiet erosion. This erosion does not register as failure until it is advanced. By the time outcomes shift, the system has already taught people what must not be said, what must be absorbed, and what must be carried silently for continuity to be maintained.

This book has addressed Drift as it appears in the absence of architecture. It has shown how organizations collapse when structure is unclear, when accountability is shared, and when performance is sustained through personal sacrifice rather than design.

It has not resolved what emerges after Permanence is established.

That omission is deliberate.

Because once architecture governs, responsibility does not end. It sharpens.

The responsibility is no longer to create order from chaos. It is to observe what order requires. To examine whether continuity is being maintained through explicit design or through unspoken human compensation. To notice when stability is preserved by narrowing acceptable variance rather than by governing demand.

Design is not vigilance alone; it is the active governance of demand through enforced limits.

These questions cannot be answered by intention. They cannot be delegated downward. They cannot be resolved through culture statements or values language.

They require design decisions that treat human constraint as a governing input rather than an inconvenience.

Any system that functions only when people suppress signals of overload, uncertainty, or misalignment has not escaped Drift. It has relocated it. Drift, in this form, is quieter, more disciplined, and far more difficult to confront precisely because performance appears intact.

Architecture makes systems governable.

Design determines whether that governance extracts silently or sustains responsibly.

This distinction matters.

Organizations often fail loudly when architecture is absent. They fail quietly when design is neglected.

The temptation, once Permanence is achieved, is to codify success and replicate it without examining its cost. To assume that what can be carried now can be carried indefinitely. To mistake continuity of output for continuity of capacity.

That assumption is itself a form of Drift.

This book does not provide comfort against that risk. It was not written to. Its role is to establish law where personality once stood, and to remove denial as a governing strategy. It ensures that failure can no longer be attributed to effort, motivation, or character.

What it leaves unresolved is what no architecture alone can resolve: how systems that hold must be designed to acknowledge the humans they govern.

That question does not announce itself as urgency. It appears after success. After stability. After confidence sets in. It emerges as a subtle tension between what the system requires and what it silently assumes will be absorbed.

The architecture stands.

What remains is whether the Continuity of that architecture is sustained through deliberate design, or through invisible human cost.

That responsibility does not belong to individuals.

It belongs to the system.

And it does not expire once Drift is contained.

The Three Laws

Excellence is engineered.
Structure shapes behavior.
People are the structure.

Architectural Maxims

Design is destiny; Drift is surrender.
Performance without engineered resilience guarantees collapse.
Learning without alignment fractures into noise.
Collapse is permitted; adaptability is architectural.
Structure shapes behavior; architecture delivers mastery or collapse.
Structure enforces culture; it determines whether people excel or collapse.
Excellence is engineered. Drift requires neglect.
Resilience is the net; Drift is the fall.
Mastery forges mind and body into the permanence of excellence.
Mastery drives behavior; personality anchors potential.
Trust is the architecture converting human promise into structural integrity.
Meaning humanizes resistance.
Validation is the architecture of permanence.
Continuity is architecture surviving the architect.
Adaptation rehearses permanence before change arrives.
Propagation is architecture self-teaching; permanence is mastery without the master

www.ingramcontent.com/pod-product-compliance
Lightning Source LLC
LaVergne TN
LVHW062146200926
848484LV00007B/1867